BE (LIQUID) COOL

52 Weeks of Witty, Pithy, and Profound Sci-Fi-Based Inspiration

For Positive Thinking, Planning, and *Action!*

AUSTIN DRAGON

Copyright © 2023 by Austin Dragon

All rights reserved. No part of this publication may be reproduced, distributed, or transmitted in any form or by any means, or stored in a database or retrieval system, without the prior written permission of the publisher.

BE (LIQUID) COOL

52 Weeks of Witty, Pithy, and Profound Sci-Fi-Based Inspiration

For Positive Thinking, Planning, and Action!

978-1-946590-28-2 (paperback)

978-1-946590-98-5 (ebook)

http://www.austindragon.com

Published by Well-Tailored Books, California

This is a work of fiction. Names, characters, places, and incidents are the product of the author's imagination or are used fictitiously. Any resemblance to actual persons, living or dead, events, or locales is entirely coincidental.

Table of Contents

INTRODUCTION 1

About Liquid Cool 2

About This Book 5

How to Use This Book 9

FIRST MONTH | January | Classic Sci-Fi Actor Birthdays 14

PRE-LAUNCH MINDSET 15

The Planners 23

Who's Cruz? 29

Week 1: Know the "Why" 32

Who's Run-Time? 35

Week 2: No Mind Gutters 38

Who's PJ? 43

Week 3: We All Got Problems 46

Who's Dot? 50

Week 4: Believe Me, Others Have Had Worse Tragedies Than You 52

Who's Wilford G.? 59

Week 5: Or Would You Want to Switch Places 61

SECOND MONTH | February | Classic Sci-Fi Actor Birthdays 65

THE ACTION MINDSET 67

The Planners 72

Week 6: Be It 77

Week 7: Get Out of Your Comfort Zone (Or, at Least, Don't Let It Get In Your Way) 81

Who's Phishy? 87

Week 8: Pick Your Associates Wisely 89

Week 9: Have the Right Tools 95

THIRD MONTH | March | Classic Sci-Fi Actor Birthdays 103

THE ZEN MINDSET | Mind, Body, and Soul 105

The Planners 108

Week 10: Eat Right 113

Week 11: Movement 122

Week 12: Sleep 128

Week 13: Meditate 133

Week 14: A Day to Unplug 136

FOURTH MONTH | April | Classic Sci-Fi Actor Birthdays 140

THE PEOPLE POSITIVE MINDSET | Positivity Empowers 142

The Planners 144

Week 15: Respect 149

Week 16: Humility 154

Week 17: Don't Be Rude 159

Week 18: People Don't Like Negative People 168

FIFTH MONTH | May | Classic Sci-Fi Actor Birthdays 173

THE ENGAGEMENT MINDSET | About Engagement 175

The Planners 178

Week 19: Hard Work 184

Week 20: Don't Forget the Family 190

Week 21: Build Your Tribe 196

Who's Compstat Connie 201

Week 22: Mentors 203

Week 23: Be Cool 208

SIXTH MONTH | June | Classic Sci-Fi Actor Birthdays 212

THE ADMIN MINDSET | About Admin 214

The Planners 220

Week 24: Have A System 227

Week 25: Set Aside Time to Plan, Assess, and Adjust 231

Week 26: Big Rocks versus Small Pebbles 235

Week 27: Priorities 237

Week 28: Research 239

SEVENTH MONTH | July | Classic Sci-Fi Actor Birthdays 245

DON'T BE YOUR OWN ARCH-ENEMY | About Self-Sabotage 247

The Planners 249

Week 29: Keep Your Ego In Check 255

Week 30: Avoid Drama 260

Week 31: Resist the Urge to Be Stupid 268

Week 32: Do the Right Thing 274

Week 33: Manage the Negative Emotions 278

EIGHTH MONTH | August | Classic Sci-Fi Actor Birthdays 294

DON'T PANIC. LIFE'S SUPPOSED TO BE UNEXPECTED | About the Unexpected 296

The Planners 299

Week 34: The Unexpected 304

Week 35: The Ridiculous 311

Week 36: Don't Be Afraid to Ask For Help 325

Week 37: You'll Have Setbacks, Just Keep Moving Forward 329

NINTH MONTH | September | Classic Sci-Fi Actor Birthdays 333

DON'T OVERTHINK IT | About the Simple Things 335

The Planners 336

Week 38: A Purpose-Driven Life 341

Week 39: An Enjoyed Life 345

Week 40: Use Time Wisely 349

Week 41: Accept The Gift 352

TENTH MONTH | October | Classic Sci-Fi Actor Birthdays 357

GIVING BACK (WHEN YOU CAN) | About Giving Back 359

The Planners 362

Week 42: Encourage Others 367

Week 43: Be Classy 372

Week 44: Help Others 377

Week 45: Be a Mentor 384

ELEVENTH MONTH | November | Classic Sci-Fi Actor Birthdays 393

DON'T FORGET THE FUN | About Fun 395

The Planners 398

Week 46: Don't Forget Family and Friends (Part II) 403

Week 47: Don't Be So Serious 412

Week 48: Schedule Spontaneity 417

Week 49: Vacations! 423

TWELFTH MONTH | December | Classic Sci-Fi Actor Birthdays 432

THE FINAL STRETCH | Almost There! 434

The Planners 435

Week 50: Accomplished 439

Week 51: Perseverance 441

Week 52: Celebration 448

BONUS | "The Box" 451

APPENDIX 455

More Blank Planner Pages 457

REVIEW REQUEST 460

ABOUT THE AUTHOR 462

Special Mention

SPECIAL THANKS TO OUR (Futuristic) Contributors

Cruz, our Favorite Sci-Fi Detective With An Attitude, and Company

INTRODUCTION

About Liquid Cool

THE INSPIRATION FOR This Inspirational Book

"For me, science fiction is a way of thinking, a way of logic that bypasses a lot of nonsense. It allows people to look directly at important subjects." — Gene Roddenberry, creator of Star Trek

THIS BOOK IS ABOUT Positive Thinking, Planning, and—most importantly—Action! We'll begin with a real-life person as an example of results—myself—since I'm the one person whose story I know best.

I started my adult life strongly rooted in the ethos of helping others, including joining the US Army right out of high school. If my journey can humbly help you in yours, then more power to us both. Others helped me get to where I am and become the person I am today. I wish all of us had those mentors and role models throughout life—at the top of the list being my parents—to look up to, emulate, and learn from.

You may have picked up this book hoping to find valuable nuggets of inspiration and encouragement in your quest for self-empowerment. Is the goal to make a "new you" and change your life significantly? Is it to accomplish something you've procrastinated about for a long time or never thought of? Maybe you want to achieve overall happiness or just be more content in life with all its challenges.

A person can be many things in life, either as a vocation or a hobby. I wrote my first book at three—yes, the power of early literacy should be the primary domestic policy of every society on Earth. It was only a few pages with big lettering and bigger drawings, but it was the first. So, right from the beginning I was a creative. That talent manifested itself in drawing primarily, but later the writing consumed all my creative energies. By middle school, I was writing full-length mystery detective novels on my favorite manual typewriter. Yes, these contraptions were real and used daily around the world. Then, all my writing stopped when I graduated from high school, enlisted in the US Army, and adult life began. I wouldn't write another word of fiction in almost twenty years!

In all that time, I didn't cease being creative. In fact, those creative juices were always creating something in the universe of my mind. I was just too "busy" with life. Then, in 2010, I walked away from the activities that consumed most of my free time outside of my career—bringing about quality inner-city public education. I became disillusioned with the entire political landscape and was done.

Every year, I picked one or two new things I'd accomplish for the year. One time, it was learning salsa; another time, it was traveling to a particular country for the first time. One fateful year in 2011, the goal was to publish one book (emphasize the word "one"). Without realizing it, I had uncorked the bottle—a bottle that was bigger on the inside than it appeared from the outside—and my creative energies flooded out. They were "free at last" as the dam of excuses and distractions was gone. I didn't publish one book. As of 2022, I've published thirty, with five distinct series in science fiction, epic fantasy, classic horror, and more on the way.

The first of those series was a very heavy sci-fi, international thriller chronicling the events leading to World War III. Already it has predicted quite a few things that weren't true at the time of their release, but have since come to pass or we're in the middle of now as a society. Bottom line: this was a very serious work. I like serious, as I am part intellectual, but only part. The other half of my personality is definitely that of a jokester. I needed another series to represent that side of me. In Star Trek terms, I am Spock and McCoy in the same body, and both my intellect and emotions power my creativity.

In 2015, I mapped out four new series. I have always loved mysteries and private detective stories. So, for the first of the new series, why not merge that with my love of sci-fi? Liquid Cool was born! My homage to the classic Ridley Scott movie, Blade Runner, inspired by the novel, Do Androids Dream of Electric Sheep by classic sci-fi author Philip K. Dick.

On August 1, 2015, I released These Mean Streets, Darkly, the prequel short story to the upcoming Liquid Cool series. Oh, my goodness! You should have heard the howls from my Readers' Club members. "Where's the rest of the story, Austin?" "I want to read this now, Austin." "Do you hate us? Where's the book, Austin?" It continued from there.

Book one of Liquid Cool: The Cyberpunk Detective Series was officially released on February 16, 2016. We're introduced to Cruz, our favorite sci-fi detective with an attitude, and his eclectic band of family, friends, and associates. He solves cases on the rainy, mean streets of the supercity of Metropolis. The prequel may have been less than 50 pages, but the debut novel was over 400! As of 2023, the series has ten major novels, a mini-series of three novels, four box sets, and another companion case short story. Two novels and another box set are on the way.

My Liquid Cool fans are happy.

With the approach of the New Year, I came up with the idea to create a non-fiction weekly planner using the characters of Liquid Cool as an inspiration. Our main protagonist, Cruz, fell into being a street detective. However, he wouldn't have lasted past his first case if he hadn't seized the opportunity. He became the famous detective we know and love today with the support of friends, hard work, natural talents, and overcoming his fears.

Cruz, with his family and friends around him, has quite a lot of wonderful life lessons to share.

Let's get into **Be (Liquid) Cool.**

About This Book

THE NEVER-ENDING, AGE-Old Human Quest to Improve

"Look up at the stars and not down at your feet." — Steve Hawkins, theoretical physicist, cosmologist, and author

YOUR MOTIVATIONS

Want to improve? Something specific or an overall aspect of your life, character, or personality? Or just do something new for the year!

End bad habits? Reverse bad choices? Go beyond the tired perennial New Year resolutions?

Begin visiting all those countries around the world you've been putting off? Do something crazy like switch to a completely new career? Do something big?

Feeling blue, bored, or aimless? Want to be empowered and take control of your life?

How Big Is the Market?

Every year, billions are spent on motivational self-help, self-esteem, inspirational, and assorted daily and weekly planner books. People wanting to improve themselves or their lives are as old as humanity itself.

It's a $10.4 billion self-improvement market!

According to Market Research.com (2021), "Market data estimates that the U.S. self-improvement market alone was worth $11.6 billion in 2019, and forecasts 6.0% average annual growth to $14.0 billion by 2025."

The numbers are not merely about the number of books bought. It shows the immense, ongoing interest in the subject. That's a good thing!

It's a noble endeavor to want to improve for the better, continue to grow in life as a person, or positively impact those around you or in the world. So is having a more rewarding relationship with family and friends, or being more successful in life or work. Above all, it's about being happy and content with our lives in the universe.

About Humans

"What a piece of work is a man! How noble in reason, how infinite in faculties! In form and moving, how express and admirable! In action, how like an angel! In apprehension, how like a god! The beauty of the world, the paragon of animals!" — The Tragedy of Hamlet, Prince of Denmark by William Shakespeare, 1599-1601

"O wretched man, wretched not just because of what you are, but also because you do not know how wretched you are!" — Philippic by Cicero, orator and philosopher of ancient Rome, 43-44 BCE

Two quotes from totally opposite ends of the spectrum. In fact, you couldn't get a stronger contrast. We strive for the former and clearly don't wish to be the latter or anywhere near it.

About Be (Liquid) Cool

I divided the book into 12 months, each with a different theme. Each month has four to five lessons—totaling 52 weeks, each with its own subject.

The major work is on the week-to-week level.

Chosen monthly topics are meant to only touch upon a major theme. We all have subjects we wish to delve into more with further reading. Which subjects those might be depend on you, and can occur over a lifetime. We definitely encourage you to go further if you wish.

The purpose of the book is not to overwhelm but to guide. It simply touches the tip of the proverbial iceberg each week with a different topic in a fun way and, hopefully, a poignant one, too.

The Chapters

The month kicks off with the Birthdays of the Month page of selected classic television and movie sci-fi actors and creators from the last fifty years (the 1960s to 2000s). I consider this period the "golden age" of modern science fiction entertainment. This is a sci-fi-inspired book.

Readers get inspirational quotes and a preview from a Liquid Cool novel featuring Cruz or his supporting cast of characters at the start of each week. The selected excerpts from Liquid Cool novels are to instruct, inspire, and, sometimes, give you a chuckle.

We're all different. Some chapters will resonate more with you than others based on our own unique circumstances, interests, goals, and objectives.

Themes Touched Upon

Confidence	Family	Quiet Time
Positivity	Friends	Faith
Happy	Relationships	Movement/Exercise
Contentment	Food	Read/Brain Power
Perseverance	Life	Stay Away From the Negative
Spontaneity	Distractions / "Noise"	Stay Away From the Stupid
Work	Gratitude	Try Something New
Play	Appreciation	Become Something New

Appendix

Besides blank monthly and weekly planners, it includes additional topics for consideration.

Closing

Ultimately, this book is not about Liquid Cool. It's about you or helping you become the best version of yourself.

Plan. Act. Stay Consistent. Achieve! Transform!

How to Use This Book

GOOD THINGS TAKE TIME...One Day at a Time

"I've seen things you people wouldn't believe." — Roy Batty in Blade Runner (Original Movie) played by Rutger Hauer

BE (LIQUID) COOL IS all about self-improvement. Whether your goal is to change something or do something, the book is geared for work month-to-month, then down to the week-to-week level. Positive Thinking is the mindset. Planning is the start. Action is the work.

How do you personalize your journey? Each section of each month has both monthly and weekly planners to use or copy. At the back of the book, in the Appendix, are additional blank Monthly and Weekly Planners. You can also download the pages from my author website for free. At the top of the planner is space to write the month and week of the specific week based on when you start. The blank planner has space for you to write your plan and any notes.

We recommend you set a broad monthly goal to accomplish, then map out specific objectives for each week. As you go, assess your progress and, at the end of each week and month, take stock of your progress, accomplishments, and any setbacks. Include any adjustments you need to make to next week's or the month's goals.

There is no right or wrong way to effective planning and overall time management. It's a matter of what works best for you to move towards your goals, and can remain consistent with whatever approach you choose.

"In Order" Versus "Out of Order"

You don't have to start in January only. Maybe you got this book months before January or some other month. Start with any month you like and follow it out for twelve months.

Projects versus "Permanent"

A key question to answer from the start when you sit down to create your plan is: Are you embarking on a short-term goal or a major life/lifestyle change? Those not new to life planning know that it almost always takes more time to accomplish something than you originally planned. However, the more you do, the better you get at your time estimates.

Goals Versus Objectives

A goal is the overall outcome you want to achieve, while an objective is a specific and measurable action that can be reached in a short amount of time toward the goal. Goals are typically broad statements and are often long-term endeavors when written out. Objectives are the step-by-step processes or action steps to achieve those goals.

A good way to remember the difference between the two is: the goal is the destination; the objective is how you get there.

Avoid "Planning Paralysis"

Each month and week has a planner to map out your goals and objectives, track your progress, and assess accomplishments and setbacks. But the exercise shouldn't overwhelm or distract you. The exercise should empower you by keeping you focused and on track. The goal is the work, not spending all your time planning and writing about the work you plan to do, which is called "planning paralysis." It's a disease to avoid.

Avoid the "Busy-Work Hamster Wheel"

Planning is the most important step in preparing to reach your goals and actually get things accomplished through action. You must also remember the hierarchy between the big things ("Big Rocks") and the little things ("Small Pebbles"). Anyone can make a to-do list and feel very satisfied checking things off at a steady pace. However, are these things essential? Do they add up to the big thing you're trying to accomplish, or are they only "make-work" tasks that won't really impact your ultimate goal? If the little thing doesn't lead you forward to your big thing, it shouldn't be on your action plan list. "Busy Work" is the other disease to avoid when planning effectively.

Plan and Write

At the beginning of each month, write your goal for the month and for the first week. Only you know your daily and monthly routine and the family, work, and personal obligations you must plan for. Your own monthly and weekly plans will reflect this.

Also, don't do too much at once, especially at the beginning. How many new things can you realistically do in a given week? Can you really accomplish that big thing in one month, or should you divide it up in stages over a month or more? Learn as you go.

Weekly plans shouldn't be stressful, boring, or a chore. You can be serious about your goals but have fun too.

Method of Work

Two ways to reach your goals are to set personalized objectives and learn from inspiration in quotes. The strategy is:

- Plan and write out your specific Monthly Goal (i.e., begin writing my "great" novella)

- Read the Witty, Pithy, and Profound Sci-Fi-Based Inspirational lesson for the month and/or week

- Plan and write out your goals and objectives for the week (tied to your Monthly Goal) (i.e., outline the entire book and start chapter one)

- Action! Make it happen over the week (i.e., write a few pages or a specific number of words each day)

- Assess and adjust (as needed) (i.e., Won't be starting Chapter One this week. Still working on the outline. And still can't come up with a cool name for my protagonist)

- Repeat

Action!

Yearly and monthly goals are great. However, the most decisive goals you make will be your weekly ones and, especially, what you can accomplish day-by-day. Even baby steps over time consistently will get you to a mile in the end.

Create Good Habits

Habit: (definition) — a regular tendency or practice.

Create good habits to succeed by replacing the bad habits that hold you back, take you in the wrong direction, or have you standing still doing nothing.

Assess

Once you start, stick to it. You can assess and adjust as you go.

Assess how you do every week. After every four or five weeks, there is a section for you to assess the month. These regular spot checks can be so helpful in keeping you on track with your goals.

Also, as you track progress, highlight accomplished milestones as you go!

Make it a Team Effort?

Some of us are very self-motivated. Others need a nudge or two from a family member or friend. If the latter is the case, then enlist that person to help you stay on track. If you're the former, march onward.

Words For Success

Plan. Act. Achieve. Transform.

Stay Focused. Be Consistent. Be Adaptable.

Are You Ready?

Let's begin Week One of your 52-week journey and start piling up some accomplishments to be proud of!

FIRST MONTH
January
Classic Sci-Fi Actor Birthdays

CHARACTER (ACTOR) TV Show/Movie

January 5: John Sheppard (Joe Flanigan) Stargate Atlantis

January 6: Talia Winters (Andrea Thompson) Babylon 5

January 10: Sebastian (William Sanderson) Blade Runner (Original Movie)

January 12: Saavik (Kirstie Alley) The Wrath of Khan (Star Trek)

January 17: Darth Vader (voice) (James Earl Jones) Star Wars: Original Movies

January 19: Teyla Emmagan (Rachel Luttrell) Stargate Atlantis

January 20: Dr. Leonard McCoy (DeForest Kelley) Star Trek: The Original Series

January 22: Kane "iconic chestburster victim" (John Hurt) Alien

January 23: Colonel/General Jack O'Neill (Richard Dean Anderson) Stargate SG-1

January 23: Batty (Rutger Hauer) Blade Runner (Original Movie)

January 27: Zefram Cochrane (James Cromwell) Star Trek: First Contact

January 27: Na'Toth (Julie Caitlin Brown) Babylon 5

PRE-LAUNCH MINDSET

METROPOLIS

A Hi-Tech, Low-Life World

A supercity of fifty million people. Ubiquitous hovercars, laser gun-toting gangsters, neon cyborgs, corporate samurai soldiers, uber-rich tycoons from off-world colonies. This is the world Cruz lives in—born, raised, and scraping out a living.

What's your world like?

Excerpt From: *Liquid Cool: The Cyberpunk Detective Series (Book One)*

Metropolis.

Everything that was seen or heard, every smell, and almost every feeling belonged to it. Skyscraper monoliths with their side lights rose into the near-perpetual overcast sky one way, blink-blink, and the lukewarm downpour fell onto the neon urban jungle the other, drip-drip. From the ground, looking up, on those days that were as clear as it could ever get, buildings seemed to have their own halos, courtesy of the rooftop lights. On "normal" rainy days, that same illumination gave the sky a faint glow. Also, from the vantage of the streets, the city's lighted buildings pulsated in all the many psychologically-tested and focus-group-researched colors to mitigate the street's base griminess, despite the ever-rain. The flashing neon signs screamed every second of every day; their soft-sell, quasi-hypnotic consumerist cons of Big Bad Business and government public service "aggravations" (PSAs) of Big Bad Government. But people were numb to it all, no matter how outrageous or provocative.

The crowds on the streets moving about were like a collective life form. Everyone clad in their gray-toned or black slickers, and for those carrying them, umbrellas with glowing-colored handles. Most had their ears covered with headphones, their heads covered with hoods, and everyone had their eyes covered with glowing-colored glasses. The masses were in the world, but mentally someplace else—away from it, never a part of it, unless there was a reason, and there rarely was a reason. Tech tricksters, analog hustlers, and digital gangsters, at least, had a purpose. The masses had only one concern—to exist, get to the end of the day unscathed, and then do it all over again the next day. Maybe smile a real smile a time or two in life. Escape was only possible if you could buy or trick your way Up-Top or, of course, when the Grim Reaper came a-knocking. 'Til then, for most, there was plugging the ears into the music and the eyes (and brain) into the virtual television. For too many others, it was also about jacking the body into the drugs or the mind into the cyber-games. Everything was an attempt to stave off the dark emotions and conventional madness that accompanied the daily grind of life in the 50 million-plus supercity of Metropolis and the many, many other metropolises exactly like it, though smaller, on Earth.

Start with the Plan

I know the "universe" that Cruz and company inhabit. Only you know the personal "Metropolis" that you live in. When you quietly sit down to map out your pre-launch plan, there's you and your "world"—the people and places around you.

To begin, you will…

I. Decide what you want to do or accomplish

- Write down these goals and priorities

- Determine how you will achieve these goals

II. Set your long-term and short-term goals

- Set specific deadlines (even if you change or adjust them later)
- Create the Plan

III. Execute

- Begin the Action
- Track your progress as you go
- Make any needed adjustments as you go
- Recognize accomplishments and milestones along the way

Of course, there are other considerations...

About Problems

The forever-present obstacles of life, however...

IN LIFE, MANY PEOPLE feel aimless, unfulfilled, overwhelmed, or unproductive, especially in these times. Many say it's a problem with time. But often, it's not a lack of time but a lack of focus, commitment, and the wrong mindset. A key first step to change this includes preparing to act (the plan) and then acting with purpose (the execution of the plan).

Always remember you control your frame of mind, not the problem. Problems in life are as normal as stars in the cosmos, so there is no need to despair. The question is how you handle them—with a frown, with sadness, or a big, wicked smile. We, of course, recommend smiling. But not 24-7, or people, us included, will think you're crazy. So, no inappropriate smiling.

Positive Mindset Thinking

"Do not try and bend the spoon; that's impossible. Instead, only try to realize the truth. There is no spoon." — The Boy in the Matrix (Original Movie)

KEEP IN MIND THE FOLLOWING:

- You are more capable than you think you can be
- You can be braver than you believe you can be
- You can be stronger than you think you are
- You can be smarter than you give yourself credit for

The potential of all these things and more is within yourself if you work to bring those aspects of yourself out into the open.

Negative Mindset Thinking

"I'm sorry, Dave. I'm afraid I can't do that." — Hal, 2001: A Space Odyssey

---

- I can't do this
- I'm not good at this
- I don't have time
- This is too hard
- This is good enough (even though I know it's not)

TO CHANGE YOUR THINKING, change your words and mindset. Negative words lead to negative results. Negativity will never lead to positive action.

Whether for good or bad, whatever you think about yourself will become a reality for you. That's why positive thinking is so powerful. What goes through your mind can manifest itself in some way. So, ditch the negative and amplify the positive.

Master Your Mind for Growth

"Use the Force." — *Ben Kenobi, Star Wars: The Original Movies*

- With effort and practice, I can get good at it
- Everything is hard before it is easy
- The more I work at it, the better I'll get
- Mistakes help me do better next time
- I can always keep learning
- I can change my whole life
- A little progress each day adds up to big results
- Build good habits and break bad ones to achieve my goals
- Build a life you don't need a vacation from

WHATEVER THAT DRIVING "force" is for you—religious, spiritual, or something else—use it!

About Distractions

Distractions, or a Minor "Speed Bump"?

AS YOU IDENTIFY YOUR goals and objections, always remember that things will arise to break your focus. Don't allow either major obstacles or minor distractions to win out. Either prevent them, go around them or ignore them altogether—whichever makes the most sense.

Questions to Consider

As You Create Your Pre-Launch Mindset

GRAB A PEN AND PAPER or get comfortable at your laptop and map out your next month, three months, six months, or more. Whether you decide to map out the year all at once or in smaller slices of time, you will have your 52 weeks. Peek into the future a year from now. What is it do you want to have accomplished after the 52 weeks?

Is it something big? Then it could take all year. Work backward, month-to-month. What will you tackle in each of those twelve months to reach your year-end goal?

Or is it something on a smaller scale of time? That's fine too. Maybe it'll take only six months or 90 days. It's your plan. The length of time is whatever you choose, but do set specific time deadlines. It forces you to meet those objectives builds your discipline, and is how you track your progress and accomplishments.

(Non-Sci-Fi) Quotes About Planning

"Before anything else, preparation is the key to success." — Alexander Graham Bell, Scottish-born inventor, scientist, and engineer credited with patenting the first practical telephone

"By failing to prepare, you are preparing to fail." — Benjamin Franklin, Founding Father of the United States and inventor

"Give me six hours to chop down a tree, and I will spend the first four sharpening the axe." — Abraham Lincoln, 16th U.S. President

"Always plan ahead. It wasn't raining when Noah built the ark." —Richard Cushing, Catholic Archbishop of Boston and later cardinal.

"Good planning without good working is nothing." — Dwight D. Eisenhower, 34th U.S. President

"Plan your work and work your plan." — *Napoleon Hill, famous American self-help author*

Six Guidelines to Consider in Creating Your Plan: The 5 Ws + 1 H

- Who
- What
- Where
- When
- Why
- How

Questions to Consider in Creating Your Plan

- What is the problem you want to solve?
- What is the thing you want to change?
- What do you want to do in life? (This year)
- What do you want to change in your life? (This year)
- Try something new?
- Become something new?
- What is it you want to accomplish?
- What are your goals? (i.e., run a 10-mile marathon)
- Is it regarding health and wellness, relationships, family, career, or something else in your life?
- What are your steps to achieve it?

- What research have you done on the topic?

- Do you need to talk to a significant other to create a realistic plan?

- Is it a one-time thing? (Run a marathon)

- Or is it a lifestyle change? (Run or walk 30 minutes each morning as part of my new healthy lifestyle)

- What is it you wish to change in your life?

- What are the major obstacles to achieving your goals?

- How do you plan to do this?

- Do you have or need support? (i.e., family, friends, religion, etc.)

- When are you going to get started?

Just a little progress at a time, at a steady pace, can lead to big results in the end. Life's a marathon, not a sprint.

The Planners

BE (LIQUID) COOL/MONTHLY PLANNER

MONTH:

SUN	MON	TUE	WED	THU	FRI	SAT

TOP PRIORITIES / GOALS

PEOPLE TO SEE / PLACES TO GO / REMINDERS

NOTES

RATE / ASSESS THE MONTH:

BE (LIQUID) COOL
WEEKLY PLANNER

WEEK: M T W H F S S

MONDAY

TUESDAY

WEDNESDAY

THURSDAY

FRIDAY

SATURDAY / SUNDAY

WEEK'S PRIORITIES / TO DO

NOTES

RATE / ASSESS THE WEEK:

BE (LIQUID) COOL
WEEKLY PLANNER

WEEK:

| M | T | W | H | F | S | S |

MONDAY

TUESDAY

WEDNESDAY

THURSDAY

FRIDAY

SATURDAY / SUNDAY

WEEK'S PRIORITIES / TO DO

NOTES

RATE / ASSESS THE WEEK:

BE (LIQUID) COOL
WEEKLY PLANNER

WEEK:

| M | T | W | H | F | S | S |

MONDAY

TUESDAY

WEDNESDAY

THURSDAY

FRIDAY

SATURDAY / SUNDAY

WEEK'S PRIORITIES / TO DO

NOTES

RATE / ASSESS THE WEEK:

BE (LIQUID) COOL
WEEKLY PLANNER

WEEK:

| M | T | W | H | F | S | S |

MONDAY

TUESDAY

WEDNESDAY

THURSDAY

FRIDAY

SATURDAY / SUNDAY

WEEK'S PRIORITIES / TO DO

NOTES

RATE / ASSESS THE WEEK:

BE (LIQUID) COOL
WEEKLY PLANNER

WEEK:

M T W H F S S

MONDAY

TUESDAY

WEDNESDAY

THURSDAY

FRIDAY

SATURDAY / SUNDAY

WEEK'S PRIORITIES / TO DO

NOTES

RATE / ASSESS THE WEEK:

Who's Cruz?

"I'M CRUZ. WHATCHA WANT?"

Our favorite sci-fi detective with a wife, two kids, a classic vehicle, and a cool hat! (But he didn't have the wife and kids yet when we first met him.)

These Mean Streets, Darkly may have been the very first work in the Liquid Cool Series, but our main protagonist, Cruz, made his full debut in Book One.

In Cruz's own words: "I'm the guy. President, CEO, COO, and detective on the go. I don't pass you on to any flunkies. I handle your business directly because I want your business."

Locations

He lives in Rabbit City, which is far from being a working-class or upscale neighborhood, but it wasn't the dumps. His place of residence is the Concrete Mama—a giant mega-tower apartment complex like a chunk of granite set down on Earth from space. If there was ever a planetary shockwave from a nuclear blast or an asteroid crash, you could bet the Concrete Mama would still be standing. It was ugly, but it would be here until the end of time in its ugliness.

His Liquid Cool offices are located in the business district of Buzz Town on the 100th floor of the tower on Circuit Circle—some people call it the Circuit; others, the Circle.

Vehicle

Cruz drives a bright red, classic Ford Pony. A high-performance, super-charged, advanced nitro-acceleration hydrogen engine. A sleek, bright red muscle-vehicle coupe to make the average person gawk and the mouths of the genuine hovercar enthusiast and collector hang open.

Cruz: "I had found the shell in a junkyard over fifteen years ago when I was in middle school, and it took me a few years to build and restore it, spare part by spare part. I had been upgrading it ever since. No one believed I found and built such an expensive muscle hovercar from scratch, but it was true, and I drove it every day. It was considered a true classic and got me solid offers to part with it almost every week, but you don't sell a classic Ford Pony; it's a purchase for life—like a legacy house. My Pony had been featured (without my permission) in so many hovercar magazines that I lost count."

Weapon of Choice

He carries an off-world omega-gun, courtesy of his slider/gun dealer friend, Phishy.

"It's the gun to end all private guns. That's what it says in the manual. And the shotgun. Now you're ready for the mean streets. And the omega-gun comes with accessories if you want to use its digital features. There's this cool piece that lights up you wrap around your leg. You'll see."

Medium-yield plasma discharge rounds. I needed something to practice on to see their effectiveness. The mayhem commenced. Lucky for them, it was not set to kill; unlucky for them, they would be showered with burning, excruciating painful rounds.

OCD-tendencies (Recovered)

Cruz has come a long way from his nearly full-on obsessive-compulsive disorder days:

I was the OCD guy who checked the front door to make sure it was locked five separate times before I went to bed.

My first stop would be the main Disease Control Center to sterilize my clothes and give me a full anti-biohazard shower. It was something the average citizen didn't know about, but it was all covered by medical insurance.

I was always of two minds inside a hospital. On the one hand, it was a shining example of society's amazing technology, which was for nothing less than to make people whole and save lives. But on the other hand, since anyone off the street was sent here first, it was a breeding ground of nastiness: germs, bacteria, viruses, and disease—a place only slightly better than the meat morgue.

I took out a bottle from my pocket and sprayed a shot up each nostril when no one was looking. The immune system booster product probably was a complete waste of my money, but it made me feel better since I couldn't put on a full biohazard suit.

Week 1: Know the "Why"

CRUZ: PONDERING LIFE in a Particularly Morose Way

EXCERPT FROM: *Liquid Cool: The Cyberpunk Detective Series (Book One)*

I felt trapped, like a bug in a spider's web. Everybody followed this system of life, from the littlest guy shuffling to and from his nine-to-five, all the way to those god-like guys living above us all, consumed by their own power and fortune. We all had the same basic concerns, but in the end, we all ended up at the same place—meat at the morgue. The masses did a lot in that in-between time to go about life in the rain with style—designer Goodwill wet-wear clothes and colored neon shades—to blot from the mind the fundamental drudgery of it all. To survive to your ultimate destination, you had to know your place to not upset the order of things. You either worked for the international, multinational megacorps, or you worked for uber-government, the "state," and, though you'd never get Up-Top, you could retire free-and-clear for your last decade or two of life. It was the unsaid, universal contract that most accepted.

Perspective

Cruz: The Desire for a Life Change Was Always There

EXCERPT FROM: *Liquid Cool: The Cyberpunk Detective Series (Book One)*

But I had tried to make my futile mark on the cosmos with my contrarian self. I avoided umbrellas; instead, I wore my tan fedora. I didn't wear neon shades, and I didn't wear dark-colored slickers; instead, I wore my favorite tan coat. Everyone had dark-colored hovercars; I drove a bright red, classic Ford Pony. That's what I did to separate myself from the masses—pathetic and pointless, but I did it anyway and could do no different.

What the hell have I even accomplished? If I clocked out of life, what exactly would be my legacy? I hated my birthdays. My parents told me I hated them, even as a kid, the time you're supposed to be the most optimistic in life, even despite all the sweet birthday cakes and presents from every known relative on the planet. My girlfriend said I needed to stop my annual "morose period." "There are people in the world with no food to eat or born with no eyes or limbs, or born mentally retarded. What is your complaint?" she'd say to me. "An innocent kid was shot in the head today and will be brain-dead for the rest of his life, or a woman had her kid crushed by a drunk driver in a hovercar," she'd add.

True, I had no serious tragedies to complain about. No great losses. No disabilities. I had all my fingers, toes, limbs, and other natural organs—not a bionic part anywhere. Metropolis hadn't been bad to me.

Everyone simply had to accept it all. I did. But this was an especially bad year of reflection for me, which is why I was here sitting in my red Ford Pony, hiding out on a street I've never been, far from any part of the city I had ever been, so I could just sit, stare at the falling rain, and simmer in my own perennial moroseness and not be bothered by the girlfriend, friends, enemies, frenemies, the sidewalk johnnies, hustlers, or any strangers.

Recap

Why do you want to embark on your new plan to change yourself or an aspect of your life or do something you always wanted to do? It'll distract you the most, if you can't explain why you're doing something.

Motivations matter, and knowing them helps you stay focused on your journey. The answer could be very simple: "live healthier," "cross it off my bucket list," "time for a change." But whatever the reason is, know it before you start, as it will shape your overall plan.

Cruz was a simple laborer in the supercity of Metropolis, meaning he did odd jobs to pay the bills. However, he wanted to do more and be more—it was that simple for him. The desire to change was always there, but he didn't know how to go about it. However, he knew the "why."

Who's Run-Time?

"CAPITALIZE," I HEARD Run-Time's voice in my mind. "Capitalize on your opportunities, or someone else will."

CRUZ'S CHILDHOOD BEST friend and mega-millionaire founder, President, and CEO of Let It Ride Enterprises.

Run-Time was a hovercar mechanic at thirteen, valet attendant at fourteen, hovertaxi driver at seventeen, hovertaxicab owner at nineteen, buying three more at twenty-one. He became a millionaire at twenty-two, started Let It Ride Enterprises at twenty-five, and mega-multi-millionaire by thirty. Run-Time and Cruz became friends when they were both kids in middle school.

Business

Run-Time is a "Who's Who" among the wealthy elite of the supercity of Metropolis, and he wasn't even forty yet. But there was nothing "elite" about him. He owned all the top car washes, hovercar body shops, hovercar rental shops, hovercycle rental shops, hovertaxicabs, and hoverlimousine services in the city. Anything that had to do with private transportation, Run-Time had his hands in it.

But the operation that surpassed every other line of his businesses was his mobile hovercar security services. The hovercar remained the top luxury item in the city, despite ubiquitous public transportation and commercial hovertaxicab services. With virtually every city resident in some type of legacy housing, it was hovercars that people spent virtually all their discretionary income on. Such an investment demanded some kind of protection, and Run-Time was there to fill the need. Call Let It Ride, and a rep would descend from the sky via jetpack to guard your precious investment hourly, nightly, or daily. No one messed with your car when Let It Ride was protecting it.

Cruz had been a client of Run-Time's for years, one of his premium customers and, long before that, a best friend. Run-Time realized the hard way: the higher up the wealth ladder one went, the smaller the number of people one could genuinely call "friend." In all the years Run-Time had known Cruz, Cruz never once asked for a favor or money.

Dress

Run-Time never wore sweats or hoodies. Monday to Thursday, he wore his slim-fit business suits and slim ties, and on casual Fridays and the weekends, if he came in, he left the tie at home. The only casual thing he wore was his trademark flat cap. You'd never see his head without it, and you'd never see him wearing it backward. He didn't have to work as hard as he did now that he'd "made it"—he could hire people to run his business for him, while he lived the pampered, human vegetable, booshy life, but that wasn't in Run-Time's DNA. He was the hardest worker around among his fifty-five-thousand-plus-employee corporation. His people worked hard, and he paid them well for it.

Locations

Peacock Hills was one of the premier business districts in the city. From a distance—a long, long distance—the monolith buildings looked like gargantuan fingers extending into space through the city's rain cloud cover. Each was illuminated in the conservative colors of white, light yellow, and blue. As with most of the city's buildings, the roof lighting of each structure reflected off the sky, giving them the appearance of having angelic halos.

Run-Time exited the elevator on the penthouse level, two hundred and fifty floors up, and did as he always did. "Good morning, good ladies," he greeted.

He was not a boss who demanded that staff snap to attention at his arrival. His philosophy was, "If you can't give me a high-five fist bump, or shake my hand like a normal person, then you're working at the wrong place. I'm just a guy, not a dictator or the Second Coming."

Three women sat at the reception desk, evenly spaced apart from each other. "Good morning, Mr. Run-Time," the receptionists responded in unison.

Week 2: No Mind Gutters

RUN-TIME: "KEEP OUT of the Mind Gutter" and Take the Encouragement, or Encourage Yourself, For the Long Journey

EXCERPT FROM: *Liquid Cool: The Cyberpunk Detective Series (Book One)*

Cruz and Run-Time sitting in the hovercar, talking about life.

"Nothing." I sighed loudly. "All I want out of life is to get ahead and be content with what I've accomplished. All I can say at this stage of my life is that I'm a laborer. That's my listed occupation—laborer. That was my listed occupation when I was in high school, so I've accomplished nothing."

"Cruz, why would you say that?"

"Because it's true. I've been so principled. I wouldn't work for the government or some multinational, sitting in some cubicle. Yeah, and all my friends who did are managers and supervisors, and I sit in my little red vehicle as a laborer. When do I get my break? How long do I have to wait for my one break? I'm getting so tired."

"Cruz, everybody is struggling. Don't be fooled. You want to be them, and they want to be you. Everyone always thinks the grass is greener on the other side. Be patient. Your ticket will come.

"I know it looks nice on my company biography. The 'Run-Time rags-to-riches' story. I didn't drop out of middle school at eleven to begin my path of becoming a self-made millionaire. I dropped out because I realized it was all pointless. Stay in and get good grades and amount to not much, like my father and so many others. Turn to crime like my uncle and so many others, and end up dead or in jail. Those were my choices, I asked myself. Who makes up these rules? They say you have to be able to figuratively bend a spoon with your mind to make it in Metropolis. Says who? I said there was no spoon. I said the system is rigged, but not by the powerful. It's rigged by the powerless trapped within it. The power to be either the powerless or the powerful is and has always been in my hands alone. I knew the cards the cosmos had dealt me from birth. This was my path in life, but was it my true destiny? No. That's exactly why I seized the opportunities I did. Because I knew what the future was, so why not make a different one? There's not a single, solitary thing to lose.

"Cruz, keep your nose clean as you always have, and your ticket will come. That much I can promise you. Don't mess it up now. You have too many years invested. You and I both have seen what happens to those who went for the quick fix or supposed sure thing, instead of being patient."

I always liked talking to Run-Time. He was a born motivational coach and life counselor. It's why we were friends for all these years. He talked the talk, and he exuded positivity. That's what I needed. I was too much of a glass-half-empty kind of guy. I needed to surround myself with the Run-Times and Dots of the world to pull myself out of the mind gutter.

"Yeah," I agreed soberly. "It's hard to be patient when everyone is passing you by. An endless rat race, but I'm not getting anywhere."

"You got solid legacy housing, an amazing girlfriend, and a classic car that everyone wants. The housing and the car are just things, but don't discount Dot in your life. You got a lot more going for you in life than you're acknowledging. Here's the thing, Cruz. Just because people are passing you by doesn't mean they'll finish the race. Just because they're passing you by, doesn't mean they're going anywhere. Just remain Cruz, the cool cat that you are, and your ticket will come."

Perspective

Encouragement Can Make All the Difference

Excerpt From: Liquid Cool: The Cyberpunk Detective Series (Book One)

Cruz met up with his friend at the Let It Ride headquarters after finishing his first-ever job as a detective for hire.

"Run-Time, I can't take all that money for just a few city stops in the Pony."

"Cruz, the money is yours. I'm satisfied. Nat's satisfied. What do you plan to do now?"

"I'm not sure. I have a few construction gigs coming up and a big car restoration job at the end of the month."

"You can still do those. What do you plan to do career-wise?"

"I don't know a thing about being a detective."

"What's to know? It was like asking me what there's to know about being a company CEO. You do it, and you do it long enough; you become it. And it would seem you already have a head start on the promotion front."

"What do you mean?"

"Who's this guy called Phishy?"

"That Phishy!"

Run-Time laughed. "He could be your marketing genius, so be nice to him."

Run-Time was all about encouraging people to do more in their lives. I had seen him do so a million times, so this was my turn. As a legacy baby, I did have more free time than I knew what to do with.

"I'll give it a whirl and see what happens."

"Get some business cards."

"Business cards?"

"Everything becomes real when you have some snazzy business cards. People take you seriously because serious people, at the very least, have business cards. You know that. Sidewalk johnnies have business cards."

I laughed this time.

"That they do," I said.

I stood from my chair and did a patented Run-Time handshake. Shake the hand, but don't let go until you finish what you have to say.

"I really appreciate your faith in me on this. I know how serious it was and how serious it had the potential to become. I won't forget it. I owe you one."

"You owe me nothing. We've been friends for years, and that's what friends do."

I let go of his hand and said no more. He gave me a playful pat on the shoulder and this time, he walked me to the elevator capsules.

Recap

We cannot underestimate the power of encouragement. Some of us can be our own motivators; others need the help of others. Cruz simply needed some encouragement and help from his friends. That turned out to be Cruz's biggest asset in his quest to change his life. As negative as Cruz was about life, he only hung around positive people who were successful doers in their own lives. You are who you surround yourself with.

Also, be the encouragement for yourself. An old saying is, "Your Attitude Determines Your Altitude." Believe you can do it. If you don't believe in your own success, then you'll definitely achieve failure.

One day, success did rub off on Cruz. They gave him his chance at something more, but he was the one who recognized and seized it. No one can do that for you. He did the hard work to make his new life a reality to the cheers of the working class of Metropolis—and the curses of the criminal class. The Liquid Cool Detective Agency was born.

Who's PJ?

"I HATE LONG SLEEVES. Long sleeves are for squares. I got nice (bionic) arms, and they deserve to be shown off. If punks see these muscles, they won't be quick to cause any trouble."

CRUZ'S CYBORG SECRETARY who's promoted herself to VP of Client Services.

My one employee had the street name of Punch Judy. When you knew she was a cyborg with two very impressive bionic arms, that made sense. But she was Punch Judy even before her "accident." My ex-felon, cyborg secretary, was a soldier in the punk-posh gang Les Enfantes Terribles in Neo-Paris, France. She got her street name because she liked to punch people and was quite good at it. Now, she could even punch a three-hundred-pound cyborg through a steel and concrete wall—and had. She only wore sleeveless tops to show off her buff bionic arms.

Today, PJ had short, crimson hair and a simulated mole—a dot above her lips, matching her crimson lipstick-covered lips. Hip, female business suits were what she wore nowadays—sleeveless tops, knee-high skirts, heeled leather boots. We started out as frenemies, but she was my respectable second in command these days.

I walked through the front door and was met by her French ska music playing.

Past Life

Back in the day, Judy was a soldier in the punk-posh gang, Les Enfants Terribles in Neo-Paris, France. Haute-couture designer clothes—the most expensive right off the racks of Goodwill—with fashion-matched combat boots, knuckle-studded leather, half-gloves, and Devo-style half-helmets on their rainbow-colored, punk hair. They were "royalty."

But then, the gang got greedy, and it all went wrong. They started to believe their own hype and tried to extend their territory way beyond the French quarters. Posh gangs never do well in direct confrontation with feral gangs of chaos or long-game, Moriarty-planning, brainiac gangs. It was like the Fall of Old Paris all over again. Les Enfants Terribles, The Terrible Children gang, was decimated in mere days by rival (real) gangs in one show of unity. The gang war left many parts of Neo-Paris burning and most of the Les Enfants Terribles dead.

PJ was crazy, even then, when it came to loyalty. She could not let it go and went to war with all of them by herself, tracking key leaders outside of the country. A murderous chase through the streets of Metropolis in her self-made death mobile led to a horrific accident, pinning her body in a burning wreck as enemy gang members stood and laughed nearby. Then Cruz happened.

Her Domain

My office was my domain. I did all the decorating, had the furniture moved in, had stupid pictures on the wall to cover it, and all the secret stuff, like hiding my big shotgun underneath my main desk where I could get to it easily.

PJ ruled the reception area. It would be like an ex-posh gang member to have an haute couture interior design decorating sense. With her punk rock playing in the background on an infinite loop, she had turned the barren space into some hipster, scenester receptionist-waiting room of the stars. Psychedelic posters on the wall, her fancy "modern" glass desk with see-through glass drawers, and a boombox on top, along with her own mobile computer. All of her workstation was behind a metal barrier, but it didn't look like a barrier with the decorations. The waiting area had these geometric, purple couches around a glass table on a shimmering, neon powder blue rug. The reception table had French fashion magazines, which

I thought was stupid because how could people read them, but then I realized—fashion magazines—so that meant lots and lots of pictures with few words, so it didn't matter, and numerical prices were universal.

Now, she was working on her own do-it-yourself neon light sign. I don't know where she found it, but she was busy at work, making a LIQUID COOL sign for the space she designated right on the wall behind her, outside my office. It would be the first thing people would see. She even had another box in smaller neon letters to make DETECTIVE AGENCY. I was impressed.

Week 3: We All Got Problems

TO PJ: "*WE ALL GOT problems, Punch. Every last person in this city has problems, even the ones who pretend they don't.*"

EXCERPT FROM: LIQUID Cool: The Cyberpunk Detective Series (Book One)

Four of the local sidewalk johnnies watched her.

"I'm sorry," she said to them.

"I thought you were one of us, Punch," one of them said.

One could see the men were dressed decently under their gray slicker coats. It must have been a multi-buy sale because the slickers were identical and all had their hoods covering their heads. Their faces were another matter. Weathered faces with scraggly mustaches, beards, and heads of hair. This particular crew of sidewalk johnnies wore subtle yellow shades.

"I am one of you," she answered, standing to her feet.

"That's not how it sounded when you were talking on the mobile, Punch. It's like you're ashamed of us," another man said.

"No, that's not true. She was disrespecting you, not me. I'm an adopted sidewalk sally. You know that. I have problems. You know that."

"We all got problems, Punch. Every last person in this city has problems, even the ones who pretend they don't."

"Absolutely true." She walked down the steps towards them and could see in their expressions that they were not happy with her. "No hard feelings. I'm always here with you. We look out for each other. Isn't that true?"

"Yeah, but if you don't want to associate with us anymore—"

"No! I won't hear any more about it. We are the guardians of the streets. We know better than anybody what the street is capable of. We must stay united because the street can get angry. We're the line of defense against that. Besides, you know I say all kinds of things. That's why I try to keep from talking. When I talk, fifty percent of what comes out of my mouth will be stupid. Isn't that true?"

The men smiled.

"Okay, Punch. Everyone deserves another chance," one of them answered.

Perspective

When You Have the Wrong Mindset, Everything is a Problem

EXCERPT FROM: LIQUID Cool: The Cyberpunk Detective Series (Book One)

PJ placed her cigarette in the corner of her mouth as she reached into her jacket pocket. As soon as she flipped it on, it rang. She looked at the outside display screen but didn't recognize the number.

She answered it and saw the tiny face of China Doll on the display.

"How did you get my number?"

"Where's Cruz?"

"Why are you asking me?"

"Maybe because you're the sidewalk sally who sits in front of his building all day long."

"I am not a sidewalk sally!"

"Where's Cruz?"

"I don't know, and I don't care, and I wouldn't tell you if I did know and care."

"Tell him I'm looking for him."

"No, I won't."

"And call me immediately."

"No."

"As soon as you see him."

"No."

"Now you can go back to doing whatever nothing you were doing, you sidewalk sally."

"I am not a sidewalk sally! I live in this building!"

"Whatever."

"I am—"

It clicked before she could finish. She cursed in French and crushed the mobile phone to pieces with her bionic hand.

Recap

The irony is that Cruz and PJ lived in the same building but started out hating each other. PJ resented him for saving her life in Neo-Paris. Cruz resented her for resenting him. But credit goes to Cruz for looking past all that and recognizing in her the potential to be the very person he needed for the job—his first Liquid Cool Detective Agency employee.

But nothing is ever that easy. PJ yelled at him, called him names, and flatly turned down his job offer—all out of anger. But PJ had been doing the same thing Cruz had been doing for years—hiding from life. She no longer lived in Neo-Paris, wasn't a top person in her gang, and still couldn't forget the accident that made her a cyborg despite boasting about her bionic arms. She couldn't move forward with life because all she saw were her problems. Then Cruz came along.

He hired her as "secretary" but has been self-promoting herself seemingly in every book.

Who's Dot?

"I'VE KILLED PEOPLE with these boots!" (joking) (maybe?)

CRUZ'S GIRLFRIEND, then wife and second-in-command fashionista at the renowned Eye Candy Salon.

She went by China Doll, but women who knew her called her China; men called her Doll. Only her family and Cruz called her by her real name—Dot.

Business

She was the consummate fashionista, with every piece of clothing, every accessory, and every piece of jewelry being the trendiest and the most stylish. Leaving all that aside, they made her look "film quality." Today, she was adorned in a luminescent halter top under a glossy leather jacket, a sapphire blue pearl belt wrapped around her waist, black skin-tight pants, and topped off with black heels adorned with faux-diamond glitter. Her hair was tied back, with the ponytail carefully resting on one shoulder, always a colored neck scarf—today in basic black—and her makeup was always perfect and never overdone. Every finger had a colored ring, and each wrist had multiple bracelets.

Eye Candy Image Salon was always packed with customers from the time it opened until its late-night closing. Women came from every corner of Metropolis to be made to look like movie stars with its "fashion police" of makeup artists, hairdressers, manicurists, pedicurists, skincare techs, tattoo artists, wardrobe stylists, and even dressers to assemble their wardrobe if needed. The establishment was owned by Prima Donna, the Matron Queen of Metropolis fashion, who still had the magic touch after so many decades and personally tended to their oldest and highest-tipping clients.

China Doll was Prima's number one and was boss in her absence. Like every other fashionista employee, she wasn't some by-the-hour laborer. This was a coveted and highly competitive career, and everyone who worked in the parlor had advanced degrees in beauty and skincare, fashion and style arts, health, and nutrition.

The interior of Eye Candy was designed like a beehive design, and every section was visible due to its transparent walls, to every other section, except the break room, full body baths, and the bathrooms. Eye Candy was nothing but carefully coordinated chaos—women sitting on chairs getting their hair and makeup done in one section, their nails and toenails in another, facials in another, tattoos in another (always temporary to change according to current fashion trends), skincare consultations in another, and style analysis wardrobing in yet another section.

Week 4: Believe Me, Others Have Had Worse Tragedies Than You

CHINA DOLL/DOT: "MRS. Fancy, come on down and get that cougar self in my chair."

EXCERPT FROM: *You'll Never See Starlight Again (Liquid Cool, Book Ten)*

That's how I met China Doll—real name Dot. And the future Mrs. Cruz.

As the months went on, our Phobias Anonymous Support Group class would finally get up to its thirty-five court-appointed attendees, but we'd learn none of us had anywhere near the phobia of China Doll. We were a group of people afraid of water bugs, mirrors, and silly things. We should have been ashamed of ourselves. Dot, however, had been a professional, amateur hover-go-cart racer as a little girl with a competitive streak to match any seasoned race driver three times her age at the time. One fateful day of racing, she pulled ahead of her two rivals before going under a bridge, but she was going too fast. She didn't react as she should have; she didn't duck down enough. Her vehicle and body went under the bridge... but her head didn't. The stars were aligned in her favor that day because medics happened to be standing right there. Dot became a cyborg that day—neck, top of shoulders, and spinal column all bionic. However, the nightmares of such a horrific freak accident haunted her into adulthood. She had been conscious the entire incident. Wouldn't you be scared of bridges, too, if that happened to you?

After meeting China Doll, I decided to put an end to my phobia demons right then and there. The whole class did. Our phobias could never compete with hers—not even close.

Perspective

Trauma is a Real Thing

EXCERPT FROM: *Liquid Cool: The Cyberpunk Detective Series (Book One)*

Getting a hovertaxi was like playing Russian roulette. You never knew what you'd get. Would you get a driver who knew the city and would get you where you wanted fast? Would you get a scammer who'd take the longest possible way to charge you absolutely the most he could get away with? Would you get the idiot newbie who had no clue where he was going? Dot and I got none of that; we got the rudest bum possible.

Why didn't I call Run-Time? One of my corporate clients (who paid his bill promptly) had an uncle. The uncle owned this hovercab company, and it was part of my arrangement to get a good review and more referrals. So here Dot and I were—the first and last time.

"Driver," I said.

Dot didn't see it, but I did. There was no reason we should have been in the sky-lane we were in. The guy was either lost or trying to gouge us on fares. We were heading for a bridge, and I knew if I didn't get control of the situation fast, things were going to get very bad.

"Driver," I repeated. "I need you to slow down and pull to the side."

The driver either was ignoring me or had music playing in his ears.

Dot saw the approaching bridge and screamed out. The driver reacted and glanced back at us.

"Pull the cab to the side and stop!" I yelled.

"What's happening?" he yelled back.

Dot's eyes were closed tight, her teeth were clenched, and she was in the beginning stages of a violent fit.

"Pull the cab to the side!"

"Why? What's happening?"

My anger took me, and I pulled my piece from my jacket and pounded on the glass partition between the driver and the passenger seats. I grabbed it and slid it to the right so the only thing separating us was his seat. In the rearview mirror, I saw the driver's eyes had opened to the size of baseballs, as he knew what I was about to do. He jerked the steering wheel to the right and took the hovercab out of the main sky-lane to the side, and stopped just as I was about to yank his head back through the space between the front and back.

"Move into the passenger seat!" I yelled.

"Are you crazy? We're three hundred feet in the air..."

"Put it in park!"

He continued to protest, but I had already opened the passenger door and was out, my foot on the side steps. I clung to the hovercab as I looked down, then kept moving. We were over thirty stories up, hovering in the air, as every kind of hovercar and van whipped past us. I opened the driver's side and was ready to pummel him, but he was already in the passenger seat.

"Don't shoot me, mister. You can have the hovercab."

I jumped into the driver's seat and fastened the seat belt. "You bum! Why didn't you do what I said?"

"I'm sorry."

"I should shoot you."

"You can take it."

"I own a classic Ford Pony, free and clear. Why would I want your dirty ol' hovercab!"

"You can take it."

I disengaged the air-brake, looked into the traffic, and pushed the cab into drive. I took the cab down to the lowest sky-lane—one story up, then moved to practically touching the ground.

"Dot!"

The driver looked at me and then to the backseat, where Dot was fighting a complete mental collapse.

"It's okay. We stopped, and we're close to the ground. We're close to the club, so it makes no sense to turn around now. Come up to the front and get in your position." I leaned towards the driver with menace and yelled, "Get in the back!"

The driver leaped out of the seat and climbed over the seat into the back.

Dot took a while to calm down and slowly come out of it. Finally, she opened her eyes and looked around. The driver was quiet as a mouse but watched both of us. Dot climbed into the passenger seat next to me and reclined it as far back as it would go as the dumb driver moved behind my seat.

"It's okay," I said. "I'm putting it in drive, but I'll go slow."

The one thing drivers in this city hated more than hoverbikers was slow drivers. They hated them with a passion. They'd shoot them out of the sky or have someone else do it if they could legally get away with it. We were the slow driver. I never exceeded fifty miles an hour with an uproar of honking hovercars all around us. We were far from the fast lane, but it didn't matter. We were a moving hazard.

As we passed under the bridge, Dot closed her eyes again and gripped the armrests with all her might. We were under, through, and out. Dot's eyes opened slightly, and her breathing started to get back to normal. When we were far enough away, I put it in gear, and we were off. I was up and into the fast lane. We made it to Booty Shakers in no time.

Booty Shakers wasn't just a dance club. It was one of the platinum dance clubs, and you didn't set foot inside unless you planned to dance all night long nonstop and have obscene amounts of fun. No one ever left there unsatisfied, and when you did, you were ten to twenty pounds lighter from all that sweating on the dance floor.

I pulled up to their valet service. Self-park was not allowed, and I immediately got out before the valet could get to the driver's side and opened the back passenger door. I yanked the driver out.

"Please don't shoot me. You can take it."

I leaned close to him. "When my girlfriend was a little girl, she was a go-cart champion. Won races all over the country. At one of those races, they had this brand-new course, the hardest course ever for the kiddies. One of the obstacles was a path that went under a bridge. Well, you can see where I'm going with this story. Those kiddies were going around the course at 80 miles per hour. My girlfriend was in the lead, but she had to win and pushed her go-cart to 100 miles per hour. Her go-cart hit a bump and jumped the course just as she went under the bridge. She was decapitated. Lucky for her and me, there was a medical team right there, and they were able to save her. Her neck and all down to her shoulder is bionic. So you can imagine what such a trauma like that would do to a child, especially when you clearly remember your head lying on the ground and your entire body in the go-cart ten feet away from you. You can imagine what going under any bridge as an adult could do to you. You could imagine what a driver not stopping his dirty hovercab and ignoring her boyfriend's call to pull to the side and stop could do."

"Mister, your point has been made in the clearest possible way. There's no charge for the fare."

Recap

If you're wondering if Week Four is the same as Week Three, it's not. By no means do I wish to minimize real-life trauma people have experienced. A "problem" and "trauma" are not the same thing, and we should clearly acknowledge that. You don't need to be an army veteran like me to realize this.

The Liquid Cool series has a lot of twists, turns, action, and humor, but it also deals with serious things since Cruz is a bona fide private detective on the gritty, grimy Metropolis streets facing off against some very violent criminals and clients, or "crazy maniacs" as he often calls them. But let's not forget in Dot's case—guys, she got decapitated as a kid! That's much more than a "problem."

However, Dot took a very different path than PJ. Dot never let her trauma get in the way of her life and career for one nanosecond. That was her mindset from the start. She succeeded triumphantly. Not everyone can do that, but she did, and others have, too. They are all positive role models to be recognized.

Also, she did not ignore the trauma. She got the help she needed on her own terms. Unfortunately, too many people suffer in silence, and we must do better at encouraging people not to do so. As a bonus for Dot, she met her future husband, Cruz, in that Phobias Anonymous Support Group.

Who's Wilford G.?

FROM THE TIME WE LEFT his place, and now, I was noticing his snazzy two-color loafers. The man had some cool shoes on his feet.

CRUZ'S (POSTHUMOUS) mentor in his new vocation as a private investigator.

I wished I had met Mr. Wilford G., the 92-year-old private eye. He lived and had a lot less than I had.

The book I found myself glued to was not the 1,000-page tomes of the first category or the 400 page-turners of the second, but this 60-page book titled *How to be a Great Detective with 100 Rules*. It was written by a guy who had been a private eye for 70-plus years. In fact, he died only a few years ago at the age of 92 and had worked right until the end. The book was brilliant. I had read it five times already and was reading it again. The rules seemed basic, but his one-paragraph explanation of each was packed with real insight and his own folksy, street-wise expertise. He was the real McCoy—not any fake movie-land detective. You could tell by the way he communicated. He must have led an amazing life. To live 92 years in Metropolis—the things he saw and experienced. It's too bad he didn't write a compilation of his life through his cases.

I had my trademark tan fedora and slicker. How does one replace a legend? I was a former hovercar restorer. I fell into the street detective business like a drunk tripped over his own feet to fall onto the wet pavement. There was no plan. It just happened. I felt so…inadequate since then. I was the heir to Wilford G.? That didn't seem right somehow. It would be like someone saying they had *the* replacement for my classic hovervehicle and then showed up on a red hoverskateboard. Seriously? A skateboard to replace a classic red

Ford Pony? I'd smack that person for such an insult. The successor to the great Wilford G. was me? It felt insulting. I was insulted.

Week 5: Or Would You Want to Switch Places

WILFORD G. TO CRUZ: "Me? You're the one fainting and running from imaginary isopods. I expected you to be at the hard-boiled, steel-grip detective level by now. Instead, you're giggling and fainting in front of me."

EXCERPT FROM: *A.I. Confidential (Liquid Cool: The Cyberpunk Detective Series, Book Six)*

Cruz and G are at G's apartment.

"Here, catch."

Wilford G. threw me a block of wood. I almost dropped it when I saw what it was—a baby isopod encased in a clear, solid resin in the middle.

"YOUR DAY IS MUCH BETTER THAN HIS—OR WOULD YOU LIKE TO SWITCH PLACES?"

I didn't even know what to do. I took his point, but I was not putting it in my jacket, which meant I'd be carrying it for the day.

"It's small enough to fit in your pocket," he said.

"I'll hold it."

"You do that, but I hope you were listening to me."

"I heard you."

"Good, then that bit is closed until the case is done. Let's get on into the Skanky Squirrel."

I laughed. Already Wilford managed to make me forget that I was angry with him. "Sketchy Squirrel."

Perspective

Gratitude is a Key Foundational Element of Positive Thinking and Action

---

EXCERPT FROM: *Liquid Cool: The Cyberpunk Detective Series (Book One)*

I had gone my entire life without ever even getting a speeding ticket. No arrests, no jail time, nothing. No trouble with police, ever. Now I had gotten shot at three times in a space of two weeks! I had to get smart fast, or I'd get dead faster. There were no other options. I was in a job industry right on the ground floor of the city's mean streets. The streets obviously didn't like me.

How did that poem go? "These Mean Streets, Darkly. With its Cornucopia of Clients and Villains, Starkly." It was the opening quote in my How to be a Great Detective with 100 Rules I had now purchased to be my industry bible on my newly chosen vocation.

I needed to think about all this carefully. This detective life "ain't no joke," as they say. This was a job that immersed you in the grime and crime of the city, and there were no two ways about it. People would shoot at me, and I'd have to shoot back at them. There'd be fisticuffs and all kinds of violence.

Mr. Wilford G. was lucky making it to 92. I, as a modern-day detective, better get as mean as the mean streets of Metropolis, or I'd be meat in the morgue. I had to decide fast. Be a detective and embrace the life, or quit it now and forever. Whatever I decided had to be final. Mr. Wilford G. said it in his book. There's nothing glamorous about this life—nothing. Some felt it was fantastic, but then they weren't private-eyeing for a living.

I took a deep sigh and made the hard decision. I would quit. I wasn't cut out for this, and I was getting married. Dot wasn't cut out for this life. A lot of people would be disappointed, but I was the one dodging bullets. If they like it so much, then they could be the detective. I'd go back to my hovercar restoration gigs.

Wait! I couldn't. I already did the full order for all my business cards—and PJ's, too. Oh, snaps! And the payment was non-refundable.

Recap

His new life had arrived. Cruz was a real detective. Then it seemed he would give it all up, but he didn't because he'd already ordered his business cards? No, not true. He had a free office, a cyborg secretary, and already a few cases. He was not about to give up any of it without a fight.

Wilford G. was a very no-nonsense, old-school street Metropolis detective. He'd acknowledge that "Life's not fair." Then he'd say "So what? Be grateful anyway."

Gratitude and thankfulness are not the same thing, though.

When you're thankful, you acknowledge and show appreciation for what someone has given or done for you. We can express this feeling with a simple "thank you." Gratitude or gratefulness is appreciating something done or received, or, even more so, it's a state of being. It's more than the feeling but a mindset.

You should mix gratitude into the center of your being, as it is a powerful, positive emotion. Be grateful for no other reason than you have the opportunity and ability to change yourself or your life, do something new or big, and accomplish something. Always remember, not everyone can say that.

Questions to ask yourself:

- What are you grateful for?

- Who was the last person you thanked?

- Why?

If you can't answer these three questions readily, that should become your task or open-ended challenge (i.e., homework assignment) until you can.

SECOND MONTH
February
Classic Sci-Fi Actor Birthdays

CHARACTER (ACTOR) SHOW/Movie

February 1: Dr. Carol Marcus (Bibi Besch) Star Trek: The Wrath of Khan

February 1: Lennier (Bill Mumy) Babylon 5

February 2: Data (Brent Spiner) Star Trek: The Next Generation

February 3: Temporal Agent Daniels (Matt Winston) Star Trek: Enterprise

February 4: Private Vasquez (Jenette Goldstein) Aliens

February 5: Sarris (Robin Sachs) Galaxy Quest

February 8: Neelix (Ethan Phillips) Star Trek: Voyager

February 12: Commander Adama (Lorne Greene) Battle Star Galactica (Original Series)

February 14: Mathesar (Enrico Colantoni) Galaxy Quest

February 14: Elim Garak (Andrew Robinson) Star Trek: Deep Space 9

February 16: Boba Fett V-VI (Jeremy Bulloch) Star Wars: Original Movies

February 16: Geordi LaForge (LeVar Burton) Star Trek: The Next Generation

February 16: Joolushko Tunai Fenta Hovalis or just "Jool" (Tammy Macintosh) Farscape

February 16: Kosh (Ardwight Chamberlain) Babylon 5

February 16: The (9th) Doctor (Christopher Eccleston) Dr. Who

February 17: Ro Laren (Michelle Forbes) Star Trek: The Next Generation

February 20: Leon (Brion James) Blade Runner (Original Movie)

February 21: Alexander Dane/Dr. Lazarus (Alan Rickman) Galaxy Quest

February 21: C-3PO (Anthony Daniels) Star Wars

February 22: Seven of Nine (Jeri Lynn Ryan) Star Trek: Voyager

February 22: Chew (James Hong) Blade Runner (Original Movie)

February 23: Nurse Christine Chapel/Star Trek: The Original Series & Luwaxana Troi/Star Trek: The Next Generation (Majel Barrett)

February 24: Gaff (Edward James Olmos) Blade Runner (Original Movie)

February 27: Spock (Leonard Nimoy) Star Trek: The Original Series

THE ACTION MINDSET

ABOUT ACTION

"Do. Or do not. There is no try." — *Yoda, Star Wars: The Original Movies*

Action plus Consistency equals Success. Don't be distracted by the setbacks or failures along the way. You reach your goals through the work, not daydreaming about it.

Excerpt From: *Liquid Cool: The Cyberpunk Detective Series (Book One)*

It wasn't Peacock Hills, where the city's biggest and best non-tech megacorps were housed (tech corps were all in Silicon Dunes). I was on Fat Street, where the second-tier companies were clawing at each other to get into the top echelons of business. It wasn't the Dumps, and there wasn't any real street crime, as it was fairly well-patrolled by police, but still, it was grimier than I preferred. Easy's sister-in-law was probably right—I was a bit booshy.

Today was my first shoe-leather day after almost a week of biz research. GW was my first real client—start to finish—and I had no one else since then, so I was on a mission, doing what all the business books tell you. Get off your butt and find your next client.

"I'm here to see Mr. Smalls," I said to the lobby receptionist.

"He's expecting you?" she asked.

"Yeah," I replied with a lie. "Here's my card."

She took the card from my hand, read it, and looked up at me.

"Detective?"

"Yes, private detective."

The woman almost seemed frightened. "I'll announce you immediately."

People-Droid had been the seventeenth company, or so I visited. I started at the first business tower on the corner and would work my way up each tower, then down the street. This was the first company on the third floor; I had 100 more floors to go, and each had six businesses, on average. I figured my shoe-leather soliciting would take me a few years to complete just this district.

"Mr. Smalls will see you, Mr. Cruz."

I knew I had stumbled into something. Every other business took my card and told me that the person I asked for would call me, meaning they'd throw my card in the garbage the second I left the office. At some point, one of them would undoubtedly call building security on me to have the "solicitor" (me) escorted from the tower.

I followed the woman down one hallway to the first office on the left, which meant either my research was faulty, or they purposely had misleading public information. If Mr. Smalls was the president, as their site said, he wouldn't be in the first office in the hallway; he'd be at the last office at the end of the hallway.

She opened the door for me to enter.

A man stood there with an annoyed look on his face.

"Cruz," I said as I extended my arm, and he reluctantly shook my hand.

"The detective?"

"Yes," I answered.

"That was pretty fast. Are your offices outside our doors?"

"I would love to play along, especially if it led to a new client, but you must have me confused with someone else."

"You're not the detective we called?"

"I'm a detective, but no, I'm not the one you called."

"Who are you then?"

"I've been checking in with businesses to see if they could use my services."

"Soliciting is not allowed in this building or any other, Mr. Cruz."

"Talking to a person is allowable on the entire planet, as far as I know. We're just talking."

"We have already called a real detective agency, so we won't be needing you."

"Big firm, are they?"

"One of the largest."

"I can understand that, but I doubt you will be happy with their system."

"System? What system?"

"For the big investigation firms, new clients are considered one-offs, so they will send in their little flunky, entry-level agents who will come in here and do more talking than listening, trying to up-sell you on all kinds of other services you don't need, rather than being interested in the situation you originally called them for. Sole practitioner agencies, like mine—I'm the guy. President, CEO, COO, and detective on the go. I don't pass you on to any flunkies. I handle your business directly because I want your business. Big firms want clients with ongoing, recurring business. That's what pays for their high overhead and exorbitant salaries. Me, no car payments, legacy office space, one employee—minimal overhead."

"Mr. Cruz, that's all well and good, but I need an established firm to handle this matter."

"I understand, but let me ask you this: Do you remember when you started your career and you were hungry?" I waited for his expression. He tried to maintain his poker face. "That's me now, not some version of myself twenty years later. I do have references, too, if it matters."

"I'm sure your references will not be of the caliber..."

"Let It Ride Enterprises, for instance."

"You've done work for them?"

"Run-Time is a personal friend."

"I don't believe you."

"You can check, but I think you really should compare my presentation to the flunkies they're about to send you. But Mr. Smalls, I understand you need to make the best business decision for your company. Here's my business card—it has my mobile on it—and if you change your mind, I'll get myself back to your office. I want to establish a good clientele of corporate businesses, such as yours."

The man took my card and glanced at it.

"I'll let myself out, but thank you for the opportunity to present."

I left the office.

I DIDN'T EXPECT TO ever hear from the man. I just consigned myself to a very, very long day of shoe-leather soliciting. That's all I could do. I had to make my own connections. No one would do it for me. Every business guy and gal I ever met said the same thing: Starting a business is brutal, but once you get your first client, number two is easier, and then comes number three, four, and five. Then you reach a critical mass where those first ones start sending you business automatically. But be prepared for the initial orgy of unfiltered, soul-crushing rejection. Well, this day was already that, except for the brief chat with Smalls.

I had already done the other offices on the floor, so it was up to the fourth floor. As I exited the elevator, I felt my mobile vibrating.

"Liquid Cool Detective Agency. This is Cruz speaking."

"Mr. Cruz." It was Smalls' voice. "You can return to my office. My boss has decided not to go with the other detective firm we called. We'll give you a chance. When can you get back here?"

"I'll be back there in a few minutes."

Recap

Give it to Cruz to jump into the deep end of the pool of his newly adopted vocation as a private detective with his best aqua-shoes right from the start. Random people, random businesses. Outside his comfort zone. But he did the work, and none of it was easy.

He got his chance. Mentally, he went from "one day, I will" to "this is day one" of the new life.

Most people don't fail because they can't be consistent or quit too soon. They fail because they don't even start.

The Planners

BE (LIQUID) COOL/MONTHLY PLANNER

MONTH:

SUN	MON	TUE	WED	THU	FRI	SAT

TOP PRIORITIES / GOALS

PEOPLE TO SEE / PLACES TO GO / REMINDERS

NOTES

RATE / ASSESS THE MONTH:

BE (LIQUID) COOL
WEEKLY PLANNER

WEEK:

M T W H F S S

MONDAY

TUESDAY

WEDNESDAY

THURSDAY

FRIDAY

SATURDAY / SUNDAY

WEEK'S PRIORITIES / TO DO

NOTES

RATE / ASSESS THE WEEK:

BE (LIQUID) COOL
WEEKLY PLANNER

WEEK: M T W H F S S

MONDAY

TUESDAY

WEDNESDAY

THURSDAY

FRIDAY

SATURDAY / SUNDAY

WEEK'S PRIORITIES / TO DO

NOTES

RATE / ASSESS THE WEEK:

BE (LIQUID) COOL
WEEKLY PLANNER

WEEK:

| M | T | W | H | F | S | S |

MONDAY

TUESDAY

WEDNESDAY

THURSDAY

FRIDAY

SATURDAY / SUNDAY

WEEK'S PRIORITIES / TO DO

NOTES

RATE / ASSESS THE WEEK:

BE (LIQUID) COOL
WEEKLY PLANNER

WEEK:

M T W H F S S

MONDAY

TUESDAY

WEDNESDAY

THURSDAY

FRIDAY

SATURDAY / SUNDAY

WEEK'S PRIORITIES / TO DO

NOTES

RATE / ASSESS THE WEEK:

Week 6: Be It

"LIQUID COOL IS A CLASSY joint with a reputation."

EXCERPT FROM: *Liquid Cool: The Cyberpunk Detective Series (Book One)*

My Pops always told me the more you pretend to be a thing, the more you become that thing and realize you're not pretending anymore. He used the word "pretend" instead of his more favorite phrase, "work so hard you bleed." No one wanted to hear the "work hard, and you'll make it" mantra.

Metropolis was stacked to the sky with people working hard but would never make it.

When I was in the box, I did more than just assimilate data. I had to think big picture. Thinking about being different is far different from being different. I couldn't yell "Oh, snaps" one day and ask to do life all over. It was a commitment, and I intended to be the best detective out there—I had to be that internally arrogant—as I had done with restoring classic hovercars. I could only do that by knowing more and doing more than the other guy. Strangely, the two professions were similar in that way. It was about knowledge. Knowing those factoids that no one else knew. Being able to see connections that not even a computer could see. As a kid, I learned every relevant and irrelevant factoid about hovercars beyond what could possibly be known, which is why my name was always bandied about in the same breath when people asked, "Who'd you recommend for my hovercar restoration gig?" Like me or hate me, everyone agreed on one thing: I knew my hovercars. I had to get to that level with this profession.

Perspective

The Mindset Precedes the Reality

EXCERPT FROM: *These Mean Streets, Darkly (Liquid Cool: The Cyberpunk Detective Series Prequel)*

Run-Time meeting with a mother in need at his Let It Ride Enterprises building...

"I will not sugarcoat anything, Carol. I tried to get Police Central to add additional resources to this case, but as you probably know—"

"I am one of hundreds," she added. Her eyes drifted from him down to the floor.

"Yes. Sad, but true. However..." Carol looked back at him. "I want you to take this." He handed her a white card. "Flash will take you home, and I do want you to go home. Get a good night's sleep. I know it will be hard, but you have to force yourself to sleep. The police may not be adding additional resources to the case, but they will at least get a call from the Chief of Police himself, and dozens of officers will be looking at the case, at least for a day, because of my call. Every bit helps. If they find anything new, they will certainly drive to your house to tell you in person."

"Thank you."

"Then, we're going to have you back here at my headquarters tomorrow."

"I'll do it, boss," Flash added.

"Flash will have you back here tomorrow, and I will have you meet with someone. I've known him for a long time, and he's not just a cool cat, but he's a solid operator. Let's see what he can come up with to find your daughter. I've already spoken to him on the phone."

"You have?" Carol's eyes opened wide.

"Yes."

"So, it will be home, sleep, and back here to meet my friend. How does that sound as a plan?"

"It sounds great."

"Good."

Run-Time, for the first time, let go of her hand as she stood. He could see the ray of hope on her face. They could all see it. The VP nodded and smiled. "Hang in there, Ms. Carol," she said. Flash walked her out of the room.

The main elevator was already waiting for them—one of the security guards held it for them and he, too, nodded at Carol.

They got in. Flash felt the hope himself. He was so glad he had come to his boss. He knew he'd find a solution.

Carol stood quietly, too. The ride was silent, but they could see the numbers count down in large digital numbers on the door. She almost forgot about it. She looked down at the white card from Mr. Run-Time.

The card read:

LIQUID COOL

Detective Agency

D. Cruz

Private Detective

Recap

It didn't hurt that all of Cruz's friends and family were on board with him becoming a bona fide Metropolis street detective. They're even handing out business cards to potential clients for him.

When you become the "new you" or start a new project, bring along those people who can help and encourage you.

Week 7: Get Out of Your Comfort Zone (Or, at Least, Don't Let It Get In Your Way)

PJ: "UMM. DO YOU STILL have the job?"

EXCERPT FROM: *Liquid Cool: The Cyberpunk Detective Series (Book One)*

I had arrived at my office and ripped down all that police crime tape in front of the door. Phishy was right; the city police put it up, but never took it down. The community or landlord was supposed to do that. It was a city ordinance, of all things.

My office had the same feel as the entire floor—empty, abandoned, uninviting. I wouldn't come here. It looked like you'd get mugged. I wouldn't come to my office. It gave off the same vibe as a morgue. There was a businessman inside of me, after all, because I was thinking the right thoughts if I planned to do this occupation for real. But only if I could address all the security issues.

I lay on the floor on my emergency work blanket from my vehicle. Again, contrary to my germophobic tendencies, right next to the tape outline of the man who got himself shot to death in my office. I had learned he was a low-level street punk. Nothing surprising about how he died. What was surprising was that it didn't happen sooner.

I heard a low knock on the door, followed by two more. Did I forget to lock the door again? Had I been hypnotized against my will not to secure my own office door?

From where I lay, I didn't even need to move. It opened, and there was Punch Judy.

Her demeanor was altogether different. I had never seen Punch Judy look amiable or humble before. She gave me a forced smile, stepped inside, and closed the door behind her. She stood there, her eyes darting around, trying to decide what to say.

"Umm. Do you still have the job?"

I looked at her from my supine position on the floor, never once answering her.

"I want the job. I need the job. You caught me off guard. That's why I was rude. More rude than French people normally are. I talked before I used my brains. I want the job. I can't live the way I'm living anymore. I can't get a job at normal places because of my psych profile and criminal record. It's not fair.

My record has trapped me. I don't want to be trapped anymore. If you give me the job, I'll do a good job."

She paused, wanting me to say something, but I didn't.

"So I'll come back tomorrow and start. My hours will be nine to six. I looked up the hours for other detective offices. That's the normal hours they have. Okay."

She waited again for me to say something, then opened the door. She stopped.

"What is the name of the detective agency, anyway?"

"Liquid Cool," I answered.

"Oh, good. Very cosmopolitan and hip. I would have hated a stuffy name or something stupid, like the Cruz Detective Agency. Liquid Cool. Very nice. I start tomorrow at nine AM sharp."

She left and closed the door.

I had a secretary. A secretary with two bionic arms that could punch a three-hundred-pound man through the wall, which she apparently did on more than one occasion, hence her psych record. Hence, her nickname, Punch Judy, rather than just Judy. Unauthorized activities as a cyborg will make you unemployable faster than being outed as a carrier of the Asian flu.

Let someone try to sucker shoot me in my own office now. We'd be ready for them.

Perspective

Satan's Robot: Citizen of Earth! Surrender! Do not resist!

Seven of Nine: I am Borg. (Nonchalantly opens its chest panel and rips out its wiring)

Satan's Robot: Surrennnnnderrrrrrr... (Shuts down)

Seven of Nine: The robot has been neutralized. May I leave now?

Star Trek: Voyager, Episode: "Night"

EXCERPT FROM: *Liquid Cool: The Cyberpunk Detective Series (Book One)*

I wondered if my fixation on the whole detective thing was because, for too long, I had nothing at all to fixate on. Idle people got excited at the most mundane. I was a laborer, a gig-worker. No permanent job, just odd job to odd job. I hated it and complained about it, but I accepted it because I did nothing to change my situation. Millions of us sat around in our legacy housing all day, and I was one of them. We were our version of the leisure class, but when you're rich, it's acceptable; when you're not, it's pathetic. Aimless was aimless no matter how much or how little cash you had in the bank. I never saw social class; I saw people who had purpose. That's why Phishy didn't annoy me and Punch Judy did. He had purpose with his crazy self, and she didn't. I didn't like her, really, because she was kind of like me.

But I had to get serious. Being a detective was to be a one-time deal. I had no money for a license, no office, and honestly, the job was dangerous. I couldn't play games—I was getting married, assuming my future parents-in-law didn't off me before then.

Yet, here I was, in the public library on 40 Winks Street. There were three left in the City. In the comfort of your own home, you could download any content you wanted to your digital book reader, but frankly, who had time for that? There were a gazillion books out there in cyberspace. Being a librarian was actually a serious profession with value; they had advanced degrees in data mining, sifting, and record compiling. Libraries sifted through all the data garbage, the clutter, the Trojan horse X-rated material, and sub-standard nonsense to present you with what you typed into your search and gave you the best of the best. Yes, libraries were also a major hang-out for the sidewalk johnnies, but they were clean and quiet. Here, I was reading book after book on...the private investigation industry.

There were only a few main categories. The first was the procedural detective books. They went into quite a lot of detail about surveillance, stake-outs, skip tracing, computer tapping, hard drive cloning, etc. Most of it was very dry or common sense, and I could see why the books didn't sell.

The second category was the best sellers—the Hollywood-style super detectives. These "true" stories were of gun battles with crime lords, beating up cops, sleeping with clients, secret consultative work with Up-Top multinationals, and more gun battles. Entertaining, but all stupid. None of it real.

The book I found myself glued to was not the 1,000-page tomes of the first category or the 400 page-turners of the second, but this 60-page book titled How to be a Great Detective with 100 Rules. It was written by a guy who had been a private eye for 70-plus years. In fact, he died only a few years ago at the age of 92 and had worked right until the end. The book was brilliant. I had read it five times already and was reading it again. The rules seemed basic, but his one-paragraph explanation of each was packed with real insight and his own folksy, street-wise expertise. He was the real McCoy—not any fake movie-land detective. You could tell by the way he communicated. He must have led an amazing life. To live 92 years in Metropolis—the things he saw and experienced. It's too bad he didn't write a compilation of his life through his cases.

I put the book on the floor, sat there, and sighed. It was the only book I checked out from the library. Here, I was sitting alone in my legacy residence, reading the accounts of a man who lived a real life, a long life, and was quite content with it. I knew that, because he kept at it until he died. Nothing stopped him—the mean streets, the meaner streets, uber-government agencies, megacorporations. He did his thing.

He had a metal heart, but back then, if you had heart disease in your genetic history, the doctors would automatically replace your regular heart with an artificial one to be on the safe side. He had bionic hips and fingers—a fall down stairs had caused the former; a nasty habit of smoking nasty cigarettes caused the latter. But again, he did his thing, his way.

I wished I had met Mr. Wilford G., the 92-year-old private eye. He lived and had a lot less than I had. What was my excuse then?

Recap

We like "comfort zones" because they're safe zones for us. We're familiar with them. Some of us do our best work within them. There are many good reasons to like them.

However, from time to time, it may be best to step out of them, especially if we've become stagnant or are stuck in a rut. If you're going to do something new, you may absolutely have to get out of that comfortable comfort zone to accomplish your goal.

But don't worry; you'll be creating a "new" comfort zone for yourself.

Who's Phishy?

PHISHY WAS STILL SPINNING around on the sidewalk, doing his chicken dance. This was how he greeted me, with some dance jig.

CRUZ'S CRAZY SLIDER associate and licensed gun dealer

Metropolis was not overflowing with life; it was choking on it. Water wasn't a precious commodity here—it was a curse, alternating between always raining or about to rain. It was space that was sacred. People were stacked on top of one another in flashing super-skyscrapers that reached into the dark skies. Hover vehicles buzzed around; jetpackers zipped around; drones gyrated around, all in the airspace above the crowds. The only real open public space was the sidewalks. That was where the spontaneous action happened daily and not from the average masses of automaton-like city citizens that passed through, going about life. The sidewalks had the real action of the people who made it the center of their universe.

However, sidewalk life had its problems, too. It was the "real hustle"—scamming and scheming for cash—that created the problem. Homelessness had been eradicated long ago, like polio and cancer; housing was mandatory for all, even for those without a legacy. But sidewalk johnnies were like the weeds you heard about that ruined a man's plush green lawn in the old days. Hanging around, watching trouble, causing trouble, hustling, looking for a hustle, but doing little of anything meaningful. They congregated, watched, chatted it up, sat around, smoked, joked, disappeared to the johns when needed, or disappeared to their sleep shack for a few hours—and repeat. At least they were harmless. Like a piece of litter—step around it and ignore it.

Dope daddies were different, perpetually pushing their "product" on an eager clientele of dope fiends itching for their daily fixes—only the rain was more persistent. Nowadays, the fiends were appropriately called dope roaches. That's what they were: come out to feed (their fix) and disappear back into the darkness. Dope daddies had it down to a science, and for every one of them the cops sent to prison camp, any of their lookouts, street corner chiefs, low-level pavement pushers, or runners would readily step up to take their place. An endless cycle of street drug life. The only way to dry up the illegal drug swamp was to get rid of the addicts. The only way to get rid of the addicts was to...get rid of people. But the cops did what they could to maintain, at least, an ordered chaos.

Then there were the in-between situations. Street hustlers, front street freddies, like Phishy. A little non-narcotic running here, a bit of courier work there, whatever scam he could get into to bring in some extra cash. Nothing illegal enough to get him a solid prison stint, but always at the level where if he got caught, he'd get no more than a mere misdemeanor situation—pay the fine and be on his way, not even a blot on the record. Cops and courts couldn't be bothered with street hustlers working non-violent, low-money scams. In a vile world, you had to set your priorities properly.

Phishy always wore a dark-colored vest and pants, but underneath was always some off-white colored, long-sleeve shirt extravaganza with colored fish all over it. He had a street name to maintain. He strutted down the street, side-stepping the sidewalk johnnies and sallies, saying hello to friends, slapping a high or low five as he went along.

Week 8: Pick Your Associates Wisely

CRUZ: "THIS DETECTIVE life 'ain't no joke.'"

EXCERPT FROM: *Liquid Cool: The Cyberpunk Detective Series (Book One)*

Since I was never a criminal myself and didn't associate with them, I had to find the next closest thing. That would be my frenemy, Phishy. He was the only friend-enemy that I tolerated and still spoke to. I didn't know why I tolerated him, but it definitely wasn't because of his assortment of colored shirts with fishes on them.

I guess it was because he also had an aversion to the hardcore criminal world, every bit as strong as mine, but he maintained a knowledge of the players and, more importantly, he kept his ear to the streets. Anything worth knowing or not knowing, Phishy would know about it or who to go to to find out.

"Easy Chair Charlie?" I asked.

Phishy was still spinning around on the sidewalk, doing his chicken dance. This was how he greeted me with some dance jig. I waited until he had sufficiently amused and tired himself out. There was no point in yelling at him to get serious. Phishy had to be Phishy first before his brain could interact with others.

Perspective

If You Don't Know the Right People to Get to Where You're Going, Find Them

---

EXCERPT FROM: LIQUID Cool: The Cyberpunk Detective Series (Book One)

As GW said, I was a psycho when I got mad. You didn't want to go there with me. I was indirectly shot at once, and a man was killed. Now, I was shot at—me—in front of my own place.

It was the fourth place I checked to find him. There was Phishy, chatting it up with his sidewalk johnny friends. I tapped my horn to get his attention. All of them looked up at me as I slowly landed my Pony on the ground. I lifted up my hovercar door as Phishy was already running to me with a big smile, but he saw my face, and he stopped; his smile disappeared.

"What's wrong, Cruz?"

I was standing and slammed my door shut. I never slammed my car door. I could feel my own fumes of anger radiating from my body. I gestured to him to approach, and Phishy did so cautiously.

"What happened?"

"What happened is that some stranger got shot to death in my new office. The police yellow-taped the whole thing, so I'm out of business before even starting. Then, to top off the day and make it even more exciting, someone tried to gun me down right in front of my place."

"In front of the Concrete Mama?"

"Yeah."

"Oh, wow."

"Oh wow, Phishy? I've never been involved with anything like this before. You know that."

"I know. I know."

"I don't do violence. You know that."

"But you're a detective now, Cruz. You have to expect that sort of thing now."

"Well, there is no now. I'm out of business."

"No, you're not."

"What do you mean?"

"If the cops yellow-tag you, as long as they don't contact you again in 48 hours, then you're in the free and clear."

"What are you talking about, Phishy?"

"That's how it works. The cops got 48 hours to escalate the case. If they don't or can't, then you can rip down that yellow tape and act like nothing happened."

"The police can prosecute you and send you to jail, Phishy, for ripping it down."

"But only before the 48 hours."

"Are you sure, Phishy?"

"I'm positive, Cruz. I know this stuff. You know that I know this stuff."

I watched him, thinking. Yeah, Phishy would know these things.

"But I'll get a reputation—"

"Reputation?" Phishy interrupted me. "There are hundreds of shootings in this city every day, Cruz. You won't get no reputation. But…was it a client who got shot in your office?"

"No, some punk stumbled into my office door, and he was armed, too."

"See what I mean. A street shootout that spilled into your office. You won't get no rep for that. But what about the other thing?"

"Yeah, the other thing. Someone trying to kill me in front of my own place."

"You know what you need to do."

"What's that?"

"Come on, Cruz. You know."

I knew.

"There's no way around it, Cruz," Phishy said. "You can be a good detective, but you have to have the tools of the trade. You're not a laborer anymore."

"Yeah, everyone seems to know that, thanks to a certain person."

Phishy flashed a smile.

"Who do I talk to, then?"

"Leave it to me, Cruz." Phishy's smile was really back.

"I'm not going to let you rip me off, Phishy."

"Oh no. I'll take care of you."

"Where? I don't want any of this near my place."

"Your favorite coffee place."

"The Wet Cabeza?"

"They have the rental offices on the top floor."

"Yeah. Okay. How do you know that? Never mind. And no scamming, Phishy. I don't like them, but I know guns."

"Yeah, I know. You even killed someone when you were five with one."

I gave him a look.

"I didn't tell anyone."

"Like you didn't tell anyone that I was a detective?"

Recap

The axiom has always been true: "You are who you hang out with." It was true when you were a kid growing up; it's true now. Peers can exert tremendous influence on you, whether you're consciously aware of it or not. Pick them deliberately and wisely.

If you want to become a runner, hanging around people who hate to even take a leisurely walk down the street probably isn't what you want to do. Hang around runners. Maybe, you want to go skydiving for the first time, learn horseback riding, or learn scuba diving. Do you want to start a new business, take on a franchise, or turn your side hustle into an actual business? Then, find your fellow entrepreneurs to network with. Do you want to learn about investing to grow your money, or simplify your life by moving to a more rural area (or the reverse—you want more bustle)?

Grow your circle of peers and new friends!

But remember, "peers" and "friends" are separate things. "Peers" is about the work. You can have friends who can be peers, if that's their specialty. You can have peers who can become your closest new friends.

Whether it was PJ, Phishy, or anyone else, Cruz looked for the best associates to do the work. Friendship was the added bonus.

Week 9: Have the Right Tools

I PULLED MY OMEGA-GUN the same time they did, but I didn't hesitate.

EXCERPT FROM: *Liquid Cool: The Cyberpunk Detective Series (Book One)*

The Wet Cabeza was my favorite, and it was one of those places I went so often that I knew everyone who worked there and the owners.

I arrived and was greeted by the staff, who I knew on a first-name basis. I had a craving for some humble pie, but I resisted. I just had a cup of silk coffee and left it at that while I waited for Phishy.

Inside, the layout of the place was a large, open cafe, all booths and barstools at the kitchen counter, with college-kid servers on hoverroller skates.

Upstairs, they had tiny conference rooms for rent. The Wet Cabeza attracted a business clientele, and offering the meeting rooms was a stroke of genius—why should hotels get all that business? It meant there was another reason to keep butts in the seats and the food and drink orders coming all the time.

It was two days later, and it seemed that he was in the same shirt with fishes, but Phishy was never unkempt or smelly. Technically, he wasn't a sidewalk johnny. He just hung with them. He was an operator. My girlfriend called him a slider, but he wasn't sliding through life; he was only sliding from one scheme or scam to the next. But with Phishy, it was never too criminal—always small time, so if he were caught, there was no real chance of jail time.

Phishy had a big, block briefcase in each hand, and he hopped up the stairs, two at a time, with a big smile. He followed me to the room I reserved, and he marched in as I closed the door. I locked it. Too bad I couldn't remember to do so at my own office.

"Okay, Phishy, I checked out what you said about the 48-hour yellow-tape, and you were right."

"I told you, Cruz. I know these things."

Phishy put the two briefcases on the small conference table and opened both cases. Guns, guns, and more guns.

"How much trouble would we get into if the police raided this room this instant?" I asked.

"None. I'm a licensed gun dealer, and none are loaded."

"What? Licensed dealer? I didn't know that. You got a cover for everything."

"I'm Phishy. That's what I do."

I looked at the assortment before me, but he stopped me before I could pick one up.

"I got something special for you."

"Phishy, I'm in no mood for scammin'."

"No. Serious. I got some pieces just for you. You're a real detective now, and you have to start building a rep."

"A rep? Am I a criminal?"

"No, Cruz. Everybody needs a rep. That's how people know if to deal with you or not. And when they do deal with you, how to deal with you."

"A rep does all that?"

"Yeah, it does. Here, let me show you. I have a pop-gun."

"Pop-gun?" I said loudly as Phishy pulled out a hidden tray of other guns in one case. "Are we like in kindergarten, Phishy? Pop-guns are what we played with when we were children."

"Not those pop-guns. These are the real thing."

"I never heard of that before."

He handed me what looked to be a metal wand attached to some kind of fabric piece with Velcro.

"What the heck is this? Phishy, I don't want kid's toys. I could have been killed."

"Come on, Cruz. Trust me."

He took my right arm, and before I knew it, the fabric was wrapped around my entire forearm. "You wear long sleeves and jackets all the time, so you'll have the concealment. Okay, let's test it. Just snap your wrist. Pop! Trust me, Cruz. Pop it."

I flicked my arm out, and nothing happened.

"You're not doing it right, Cruz. You have to be serious. Snap your forearm out as if you can throw your hand like a projectile."

I did it. Pop!

The metal wand contraption extended, and I could see it was some kind of gun barrel.

"You pop it, and it shoots one round—bullet, sonic, or pulse round. Whichever you like. No one will ever sucker shoot you ever again," he said.

My mind was changed, and I stood there admiring my arm weapon. "A pop-gun?"

"I had it made just for you. I called in real favors, Cruz."

"Okay, what else you got for me?"

"This one."

He lifted the compartment tray of the other briefcase to reveal more guns. He reached in and handed me the sweetest gun I had ever seen. It was a slim, sleek piece of black metal.

"This, Cruz, is straight from Up-Top."

"Then how did you get it?"

He laughed. "Stolen, of course. Well, I didn't, but someone did, and I'm like fifth in line."

"You're giving me a stolen piece."

"Cruz, no one will know. It's untraceable. They have their database, and we have ours. No one shares. You know that. Besides, someone who could afford a piece like that probably has a ton of them; probably doesn't even miss it or know it's gone. How does it feel in your hand?"

I couldn't lie. "Nice balance."

"See what I mean. That is the weapon of a high-class detective. It even comes with a manual."

"Manual?"

"It will take you a day to read it. And when you do, you'll be smiling, like me."

"Phishy, how much are these going to cost me?"

"Wait, I'm not finished."

He lifted up the gun trays of both briefcases and started pulling out pieces. In a minute, he assembled a shotgun.

"Cruz, nothing causes some serious fear like the cocking of a shotgun."

He did so, and its unmistakable sound was universal, and, yes, he was right. You heard that sound, and you stopped whatever you were doing to pay attention.

"All three, and you're set," he said. "The pop-gun. The omega-gun—"

"Omega gun? You're making that up, Phishy."

"It's the gun to end all private guns. That's what it says in the manual. And the shotgun. Now you're ready for the mean streets. And the omega-gun comes with accessories if you want to use its digital features. There's this cool piece that lights up that you wrap around your leg. You'll see."

"What does that do?"

"You'll see."

"Phishy, how much? They say if you have to ask the price, you can't afford it. All this seems like something I could never afford in a million years."

"Cruz, we're friends. I'll loan you the weapons, and I'll get a percentage of each of your cases. That seems fair. I know you're just starting out."

I grinned, and he grinned back.

"Phishy, Phishy. Always the angle. I amend the offer. Each percentage I give you...what percentage were you thinking?"

"Uhhh."

"Be careful, Phishy."

"Fifty percent."

"Ten percent of my cases go toward the total cost of the weapons until, and if, I ever pay off that bill."

"Ten percent?"

"Phishy! I'm sure you won't give me the ammo free, and being a detective is not exactly a no-cash-needed business. There're a lot of upfront costs. Like I have to go back to my office and turn it into a fortress, so I never get sucker shot at again. Ten percent is it. We're all going to make out on this deal. I'll even throw in a bonus if, by some miracle, I can ever pay it off."

"Bonus?" Phishy said, smiling. "That sounds good, Cruz. We're like partners now."

"Yeah, don't remind me. So, we're good?"

"We are, Cruz."

"Get me the total cost of these guns, and don't play. You know I'll check. And then we'll lock down the terms of the bonus, now, before anything gets started."

"That sounds like the plan, Cruz. I told you to trust me. Now you got the tools of the trade, like a real high-class detective. Just because we live in a low-life world doesn't mean we can't be high class."

"You were right. I have to admit it without qualification." I reached out my hand to him. Phishy almost didn't know what to do, but he shook my hand. "You came through for me, Phishy. I won't forget it."

Phishy was genuinely moved. "You're welcome, Cruz. I knew I could do it for you."

Perspective

Tools to Success Can Be Anything You Need to Be Efficient and Effective

---

EXCERPT FROM: *Liquid Cool: The Cyberpunk Detective Series (Book One)*

I strolled into Free City, and I knew the Free City gangs would try to jack me up again, and no business card would stop them this time. As I approached the tower of Easy Chair's widow, they appeared. It was the same kids; one after another they walked to me.

"It's the detective again," one said.

"I didn't think he was dumb enough to come back a second time," said another.

I was in no mood.

"Get away from me," I said.

"That's it, Mr. Detective? You got no more fake business cards to show us?"

I really was in no mood for this.

"Guess where I'm going after this?" I asked.

"Why?" one of the punks responded.

"Mad Heights."

They all laughed. "You're not going to no Mad City, you square."

"When you go to a place like that, you have to be prepared to do what needs to be done. I should practice."

Instantly, the expressions changed on their faces. They knew where I was going.

The first mistake was drawing their weapons on me. The second mistake they made was not firing at me immediately. I pulled my omega-gun at the same time they did, but I didn't hesitate. My mind was set to shoot them, not kill them—they were still young enough that they had a chance to get on the right path in life. However, I would torture them—viciously. Medium-yield plasma discharge rounds. I needed something to practice on to see their effectiveness. The mayhem commenced. Lucky for them, it was not set to kill; unlucky for them, they would be showered with burning, excruciating, painful rounds. The punks were all reduced to whimpering wrecks, bundles on the ground. They cried and begged for me to stop.

"She hired us!"

"Who?"

"She told us to stop you from coming up to her place, no matter what!" one of the punks yelled at me.

"Who?!"

Recap

Well, you don't need an omega-gun (though some of us would definitely want one, and with all the accessories). Whatever the task, project, or goal, ensure you have the right tools to get the job done efficiently, consistently, and completely. Is it software or hardware? New equipment or gadgets? It'll be different for everyone. Do what's best for you based on your own likes and preferences.

THIRD MONTH
March
Classic Sci-Fi Actor Birthdays

CHARACTER (ACTOR) SHOW/Movie

March 1: Lieutenant Starbuck (Dirk Benedict) Battlestar Galactica (Original Series)

March 2: Lieutenant Gorman (William Hope) Aliens

March 3: Montgomery Scott "Scotty" (James Doohan) Star Trek: The Original Series

March 5: Anakin Skywalker (Jake Lloyd) Star Wars: The Prequels

March 5: Sub-Commander T'Pol (Jolene Blalock) Star Trek: Enterprise

March 6: Perrin - Sarek's wife (Joanna Miles) Star Trek: The Next Generation

March 7: "Hugh" Third of Five (Jonathan Del Arco) Star Trek: The Next Generation

March 8: Teb (Jed Rees) Galaxy Quest

March 11: River Song (Alex/Alexandra Elizabeth Kingston) Doctor Who

March 11: Captain Jack Harkness (John Barrowman) Doctor Who

March 17: Dr. David Marcus (Merritt Butrick) The Wrath of Khan (Star Trek)

March 18: Dr. Stephen Franklin (Richard Biggs) Babylon 5

March 19: Commander Charles 'Trip' Tucker III/Star Trek: Enterprise & Michael -Stargate Atlantis (Connor Trinneer)

March 20: Q (John De Lancie) Star Trek: The Next Generation/Voyager

March 20: Martha Jones (Freema Agyeman) Doctor Who

March 22: Capt. James T. Kirk (William Shatner) Star Trek: The Original Series

March 22: Bryant (M. Emmet Walsh) Blade Runner (Original Movie)

March 25: D.C. Fontana - writer Star Trek: The Original Series/Star Trek: The Next Generation (created Spock and Vulcans)

March 26: Mr. Morden (Ed Wasser) Babylon 5

March 29: Deanna Troi (Marina Sirtis) Star Trek: The Next Generation

March 30: Burke (Paul Reiser) Aliens

March 30: Mouse (Matt Doran) The Matrix

March 31: Obi-Wan Kenobi (Ewan McGregor) Star Wars: The Prequels

THE ZEN MINDSET

Mind, Body, and Soul

IT'S A TRINITY. DESIGNATE Time For All Three, Not Just One or Two.

When people make life changes, they tend to think about physical health alone. Start a new exercise routine, hire a fitness trainer, and quit smoking. However, humans are not just the physical.

The Mind

"Mindfulness."

The latest word fad of the day. We humans are fond of renaming something that has always existed before.

Mindfulness, meditation, quiet inner contemplation, "alone time," the "action" of simply "doing nothing" to relax, clear your mind, and take stock of the day can benefit your overall health, too. We can get so busy with life that we sometimes forget to simply stand still, look around, and appreciate what's around us. Or, as the saying goes, "Stop and smell the roses."

Reading

Brain power!

If you have this book, you're already ahead of the game in this discipline. Sadly, reading is not as common as it should be around the globe. We exercise the body, but what about the mind?

The benefits of reading:

- Exercises the brain (mental stimulation)
- Stress reduction
- Knowledge enhancement
- Improved memory
- Improves thinking skills
- Improved focus and concentration
- Improved vocabulary and writing skills
- Entertainment

The Soul

Spirituality or faith.

They can be the same thing for some, but completely different from others. In both cases, it is the "recognition, feeling, sense, or belief that there is something greater than ourselves in the world or universe." Spiritualists believe we are part of a great cosmic whole. Religious believers, of course, believe that the greater whole is a Creator.

If you're a spiritual person, what does that mean to you? How can you grow your spirituality? How can it be the foundation for your goal to do something great or be something better?

If you're a religious believer, then that should be your foundation. How often you engage in prayer, worship, and reading of religious text is up to you. However, the questions should be the same: how do you grow your faith and how can it guide you and help you achieve your goals?

If you're neither, both can still inspire you. The quest to achieve, grow, transform, and succeed in your life goals and your inner motivation should be about more than just you.

Excerpt From: *The UFO Case (Liquid Cool: From the Crazy Maniac Files, Book Three)*

But finally, I was flying through the sky into the proverbial sunlight, thanks to my royal rocketpack. Every racer alive loved the feel of the wind across their face and the speed.

Recap

Always remember that one aspect of truly enjoying life is to actually stop to enjoy life! It's this "doing nothing" of contemplation and appreciation that can be as important as the "doing lots of something all the time."

To use an analogy of the Body, when going to the gym and lifting weights to build or tone muscle, the results don't happen as you're pumping iron. It's the period of rest that grows and refines that muscle.

The Planners

BE (LIQUID) COOL / MONTHLY PLANNER

MONTH:

SUN	MON	TUE	WED	THU	FRI	SAT

TOP PRIORITIES / GOALS

PEOPLE TO SEE / PLACES TO GO / REMINDERS

NOTES

RATE / ASSESS THE MONTH:

BE (LIQUID) COOL
WEEKLY PLANNER

WEEK:

M T W H F S S

MONDAY

TUESDAY

WEDNESDAY

THURSDAY

FRIDAY

SATURDAY / SUNDAY

WEEK'S PRIORITIES / TO DO

NOTES

RATE / ASSESS THE WEEK:

BE (LIQUID) COOL
WEEKLY PLANNER

WEEK: M T W H F S S

MONDAY

TUESDAY

WEDNESDAY

THURSDAY

FRIDAY

SATURDAY / SUNDAY

WEEK'S PRIORITIES / TO DO

NOTES

RATE / ASSESS THE WEEK:

BE (LIQUID) COOL
WEEKLY PLANNER

WEEK:

M T W H F S S

MONDAY

TUESDAY

WEDNESDAY

THURSDAY

FRIDAY

SATURDAY / SUNDAY

WEEK'S PRIORITIES / TO DO

NOTES

RATE / ASSESS THE WEEK:

BE (LIQUID) COOL
WEEKLY PLANNER

WEEK:

| M | T | W | H | F | S | S |

MONDAY

TUESDAY

WEDNESDAY

THURSDAY

FRIDAY

SATURDAY / SUNDAY

WEEK'S PRIORITIES / TO DO

NOTES

RATE / ASSESS THE WEEK:

Week 10: Eat Right

"I'M GLAD TO SEE YOU continue to eat good food, young man," the Good Kosher Man

EXCERPT FROM: *Liquid Cool: The Cyberpunk Detective Series (Book One)*

This was Woodstock Falls, and I gave the street—Graffiti Alley—one more glance in both directions. Despite its name, there wasn't, and never was, a speck of graffiti anywhere, ever. Woodstock Falls was a safe, working-class, multiethnic, but mostly Jewish neighborhood. Like similar working-class neighborhoods, residents and business owners fiercely kept the trash—human and otherwise—away. The reason why was simple—the residents didn't just work here; they lived here. The bottom half of the monolith skyscrapers were the businesses and all above to the top was residential. No hovercar, taxis, or bullet train are needed for them. Transportation for them was a simple stroll down the hallway to the elevator capsule.

Graffiti Alley may have had no graffiti, but it should have. It was secluded and dark, and though it was a main street, it had the feel of an out-of-the-way back alley, where bad things were supposed to happen. There was never a lot of traffic, and the foot traffic was always sparse. I wondered how the businesses were able to stay afloat financially.

I wondered that about every business except one. Good Kosher.

The only reason to go to Graffiti Alley was The Good Kosher Market. After all these years, I couldn't tell you the name of any other business on the street. Good Kosher took up the entire length of the street, and that's saying a lot since streets were ginormous in Metropolis. Food came in three categories—processed (practically everything sold on the market), organic (supposedly the "healthier" alternative"), and natural—or, as I would say, "straight from the dirt." I never shopped anywhere else. I didn't eat processed and felt the whole "organic" thing was nothing but a scam (by the unholy coupling of government and megacorps) to overcharge people for food. I only ate natural food, and Mr. Watts and his five sons had been serving nothing else for more than a century. It was like many generational businesses. I was a devoted customer and member of its select clientele for the last twelve.

Graffiti Alley may have been practically empty, but inside, Good Kosher was packed. I always felt people were teleported into the store by Scotty's grandson because my words when entering were always, "Where did all these people come from?"

Inside, it looked like an underground football stadium with neon rows of products. People zipped around on hovercarts of all sizes. In traditional markets, the products came to you. Here, you got your own stuff. Other than the hovercarts, there really wasn't any machination of any kind, which was rare for any modern store. But it was a "natural" market, so the presence of robots might clash with the store's image. The sons, however, wore mech-gloves with store inventory displays on the wrist area, and the hand section was telescopic to pull down things from the top shelves, without ever having to get a ladder. The gloves probably had a million other uses, like a Swiss Army knife.

I grabbed a small hovercart near the entrance, sat in the small single seat, and began my spree. The other thing that made the store so popular was precisely because nothing ever changed—fruits and vegetables were on aisle 20, juices and milk products on aisle 15, teas and coffees on aisle 16, meats on 5 and 6, etc. No one needed to ask where anything was, because everyone already knew. Good Kosher was not into anything gimmicky or faddish. Mr. Watts would say, "Nothing gets on my shelves that hasn't been in the general market, and people have been eating for at least a thousand years." Funny, but true.

"I'm glad to see you continue to eat good food, young man," he said to me as I leaned on the main counter opposite him. "More young people need to embrace that. The human body is a machine, and it always needs the best power to be put into it. I'm glad to see your hovercar enthusiasm has shown you the way to live a long life. Good fuel, car lasts forever. Good foods, human body lasts a little less than that."

I nodded. "My favorite power station for my Pony. Good Kosher for me."

"I see a question on your tongue. Mr. Cruz."

Mr. Watts knew me too well. "Is it customary to get a future mother-in-law something? Like flowers?" I asked.

When you were a fixture of a neighborhood for so long, owned such a popular business for so long, employed the same workers, and catered to the same clientele, it didn't take long for everyone to feel like you truly were family. Every family had a sage—the wise, ol' uncle or wise, ol' grandmother. Mr. Watts was our sage. You did your shopping first, one of his five sons rang up the order at the cash register, and then you spent however long chatting it up with the Good Kosher Man himself.

I didn't know how old Mr. Watts was, but he had to be in his late fifties at least, but there was nothing old about him. He had a full beard and mustache, with the hair graying at the temple and the edges of his beard. Like his sons, the uniform was a khaki jumpsuit with a fully equipped utility belt, beaded strings around the neck, and a pointed Chinese bamboo hat to protect from the constant exposure of the artificial daylight ceiling lamps, on which all its indoor natural plant life depended. The skin techs at Eye Candy, where Dot worked, would be proud. He probably had the rare hats shipped directly from the Southeast Asia territories back when they were affordable. No rice paddies here, but Good Kosher had its own interior gardens in the back and off-limits to customers, growing a wide variety of roses, tulips, and other flowers. Watts and sons would go back into that room, with its steady rain mist falling, and handpick bouquets for customers. Good Kosher was a secret flower shop too, and no one had better—if you wanted real ones and not synthetic "garbage" that everyone else sold that could survive a nuclear blast.

"Mothers-in-law don't get flowers, even if you like them. And even if they did, they surely wouldn't qualify to be a future one. The future doesn't exist—there is only the present."

"Are you sure?" I asked as one of his sons finished ringing up my order, and I handed him my cash card. "It's very important I get on their good side."

Mr. Watts made a laughing sound. "They? So, it's both the mother- and father-in-law. I don't envy you. First dinner?"

"Yeah."

"Dress nice and arrive before the arrival time. That's all you can do. Don't talk unless asked a question, even from the girlfriend. Just look cool."

I laughed. "I always look cool."

"Yes, you're a natural. But remember, they'll be watching you like a hawk."

"I'll be as nervous as a spaceman flying through a meteor shower. Well, as long as there are no best practices for a thing like this."

"Be yourself," Mr. Watts said. "Don't think about it. You think about it, and you'll get nervous. Think about something else."

"Like?"

Mr. Watts stopped and gave me a smirk. "Something appropriate."

I returned the smirk.

Perspective

Let's Be Clear—Enjoy Your (Good) Food

EXCERPT FROM: *Liquid Cool: The Cyberpunk Detective Series (Book One)*

"Yo, Phishy," the food truck guy called to him.

It was Dog Man. Only hovergarbage trucks were more ubiquitous than hoverfood trucks. In Metropolis, you didn't have to go out in the rain on a food-run if you didn't want to; the food would come to you. But most hoverfood trucks staked out their turf either in the air or on the ground.

Dog Man had the perfect corner, with six lanes of pedestrian traffic on the ground and the same above him in the air. His hovertruck never flew anywhere anymore; it was a permanent fixture on the corner, open twenty-four hours a day. Man! He could make a damn good hot dog. His food truck "owned" this street. In other words, he paid a wad of cash to the city to get exclusivity for his main truck here and two more at the other end of two more streets.

"What's up, Dog?" Phishy asked as he neared the truck. The aroma was like a drug itself.

"Do you know where Cruz is, Phishy?"

"What? Why you askin' me?"

"It's not me," Dog Man said. "Run-Time has the all-points out for him."

"I haven't seen him since Wednesday."

"Well, if you see him, call Run-Time. Maybe you can get some cash out of it."

"Hardly." Phishy frowned. "You have to be a customer to get anything from Run-Time. Otherwise, he's as cheap as the Scrooge on Christmas Eve."

"Meaning you tried to scam him, and it didn't go well."

"I try to scam everybody, even my friends. If I didn't, that would be like discriminating."

"If you say so, Phishy. How about a dog?"

"Oh man, Dog Man. You're worse than the dope daddies. You're selling the wiener version of hard narcotics out of this food truck. I get fat, I can't fit into my clothes, and I don't earn enough to get an all-new wardrobe."

"Half a dog won't put any fat on them bones. You can skip the sauces."

"You can't have a dog without the sauces and a beverage to wash it down. That would be just plain wrong." Phishy pointed at him. "Half a dog with my favorite sauce, spicy hot beverage, and that's it. Put it on my tab."

Dog Man started to get his hot dog. "Phishy, I don't know why you keep using that line. You have no tab with me or anyone else. Pull that cash out that I know you have, and I don't want any wet or dirty bills."

"I told you, I try to scam even my friends." Phishy reached into his vest pocket for his cash.

He could feel his mobile phone vibrate on his belt. He grabbed it.

"Phishy, Phishy, Phishy," he answered.

"Why do you do that?" the voice said. "Are you like two years old?"

"Yo, China Doll."

"Don't 'yo' me. Where's Cruz?"

"Why is everyone asking me about Cruz? I haven't seen him since last Wednesday. Do you have everybody looking for him?"

"Yeah."

"What'd he do?"

"No one can find him."

"Men need their alone time, too. Leave him alone. He'll show up when he shows up."

"I know you know where he is."

"I haven't seen him since last Wednesday. But if I do, I'll tell him he found a great hiding place and keep hiding there."

"Don't make me come down there, Phishy. Tell him he better not even think of not making dinner today. He knows how important it is."

"Dinner?"

"Yeah."

"Can I come in his place? I'll be hungry again."

"Uh...no."

"Why you got to be like that, China Doll? Phishies need food, too."

"I'll save some goldfish food for you, then. You know what you have to do. Use those street skills of yours and find him."

"You got Run-Time looking for him. Now me. Did you call the police and National Guard?"

"I don't need them. That's what I got people for."

"Do I get a few bills if I find him?"

"No, but you can have the goldfish food. Bye, Phishy."

"Bye, China Doll."

Phishy returned the mobile to his belt. "See how I'm treated, Dog Man."

His mouth watered at the sight of the hot dog on a petite plate in Dog Man's hand.

"You got something for me, Phishy."

"Oh yeah. I was distracted."

Phishy reached back into his vest pocket for his cash. He revealed a bill. "Here doggy-doggy." He slapped the bill down on the food truck service counter.

"I'll assume you're talking about the half-hot dog." Dog Man buttered on Phishy's spicy sauce and then handed him the plate. He made change quickly and, before Phishy could speak, said, "Beverage coming up." He grabbed a cup, hit the dispenser for ice, and then another for beer. "Know what I'm going to say now?"

Phishy had the entire half-dog already stuffed into his mouth. "You're going to give me the other half for free."

"Don't forget about Cruz," Dog Man said. "You get distracted easily. So where is he? If everybody is calling you, then you know where he is."

Phishy kept chewing. "I'm still thinking about it. I'm a man who reacts to incentives."

"Phishy, don't make that girlfriend of his come down here and stomp you into the pavement."

Recap

The word "diet" has gotten a bad rap over the decades, and deservingly so. It conjures images of eating "healthy" but tasteless, lifeless substances pretending to be food. Or, for many, it means starving oneself or eating types of foods you hate. Also, it has the connotation of being "temporary." No wonder so many people fail at diets.

The word you should use is "nutrition." You are changing your overall eating habits permanently. Some foods you should cut out from your meals—too much sugar, too much salt, etc. Proportion size does matter. Eating too often or too late at night matters. Not drinking enough water matters. For some, cutting out all soda and "fake" natural juices alone will dramatically move you along the path to eating wellness. For others, it's a matter of cutting out fast food if that's all you eat.

Avoid the extremes—only "rabbit food" or eating the equivalent of a complete cow each day—unless in those rare cases, it's what genetically works best for you. Research what works and test it out. This will take time, and that's okay. More protein/meat in your meals? More fish? More veggies? You don't want fads. You want healthy and what makes sense to you. Healthy also shouldn't mean expensive either.

Good nutrition is primarily about consistency. Once you find out what works best for your goals, then stick to it like Spider-Man on a building. Also, don't forget that genetics plays a big role, especially as we grow older and our natural metabolism slows down.

Why is this important to your goals? You don't want any distractions. Eating right is an integral part of a healthy mind, body, and soul.

Week 11: Movement

CRUZ: IT WAS WAY TOO much excitement for me. I ran away as fast as I could.

EXCERPT FROM: *Classic Cyborg (Liquid Cool: From the Crazy Maniac Files, Book One)*

I had PJ call Classic, and when he called back, find out where I could meet him. So, where was Mr. Classic Cyborg? He was leading a Tai chi exercise class at the Metro Senior Living Center. Right up until my hovertaxi landed, and I walked in, I couldn't believe it. However, I couldn't deny what was right in front of my eyes. An auditorium filled with exercising cyborgs of all types—none under the age of sixty—in row after row, standing on purple mats that covered the entire floor.

Classic was at the front in a white martial arts robe, showing off that bionic chest of his. Tai chi was very popular—the slow movement exercises and controlled breathing; it wasn't viewed as martial arts anymore, but pure meditation and life stress reduction.

I stood at the back, watching them. To see them all move in unison was actually quite compelling. Everyone in their colored martial arts uniforms of whites, yellows, blues, purples, silvers, and pinks made you want to join in. I could've watched them exercise all day, so I sat cross-legged on the floor to do so.

Mr. Classic finished the Chinese exercise class, did a Japanese bow, and the class returned the gesture, then the chatter erupted. The only group chattier than little kids were at the other end of the spectrum—senior citizens. Classic saw me, but he had to do his thing—shaking hands, patting shoulders and backs of his students.

"Mr. Cruz," he said as he shook my hand too. "You're here to give me an update."

"Yes."

"There's an office we can use."

Perspective

Cruz: Dot and I were dancing maniacs.

EXCERPT FROM: *Liquid Cool: The Cyberpunk Detective Series (Book One)*

Dot didn't want to go to the club, and she was in no mood for dancing or any kind of fun.

"Let's just go inside and call another cab," I said.

"Cruz, I'm not going to fall for it. I'm not dancing. I want to go home."

"I understand. Let's go inside, and I'll call Flash. He has a spotless cab, and he's probably on duty now."

"Cruz, it's not going to work. I'm not dancing."

"Yeah, I know. We'll go in and call Flash."

"Where's your mobile?"

"I left it at home. It's date night. Where's yours?"

"I'm not falling for it, Cruz. I'm not dancin', and I want to go home."

"Let's call Flash then."

We walked inside, and I immediately told the bouncers we were only going inside to make a call. They were fine with that as long as we paid full price. I handed them my pre-paid tickets, and we were in. Booty Shakers first got you with the beat. The music was so loud the sound waves practically levitated you up in the air, and the beat forced your feet to move whether you wanted to or not.

Dot and I were dancing maniacs. We each had our own separate hobbies, but this was our hobby as a couple, and we were good at it. My Pops always said that couples last longer when there is something that they can do together (besides the obvious one). Not something that either does separately, but that you do together prefer to do together, something fun. For Dot and I, it was ripping up the dance floor.

Dot had forgotten she was not going to dance. The music had transported us to the dance floor with the hundreds of other people on one of their many football stadium-sized floors. Through the night, we got to display our dance prowess with all our favorite moves: the Cold Lampin, the Dead Woman's Hips, the Flava Wave, the Peter Perfect, the Perfect Peter, the Honey Dipper, the Sucka Sipper, the Big Dippa, the Gettin' Busy... We could do the Booty Rumble, the Swing Slide, the Mad Robot, the Beat Box, the Devo, the Michael Moon Walker, and even the Tango Terminator—old and new. We knew them all.

This was how I passed my first night out of the box, with my girl, China Doll.

Special Note

"I am the Doctor" Doctor Who (1st through 11th Doctors)

EXCERPT FROM: *The Moon Is Good Place to Die: Liquid Cool, Book Eight*

The decon medical personnel on the spacecraft had given me the two shots, one in each shoulder, given me two pills to swallow, which they made sure I did, then pushed a big pacifier in my mouth.

I pulled it from my mouth. "What's this?" I asked them.

"The human body is a cauldron of germs, viruses, and bacteria. We must properly neutralize any bio-threats to the Lunar Colony. We've dealt with your blood, colon, GI, skin, and hair."

"Skin and hair? When did you do that?" I asked.

She ignored me and continued. "Spit and sperm are last."

"What did you say? What are you doing to me?"

"It looks like a baby pacifier but is an advanced medical cleansing device to neutralize any bio-threats in your mouth and its saliva. Don't eat or drink anything for an hour. After that, you may experience a lack of taste for a few days."

"What are you doing to me? What about the other thing?"

"That has been taken care of." She smiled. "Your reproductive systems were done when we did the skin and hair."

I pointed the sucker part of the pacifier at her. "I'm going to tell my wife what you did to me."

The medic laughed.

Recap

The words we use can greatly influence our ability to achieve our goals, as we learned in the "Eat Right" section. It's the same here. Some people have a negative reaction to the word "exercise." Not all of us, but a significant segment of the population. They associate exercise with tedious weight-lifting and awkward squats, mile after mile of sweaty running, or working out to the point of exhaustion and collapse. Well, if you put it that way, I'd be anti-exercise too. But that is not it at all. The goal is to have a healthy mindset and live healthy to achieve your other goals.

For those who have a negative connotation with the word "exercise," here's a far better one: Movement! No one said anything about being hostage to a gym—though if that's what you thrive on and can maintain the regime, absolutely continue. No one said anything about running a marathon every week—though if you are training for one, then that's your goal to be achieved.

Exercise can be as simple as walking ten to fifteen minutes daily or twice a day. Get out of the house or office and into the sun. You might have heard the common phrase these days "getting your steps in." As Cruz and Dot showed, dancing is also exercise! Why not biking or volleyball or tennis? These activities are enjoyable, and the list of choices is endless. You're moving literally and figuratively to a healthier lifestyle. That's the point.

Also, most of us humans spend far too much time sitting. Schedule your movement time. Get up from the computer or laptop, stand, stretch, and move around. What about a standing desk?

The other key is sustainability. Whatever you settle on, your "movement" should be something you can commit to for the long haul because too many people take on too much to start with. Something is better than nothing. You can always adjust as you progress, but it must be sustainable. Keep it going so the new behavior becomes your new habit—a new routine that you automatically do and should enjoy.

Also, it should go without saying that if you have any concerns about how diet and exercise might affect your health, consult a doctor first. The watchword is "health" not "harm."

Cruz, as a Metropolis street detective, has to be in top physical shape. He better be with all those shootouts he has to run away from.

Week 12: Sleep

I WAS A TRUE VOCABULARY virtuoso when I was half asleep.

EXCERPT FROM: *A.I. Confidential (Liquid Cool, Book Six)*

There was something quite heavenly about a warm bed when you were exhausted. I lay in my bed, half smiling at the crazy dream I had. I normally didn't remember my dreams, but the one I had was a doozy.

This isn't my bed!

I looked at the wall. It was different. I smelled smoke and sat straight up in the dark. There was a crack of light coming through a door that wasn't completely closed. Looking around, I saw I was on a twin bed, and it was a small room. In rich neighborhoods, it would be considered a closet.

When I came out of the small guest bedroom, there he was, kicked back on a couch with his feet on a faux-wooden table, watching a sports game on the wall TV, a glass of alcohol in one hand, a cigar in the other. The Man. Tan, rugged, salt-and-pepper hair, cut very close on the sides, slightly taller on the top. His shirt was unbuttoned and open, wearing boxer briefs, his pants were draped over another chair, and socks with flip-flops, a combination that always bothered me.

"What are you wearing?" I asked.

"Sleeping beauty awakes. Come on, Cruz. Clearly, you've seen a grown man with his boxer briefs on before."

"Not that. Why are you wearing a Liquid Cool T-shirt?"

He laughed as he was exhaling his cigar smoke. "How many people get to wear the gear of a student after death?"

"I can't believe you're wearing Liquid Cool T-shirts."

"Only kind I wear nowadays. Besides, there was a bulk sale."

I looked around the apartment. It was some kind of martial arts dojo or had been. I sat in a one-seater next to Wilford's couch. He was watching a competitive martial arts match.

"Wilford—"

"Cruz, there's plenty of time for the third degree. I want to enjoy my cigar, saké, and match in peace. Besides, I'm not sure I'm talking to you anymore."

"Anymore?"

"I expected you to be at the hard-boiled, steel-grip detective level by now. Instead, you're giggling and fainting in front of me."

"Says the man with no pants." He chuckled. "Maybe I'm not talking to you, Wilford! This is a downright evil thing you did!"

Wilford put the cigar in the corner of his mouth. I knew his fingertips were bionic—he had a few inorganic parts in his body, like a lot of people—but they looked real to me. He turned off the wall TV with the in-armrest remote. "Looks like I'm not going to get any peace."

"You brought me here."

"Would you have preferred I left you on the wet pavement? You have quite a fancy weapon. Where do I get one?"

"You get nothing. You're supposed to be dead. Your son, daughter-in-law, and your ex-wives were at your funeral."

"I don't care about the ex-wives, but Wil is different."

"I'm glad you agree. What's this about? Why are you back from the dead? Why are you sneaking around in the storage units you left them in the will? Sneaking around your old shoemaker, leading me down dark alleys?"

"Cruz, am I supposed to be taking notes? That's a lot of questions, and you're still going."

"I'm just getting started."

"I had to come back from the dead. I became dead for a reason, and I'm back for a reason."

"What reason? And today's your birthday. You know your son called me. You really are a bum doing that to your son. He's still upset."

"Wil's the head of the Police Union, so he better toughen up. I didn't raise him to be any other way. Hopefully, he's not given to giggling, fainting spells like you."

"How exactly does one act when you see someone who's supposed to be dead?"

"You were happy to see me."

"My brain wasn't working. Why are you back, Wilford?"

"Oh, don't say my name like that. You sound like Perl or Isis. It was so annoying."

"Why are you back?"

"I'm back because I've gone as far as I can go on my own. Today, my file goes into mandatory archive, so I'll be an invisible man for a while. We can move."

"Mandatory archive?" I was thinking, trying to remember. "It has to do with turning 95."

"At 95, the Metro central computer moves you to their archive files."

"What? Why is that important? You're dead."

"I don't need to be dead, Cruz. I need to be invisible."

"Invisible? To who?"

"Not who. It. Cruz, man, I came back for you."

"Me?"

"Yes." He smiled almost as wide as Phishy. "We're going to break wide open the biggest caper in Metropolis history!"

Recap

Cruz loves his sleep, and so should you. Some of us are morning people; others are night people. Getting enough hours of sleep every day goes hand-in-hand with eating right and exercising to live and maintain a healthy lifestyle.

If you can't wind down and stop working automatically, there's nothing wrong with scheduling your "bed time." Nothing to be embarrassed about. Many high-energy, super-achieving executives, celebrities, and athletes have to do exactly the same thing.

Week 13: Meditate

YOU DON'T NEED TO BE a Vulcan to Want Your "Alone Time"

EXCERPT FROM: *Liquid Cool: The Cyberpunk Detective Series (Book One)*

Besides the *pitter-patter* of the rain hitting my vehicle, the only other sounds were from the old monorail line about thirty feet above me. I could hear its hissing rumble every fifteen minutes. I wanted to be left alone to rain-watch and meditate or whatever I was doing in my head. My vehicle was parked on the ground in an alley, and the only people around were the scarce few who walked past the entrance to another alleyway fifteen feet from me. Other than that, there was no one to bother me—no sidewalk johnnies, no troll moles, no passing garbage hovertrucks, and no juvenile delinquents, skipping school and looking to do crimes.

My mobile phone had been off since last night. Who knows how many messages I had waiting? But I didn't care. I needed my alone time.

Perspective

"It's amazing how productive doing nothing can be." Kevin Flynn, Tron: Legacy, played by Jeff Bridges

---

EXCERPT FROM: *Liquid Cool: The Cyberpunk Detective Series (Book One)*

My sidewalk johnny's other job was to keep a pre-paid hovertaxi waiting and ready, which he did. I ran to it and jumped inside quickly. We arrived at the Concrete Mama, and I ran inside, past all the lobby johnnies to the elevator. I ran out of the elevator to my apartment—9732. When I was in, with all the locks locked, I could feel my normalcy returning.

When you have a city in a region with more water than the oceans, the government wants you to waste water. "Take five showers a day." "Take a shower every hour." I still couldn't grasp that there were still people in this city who showered only once a week, not even daily. I was not into soaking in body detergent, anti-bacterial, anti-germ suds. Whatever filth it dissolved off your skin, you'd be sitting right in the middle of it. I never understood the bath thing. My fave was a super shower of lukewarm water, shooting out of the main floor and ceiling vents and side nozzles, blasting out waves of hot steam. My super sauna shower. I knew I'd be in my bathroom for at least 90 minutes.

Was I being a big baby? Or was the danger of the day not to be taken lightly, and I was right to be unnerved? That was the internal debate I had to resolve. I was a detective now, so I had to expect to frequent bad places, like Mad Heights, occasionally on a case. I couldn't melt each time.

Who were those leather-suited people in the dark attacking me?

The question popped into my head. I had never experienced something so crazy. All these people standing in the dark around me. What the hell! I had to find out who or what they were, or it would bug me forever. Phishy would know.

My beautiful shower was over, and I got into the nicest, cleanest, fluffiest white clothes, and then I glided over to my bed. I dove in and pulled my super-fluffy comforters over me. And that was it. I was in for the day. I was not leaving this bed. I was traumatized, and I needed time to regenerate, as the saying goes.

Turn off the video-phone!

I jumped out of the bed and ran to it. It rang.

Recap

The Zen Mindset section touched on how people can reach the right state of mind to achieve their goals. However, the "mindset" must accompany the "action."

Meditation means many things to many people. Cruz got his "alone time" by driving to some back alley in his vehicle to hide away from everyone to just relax and think. He also was fond of his apartment's super shower! Your way may be to sit on the balcony sipping some Earl Grey tea. For others, it may be a morning run through the park with all the birds, squirrels, and dog walkers. Find your way, too.

Week 14: A Day to Unplug

"BECAUSE OF YOU, I'M no longer an agent of this system. Because of you, I've changed. I'm unplugged. A new man, so to speak." — Mr. Smith, The Matrix (Original Movie)

EXCERPT FROM: *Liquid Cool: The Cyberpunk Detective Series (Book One)*

True, I had no serious tragedies to complain about. No great losses. No disabilities. I had all my fingers, toes, limbs, and other natural organs—not a bionic part anywhere. Metropolis hadn't been bad to me.

Everyone simply had to accept it all. I did. But this was an especially bad year of reflection for me, which is why I was here sitting in my red Ford Pony, hiding out on a street I've never been, far from any part of the city I had ever been, so I could just sit, stare at the falling rain, and simmer in my own perennial moroseness and not be bothered by the girlfriend, friends, enemies, frenemies, sidewalk johnnies, hustlers, or any strangers.

The only interruption to the steady rain was the ubiquitous flashing neon and video signs. I paid no attention to the specific ads or messages they were peddling. It was always the same. The corporate ads wanted you to buy something, and the government ads wanted you to do something. The average citizen, on a normal day, was supposedly bombarded by no less than fifty thousand messages in the city. No wonder people were stupid. All those subliminal messages were taking up all the free space in a person's brain—the universe's ultimate disk hardware.

Perspective

"Relax. You'll Live Longer." — *Quaid, Total Recall (1990 Movie)*

EXCERPT FROM: *Liquid Cool: The Cyberpunk Detective Series (Book One)*

When I walked back into my offices fifteen days later, I didn't quite know what to expect. Half a month was a long time for the principal of a new business to be absent. They say when you start a new company, you're a slave to it for at least ten years, with no time off and no vacations. Maybe so, but I did what I had to.

The door was open, and there was Punch Judy with her arms folded with a smile.

"Well, look what came in from the rain," she said. "Is that a new hat?"

"New hat, new coat," I answered.

"When you get new things, they're supposed to be different than the old ones."

"I like the colors I had. All I needed was some modifications."

I felt different, and it was more than the new clothes. PJ could manage the office without me for a while. I was impressed.

"You look rested, too," she said. "Was that the first time you ever slept? Did you ever leave your place?"

"Not even once."

Recap

In the past, we called it "recognizing the Sabbath." However, you definitely don't need to be religious for this life lesson. Everyone can benefit.

What's the definition of a "sabbath"?

Observant religious Jews and Christians both have a day of rest where they refrain from work. Jews observe it from Friday evening to Saturday evening, while practicing Christians observe it on Sunday. The historical context is that God created the universe in six days and rested on the seventh.

Today, we live in the Digital Age, and it's not all the sunny rainbows we were told. Rest and "unplug" from the world for a day. Taking a break from technology, spending quality time with family and friends, and re-energizing for the following week is more important than ever before. No social media, no smartphones, no email. Family, friends, pets, and relaxation.

As Cruz showed from his time in "the box," he returned fully charged for his new career as a street detective. For you, you've finished one week towards your goals and now get to relax and socialize before you start again for the next week.

It's all part of a healthy Zen Mindset.

FOURTH MONTH
April
Classic Sci-Fi Actor Birthdays

CHARACTER (ACTOR) SHOW/Movie

April 1: Janice Rand (Grace Lee Whitney) Star Trek: The Original Series

April 4: Obi-Wan Kenobi (Alec Guinness) Star Wars: Original Movies

April 4: Agent Smith (Hugo Weaving) The Matrix

April 5: Colonel Steven Caldwell (Mitch Pileggi) Stargate: Atlantis

April 6: Lando Calrissian (Billy Dee Williams) Star Wars: Original Movies

April 9: Lieutenant David Corwin (Josh Coxx) Babylon 5

April 15: Kang (Michael Ansara) Star Trek: The Original Series/Deep Space 9/Voyager

April 16: Private Frost (Ricco Ross) Aliens

April 18: The (10th) Doctor (David Tennant) Doctor Who

April 18: Capt. Benjamin Sisko (Avery Brooks) Star Trek: Deep Space Nine

April 18: Rodney McKay (David Hewlett) Stargate: Atlantis

April 19: Anakin Skywalker (Hayden Christensen) Star Wars: The Prequels

April 20: Sulu (George Takei) Star Trek: The Original Series

April 20: Lambert (Veronica Cartwright) Alien

April 20: Leela (Louise Jameson) Doctor Who

April 25: Londo Mollari (Peter Jurasik) Babylon 5

April 25: Private Spunkmeyer (Daniel Kash) Aliens

April 27: Cyrano Jones (Stanley Adams) Star Trek: The Original Series

April 27: Jenna-Louise Coleman (Clara Oswald) Doctor Who

April 29: Capt. Kathryn Janeway (Kate Mulgrew) Star Trek: Voyager

THE PEOPLE POSITIVE MINDSET

Positivity Empowers

"JUST CLOSE YOUR EYES and hold your breath, and everything will turn real pretty." — Roy Neary, Close Encounters of the Third Kind played by Richard Dreyfuss

Last month's section was about internal positivity as a foundation of life. But closely linked with that mindset is how you interact and treat others. Extroverts thrive on being around people. For introverts, it's the opposite—people wear them down after a while, and they seek out solitude. Regardless of your core personality, put your most positive foot forward first whenever dealing with your fellow human.

Cruz didn't start out strong in that area at all—he was a germophobe and dealing with OCD. But he turned it all around despite getting shot at by suit-soldiers.

Excerpt From: *A Cruel Cyber Summer Night (A Liquid Cool Cyberpunk Novella)*

I picked myself up from the ground and watched the glow of the hover-RV engine disappear into the dark, rainy sky.

"Young man, are you police?" one of the sidewalk johnnies asked me. They were standing next to me, looking all around.

"No, but they'll be here," I said. "Real soon."

"That they will," the other one said. "Gunfire, explosions, hovercars falling apart in mid-air—wait till we tell the boys!"

The johnnies started laughing, and one of them patted me on the shoulder. "Young man, you should come by more often. You're loads of fun."

Recap

Positivity, like a smile, is infectious. People are drawn to positive people.

If you think, "I work from home" and don't have to deal with people. Or why does it matter? People-positivity also empowers one important person—you. Positive people are happy and content people. You'll do more and achieve more when you have a positive mindset rather than being all morose.

Let's look at two direct examples and two contrary examples.

The Planners

BE (LIQUID) COOL/MONTHLY PLANNER

MONTH:

SUN	MON	TUE	WED	THU	FRI	SAT

TOP PRIORITIES / GOALS

PEOPLE TO SEE / PLACES TO GO / REMINDERS

NOTES

_____
_____
_____

RATE / ASSESS THE MONTH:

BE (LIQUID) COOL
WEEKLY PLANNER

WEEK:

M T W H F S S

MONDAY

TUESDAY

WEDNESDAY

THURSDAY

FRIDAY

SATURDAY / SUNDAY

WEEK'S PRIORITIES / TO DO

NOTES

RATE / ASSESS THE WEEK:

BE (LIQUID) COOL
WEEKLY PLANNER

WEEK:

M　T　W　H　F　S　S

MONDAY

TUESDAY

WEDNESDAY

THURSDAY

FRIDAY

SATURDAY / SUNDAY

WEEK'S PRIORITIES / TO DO

NOTES

RATE / ASSESS THE WEEK:

BE (LIQUID) COOL
WEEKLY PLANNER

WEEK:

M T W H F S S

MONDAY

TUESDAY

WEDNESDAY

THURSDAY

FRIDAY

SATURDAY / SUNDAY

WEEK'S PRIORITIES / TO DO

NOTES

RATE / ASSESS THE WEEK:

BE (LIQUID) COOL
WEEKLY PLANNER

WEEK:

M T W H F S S

MONDAY

TUESDAY

WEDNESDAY

THURSDAY

FRIDAY

SATURDAY / SUNDAY

WEEK'S PRIORITIES / TO DO

NOTES

RATE / ASSESS THE WEEK:

Week 15: Respect

WILFORD G.: "I'M NOT impressed by your money, position, or title. I'm impressed by how you treat others."

EXCERPT FROM: *Liquid Cool: The Cyberpunk Detective Series (Book One)*

"Here, Phishy Phishy." I'm sure that was the playground tease Phishy had to endure as a child, but I never once joked about his name. I never teased anyone about their name. It was beneath me. It felt like childish stuff, and I didn't do childish stuff. I'm sure that's one reason Phishy always wanted to hang with me. I treated everyone the same, no matter the title or status. He appreciated that. And now I was partners with the crazy cat.

"Phishy!" I yelled and threw the wad of cash at him.

He was hanging on the street with his crew of sidewalk johnnies, like he always did, planning a scam, talking about a scam, or whatever. Phishy jumped in the air and snatched that wad of cash as if he had a bionic hand of steel. Then he transformed before my eyes and had a look. It was like when I threw a piece of chicken to this feral cat as a kid. The cat pounced on that piece of meat as if it had never eaten before and had this look accompanied by a low, guttural growl. The piece of chicken was in a death-lock in its mouth, and if anything came near it, even its mother, it would scratch its eyes out. Phishy's face looked like that.

I stood there, watching him for a moment, until Phishy's psychotic mood passed.

"Oh." His smile returned. "I'm okay."

"You didn't look okay," I said.

He turned around and was fiddling with the groin area of his pants—I assumed the zipper.

"What the hell are you doing over there?" I yelled.

His sidewalk johnny buddies were in a laughing uproar. Phishy was jumping up and down, his back to me, fiddling with his pants. He stopped, did something, and then looked to pull up his zipper. By this point, his crew was rolling on the wet ground, laughing so hysterically I thought for sure they'd have heart attacks.

Phishy turned around to face me. The wad of cash was gone from his hands.

"I'm really okay now," he said.

"Don't even tell me you did what I think you did."

He laughed.

"Girls hide it up there," he said, rubbing his chest. "We put it down there."

"Phishy, it's called a wallet, and it goes in your pants pocket or your jacket pocket. What's wrong with you?"

"Nah, you get robbed that way. No one's going to reach in there. Not even the police."

"Okay, enough, Phishy. I don't even want to hear about your personal body security measures."

"Give us a handshake," he said jokingly as he walked to me like a zombie with his hand outstretched.

"Get away from me, Phishy."

He kept coming, and I ran away.

Perspective

Opposite: Why Be a Jerk? (Especially with Cruz)

EXCERPT: *From Liquid Cool: The Cyberpunk Detective Series (Book One)*

I was treated like a celebrity from the moment I got out of the city hoverlimo that picked me up at my office and flew me to City Hall. Aides were fawning over me and a couple of reporters were following us, as I was led from the lobby, to the general offices, to the elevator capsules, and finally, outside the Mayor's office. There, aides turned over escort duty to the deputies.

A tall man opened the door and gestured me in. Run-Time's office was ridiculously huge. The Mayor's office was double that size. It was like a major trans-continental excursion to walk from the entrance to the Mayor's desk—no mayor to be seen—but four others were waiting. Chief Hub, the

Interpol man, and two other suits. They all were as stone-faced as stone. The tall deputy stood behind me—much too close for my comfort—as I waited.

The Mayor waltzed in with two other aides following him. He had a big smile on his face.

"Mr. Cruz," he called out and vigorously shook my hand. "Thanks for coming by. Please take a seat."

I sat in the chair in front of the desk. As soon as I sat in it, I realized I was dealing with deranged children. The chair was a kid's chair, and from the Mayor's vantage point, all he saw was my head.

"Mr. Cruz, the reason I asked you to come by is I wanted to tell you how things were going to go for you in my city going forward. You will not be getting a detective license. I'm, personally, going to make sure no one in government or any business that does business with the city will do business with you. If you are ever caught referring to yourself as a detective, it will be deemed as an illegal misrepresentation of being a member of the law enforcement industry, and you will be prosecuted and fined. You can apply all the times you want, but it will never be approved. Your gun license, which you've apparently had a long time, has been revoked. You get caught with a weapon outside of your residence, and that will be a felony, which you will be vigorously prosecuted for. I'll find out who's given you that legacy office of yours, and they will quickly find out what it's like to be on the wrong side of this office. You are not welcome in this city. You can bask in your media limelight, for now, but public attention is such a fleeting thing. The reporters will disappear, everyone will forget your name, and then you'll be a bum again, like you've always been. That's when I'm going to get you. You think we will allow an insignificant civilian to embarrass this office, my police department, and the Interspace Police? You're finished, Mr. Cruz, in this city, finished."

The Mayor should have consulted with the Guy Who Scratched My Vehicle before he said what he said to me.

I got up from their kiddie chair and left his office with my security escort.

Recap

We've all met people who thrive on being jerks and rude to everyone around them. Some of them get away with it, especially in the corporate world, politics, and Hollywood. However, it will usually boomerang back at them and hit them in the teeth one day. No one likes jerks, and no one wants to help them.

Cruz treated everyone with respect, even his frenemies. So, he had an army of people looking out for him and helping him when he needed it the most. His own good behavior towards others helped him achieve his goals and dreams.

Week 16: Humility

"TWO POSSIBILITIES EXIST: either we are alone in the Universe, or we are not. Both are equally terrifying." — Arthur C. Clarke, *English science fiction writer, science writer, inventor, futurist*

EXCERPT FROM: *Liquid Cool: The Cyberpunk Detective Series (Book One)*

Run-Time exited the elevator on the penthouse level, two hundred and fifty floors up, and did as he always did. "Good morning, good ladies," he greeted.

He was not a boss who demanded that staff snap to attention at his arrival. His philosophy was, "If you can't give me a high-five fist bump, or shake my hand like a normal person, then you're working at the wrong place. I'm just a guy, not a dictator or the Second Coming."

Three women sat at the reception desk, evenly spaced apart from each other. "Good morning, Mr. Run-Time," the receptionists responded in unison.

To look at them, you'd think they coordinated their outfits the day before. The Caucasian woman with the British accent was dressed in yellow, the Asian woman with the Southern accent was dressed in blue, and the Black woman with the West Indian accent was in red.

"Boss, your nine a.m. is here early," one of them added.

"Give me five minutes and bring him up to the office."

"He's almost forty-five minutes early, boss."

He stopped and gave her a look. "What am I thinking right now?"

"We'll send him up in five minutes, boss," she answered.

He took the steps two-by-two to his private second floor of the penthouse level and to his office at the very end of a long hallway.

Perspective

There's a difference between acting like Super Man (or Super Woman) and really believing you are.

EXCERPT FROM: *Blade Gunner (Liquid Cool, Book Two)*

I heard the front door open, and people talking, but I stood at my desk looking at the messages. When I looked up, all I saw was PJ's back to me, at the entrance to my office. She stepped backward, and then I saw the woman in front of her.

"Ma'am, you need an appointment," PJ said to her.

The woman was finely dressed in a faux-fur coat, with a black mesh veil hat. She was all in black—dress, nylons, and heeled boots, with white glowing tips. She lifted the veil on her hat.

Her eyes were locked on mine. I quickly tried to size her up to see if I needed to grab my office weapon from underneath my desk.

"You're him," the woman said and smiled.

She moved past PJ and walked to me. Her smiling face did not make me feel any better. I still had a knot in my stomach that something was off about this situation.

"You look exactly like your T-shirt."

That comment made me dislike her. Before, I had been only indifferent toward her. I'm sure from PJ's viewpoint, the woman was on the "good list." How many detectives, serious ones, were being franchised around the city by their secretary and associates with stupid Liquid Cool T-shirts with my face on them? It cheapened me and cheapened my business. PJ told me it was a legitimate revenue stream for the business, and that I shouldn't complain.

"I need you to help me," the woman said.

Now, I was concerned. She had that wide-eyed, "yes-I'm-crazy-and-off-my-meds" look.

"Maybe we can set up a good time for you to come back," I said. "I have to go out to my next appointment."

"Oh, no, Mr. Cruz. That won't do. That won't do at all." Her eyes drifted to my desk and then back to me. "I look so pale. My limbs are so pale. They wouldn't be so pale if they were real."

"Ma'am, all your limbs are bionic?"

My question was more of a code to PJ to get ready.

The woman laughed. "I'm not that bionic." Her laughing stopped, and her smile disappeared. "You're scared of me now."

"Ma'am, I'm not a cyborg at all," I said.

"That's an offensive term, cyborg. What does that even mean? It's offensive."

"It means cybernetic organism," PJ said.

"I'm a woman, not an organism. Germs are organisms. Why aren't you offended by such a word?"

"I'm not offended," PJ answered.

The woman smiled. "Your boss is scared of me, but not you. That means you're like me."

"You need to leave now," PJ said in a bossy tone.

"You need to make me."

I was about to say something. I didn't know what, but something. It was already too late. The woman extended one arm and knocked PJ across my office into the wall. I could see the anger rise in PJ's face as she clenched her teeth, jumped up, and rushed the woman.

PJ had two fully bionic arms. I was the one responsible for her getting them—though at the time, it was to save her life, which I did. There was a reason for Punch Judy's name. She loved to punch people; she was good at it, and she'd had a fair amount of trouble with law enforcement over it. But here in my office, the woman blocked every one of PJ's punches effortlessly. The woman dropped her purse to the ground, and I instinctively knew things were going to go from bad to worse. The woman lifted her arms in a boxing stance, throwing an array of punches not at PJ but at PJ's bionic arms, with tremendous force and speed.

"Oww!" I had never heard PJ get hit in her bionic arms before and cry out, "Oww!" No one had ever out-boxed PJ.

PJ dropped her arms. I couldn't believe it!

"PJ, don't—!" The woman punched PJ in the head, and my secretary crashed to the ground like a bag of old bricks, unconscious.

"Why did you have to do that?" I asked, pointing my electric rifle—my office weapon from underneath my desk—at her. "You shouldn't have done that. That's my employee you just knocked out."

"I'm sorry. My mind isn't functioning properly."

I shot her point-blank in the chest. I wasn't going to fall for the "stall for time" trick.

She stood there looking at me. "I think I'm more cybernetic than organism at this stage of my life."

This was just what I needed. PJ aside, I continued to have serious problems with cyborgs in my office.

Recap

Most of the people Cruz hung around in life, like Run-Time, shared his "treat everyone right" philosophy. His best friend built a megacorporate empire through hard work, marketing, networking, high standards, and respect for others, especially his employees.

Be humble. Be down-to-earth.

In the selected excerpt, PJ, a champion pugilist before she became a cyborg with bionic arms, didn't respect the situation and let herself get knocked out by a crazy (potential) client. Respect isn't just about people but situations. Stay alert and smart in all that you do.

Week 17: Don't Be Rude

"HEY, HEY, HEY — DON'T be mean. We don't have to be mean. 'Cause, remember: no matter where you go... there you are." — Buckaroo Banzai, The Adventures of Buckaroo Banzai Across the 8th Dimension played by Peter Weller

EXCERPT FROM: *Liquid Cool: The Cyberpunk Detective Series (Book One)*

Free City building didn't have elevator capsules—they had elevators. I only had to go to the fortieth floor, but it took forever. Matters were not helped by the elevator car being some damp, moldy, semi-dark tomb. I purposely did not look at the floor. I didn't want to vomit at what I might see.

"My name's Cruz, ma'am."

The woman who answered the door peered at me through a screen partition. She was average size, in a one-piece flannel dress with orange hair.

"How did you get here, wearing that hat?" she asked. "And you still have all ten fingers and toes. The ground floor punks let you get up here with that hat?"

"I'm wearing a classic fedora, ma'am, not a hat."

"Well, listen to the booshy talk. I suppose you don't drive a hovercar."

"I don't. I drive a classic Ford Pony. A Pony is not a hovercar; it's a vehicle."

The woman burst out laughing. "Okay, Mr. Cruz. You got a sense of humor, so you're okay."

"Are you Mrs. Easy Chair Charlie?"

"Oh, God, no. I'm her sister. Ethel!!!"

The woman's scream was like someone stabbing me in the eardrums with an ice pick.

"What?" I heard a woman's voice scream from within the residence.

"It's Mr. Cruz!"

"Let him in, then! And who is Mr. Cruz?"

The sister opened the screen door, and I walked past her and her invisible cloud of cheap perfume. My eyes were always scanning my surroundings, whether inside or outdoors. However, I never got that far as my eyes instantly locked on the trio of gremlins before me—three dirty kids in diapers.

Nothing struck horror in my heart like the sight of a dirty kid in a diaper because it meant the diaper was dirty, too. What was a diaper but strapping an unflushed toilet to your body for the day? I don't use public toilets—ever. All I could see in my mind's eye was the image of some dirty kid in a dirty diaper ripping it off and flinging it at people, people like me. Suddenly, I had an uncontrollable urge to dive out the nearest window.

"What's wrong with you?" the sister asked. "You look like someone kicked you in the stomach."

"No, I'm okay."

"I know our humble residence isn't what you booshy-class are accustomed to, but it's home sweet home to us."

"Mrs...?

"Call me, Sister. Everyone around here does."

"Sister, I've been many things, but booshy has never been one of them."

"What part of the city do you stay at?"

"Rabbit City."

The woman broke out in an "A-ha!" She moved to the three kids. "Where the booshy playboys live."

That was a first for me that someone considered Rabbit City upscale.

"How did you get up here without getting mugged?"

I turned to the new voice. "Mrs. Easy Chair Charlie?"

"Mrs. Easy is fine. Yeah. How did you get up here without a scratch? Did you have some kind of police escort?"

The other woman was a slightly older version, also in a dark-patterned flannel dress with yellow hair. She walked to me.

"It was a trick I learned when I interned for Police Central as a kid."

She stopped walking to me. "Police Central? You worked for the cops? As a kid? How? You a cop?"

"I'm not a policeman."

"Listen to the booshy playboy," Sister interjected. "Cop! Only booshy say 'police.'"

"How'd you get to be a kid copper?"

"I'm not a cop. I said: I interned with the cops as a kid."

"Interned? What's that?"

"In school. Kids go to businesses and hang for a day for extra credit for class."

"And you went to the cops?"

"Yeah."

"Why'd you do that?"

"I'm a contrarian."

"What's that?"

"I do the opposite of what other people usually do."

"That's for sure," Mrs. Easy said. "What are you then, if not a cop?"

"I'm just a laborer guy who restores classic hovercars…"

"Vehicles, you mean," Sister interrupted.

"… on the side. Not a cop."

"Policeman," Sister interjected.

"Considering the circumstances of your husband's death, I probably shouldn't have—"

"Keep your undershorts on, Mr. Cruz. I'm not about to break down sobbing. Go on with your story. How'd you get up here without a scratch from the ground floor punks?"

"Especially with that hat!"

"Fedora," I corrected Sister, and she laughed. "When I interned for the cops, I had to go into a shady part of the city, and the captain, at the time, wrote on the back of his business card: 'Cruz is my friend. See that nothing happens to him, or you will NOT be my friend, and I will come visiting to show you how much you're NOT my friend.' He told me to throw it at the leader of the local street punk gang. It worked, and I've been using the trick ever since."

"Who did you get to write on a business card for you this time?"

"Someone here in Free City, whose good graces I know they would want to remain on the right side of. The leader of a much bigger Free City gang than them."

"And why would he write you such a business card message?"

"I restore hovercars. I restored his racing hovercar for him."

"Mr. Cruz, that's a stupid story. Even if it were true, it would only work with brainy criminal-class criminals. The animal criminal-class would shoot you, even if it means they'd get shot, too. They don't think; they react. What were you packing? I know you stuck a gun in their face. They really are a bunch of cowards. Everyone knows it."

"You caught me, Mrs. Easy. I just flashed the big gun in my jacket."

"I knew it. Wait! You didn't bring your gun up in my place?"

"I left it in my vehicle with my bodyguard."

I suddenly felt a presence behind me, and there was the sister scanning me from neck to leg with a pole metal detector. "He's clean," she said.

Smack!

I jumped at the sound and glanced at the three kids. The smallest one, with only a couple of teeth in his mouth, was holding a large fly swatter in his hand. He cut the air with it and laughed. He found his mark and slammed the swatter down on the floor. His—I think it was a he—two siblings pranced about in a fit of unrestrained laughter, flapping their arms. Then, one after another, jumped on top of the fly swatter with their bare, dirty feet. "Dead!" "Dead!" Was it too late for me to dive out the window?

"Have a seat, Mr. Cruz, the detective," she said.

Every chair and couch was covered in garbage—toys, clothes, magazines, and papers.

"Sit anywhere. Just throw it on the floor."

I was uncomfortable doing so, but I did. I couldn't believe Easy Chair Charlie lived here, and this was his wife. Easy always presented himself as a class act, and there was nothing classy about this place; I saw a fly buzzing around in the apartment home.

"Wait a minute. Why did you call me a detective?"

"Isn't that what you're doing? Detecting?"

"Yeah, but what made you call me that?"

"Your associate."

"My associate?"

"Mr. Cruz, did you really believe I'd let a strange man come up to my place with my sister, little nieces, and nephew? Are you crazy? Your associate called ahead and told us you were coming. If he didn't call, you'd still be outside a closed, triple-dead-bolted, electrified door."

"Is the first initial of this associate, Phishy?"

She laughed, and her sister appeared and stood behind her, laughing too.

"Don't worry, Mr. Cruz. He said you were undercover."

Perspective

Not everyone sees the world as we do. (And we don't mean extraterrestrials)

EXCERPT FROM: *The Electric Sheep Massacre (Liquid Cool, Book Four)*

London police were not Metropolis police. We had heavy police cruisers. When I saw the London police hovercars descend from the sky, I thought I was about to be arrested by children. Their hovercars were like kiddie cars. The officer got out with their hands on their guns as they walked to me. I was just standing there holding my bag.

"Hello, sir."

"Officer."

"Did you not hear the overhead to remain where you were?"

"Sorry, I didn't."

"When there is an accident, you need to follow instructions."

The other police officer had been talking on his mobile the entire time. He flipped it closed and walked to me with a stern expression.

"Sir, you'll have to come with us to the police station," he said.

"Scotland Yard?" I asked.

"Yes, Scotland Yard."

I smiled.

The police were not amused when I asked if I could take pictures of the building for my wife. They took my bag from me and inspected it, but still wouldn't give it back. The building was not as big as Police One, but it was still a massive building. I had given them my ID, which they also didn't return.

They sat me in an interrogation room and had me wait by myself. After about five minutes, a police officer came.

"Sir, do you want anything nonalcoholic to drink?"

"Water would be fine," I answered.

"Fresh or ocean?" he asked.

I looked at him, grinning, thinking he was making a joke.

"I haven't lost the plot. Fresh is regular. Ocean is treated," he said.

"Which do you drink?"

"Ocean, of course."

"With all that salt."

"I'll bring you fresh." He left the room, but I heard him say, "American," as he closed the door.

I had my cup of fresh water I didn't touch, and after about ten minutes, two officers came and took me out of the room, down a long hall, and into an open space that seemed to be filled with hundreds of officers in uniform or in civilian clothes. It was a similar set-up to that of Metro Police Central. They took me to an office and had me sit in a chair in front of a desk. One waited with me; the other disappeared.

Excerpt From: *Liquid Cool: The Cyberpunk Detective Series (Book One)*

"I'm Cruz. Whatcha want?" That's how I greeted strangers. Though, I had to admit that it was somewhat of a rude and snarky response but hey, I didn't like strangers. I liked my friends, my frenemies, and even my enemies—all of them I knew but strangers I had no regard for. My girlfriend frequently scolded me on my bad manners, saying, "A stranger is a friend you haven't met yet." I had a far less charitable definition of them. Social scientists predicted that the bigger a city gets, the higher the anti-sociability of its people. There was no city bigger than Metropolis, and I was born and raised here, and most of my waking thoughts were about how to get out of here, so I wouldn't die here.

Recap

Above is how we were first introduced to Cruz. In those days, he was rude himself, and he knew it. But he's a whole different person nowadays.

This is a big, wide world we live in. In Cruz's universe, humans are in space, on the moon, and on Mars. But even without all that, there's a lot of diversity out there (and I don't mean skin color). Different customs, religions, points of view, nationalities, etc. Keep all this in mind. Maybe the "rude" person is just having a bad day, and your kindness, not rudeness in kind, might be the right response.

Week 18: People Don't Like Negative People

PJ: "*CRUZ, YOU ARE always a party pooper. Stop poopin' the party.*"

EXCERPT FROM: *Classic Cyborg (Liquid Cool: From the Crazy Maniac Files, Book One)*

My office was on the hundredth floor of one of many office mega-towers on Circuit Circle. From my private office, I sat at my desk, staring out at the window with a cup of silk coffee in hand. PJ was right. A storm was coming, and it was going to be bad. I had a rare, clear view of the line of monolith office towers through the tinted windows. No rain yet, but the cloud cover above was so dark and dank that it seemed all the water on the planet was building up to crash down upon Metropolis any minute.

I swiveled around in my chair to see PJ appear at my open doorway. She was hired as a secretary, though I had no idea what she had promoted herself to these days. We started out as frenemies, but now she was my second in command. She had short, crimson hair, a simulated mole—a dot above her lips, today, matching her crimson lipstick-covered lips. Hip female business suits were what she wore nowadays—sleeveless, knee-high skirts. The only reminder of her previous life were her heeled leather boots. In that previous life, she was a soldier in the punk-posh gang Les Enfantes Terribles in Neo-Paris, France. She loved her sleeveless tops to show off her buff bionic arms. PJ's street name was Punch Judy, because she liked to punch people and could, in fact, punch a three-hundred-pound cyborg through a steel and concrete wall.

But PJ wasn't just about the violence. Like me, that was only when needed. She had become the master...mistress...of customer service and "client acquisition." She had turned the main office area into a shrine to all my high-profile cases. There were framed pictures covering practically every inch of the reception area. Pictures of me at press conferences, at police scenes, with megacorporate senior executives, with the Council of Corporations president, and me shaking hands with the Mayor. But my favorites were those with just the Average Joes and Janes of the supercity, including the client from my very first major case, Carol Num, after I successfully rescued her kidnapped daughter. These were the cases that made it all worthwhile, despite all the crazy maniacs I had to deal with and getting shot. I didn't like getting shot.

"Don't I have a client?" I asked.

"He's late, but look at the weather. We're lucky anyone is leaving their home."

"But nothing's happened, and it's barely raining."

"But it's going to be bad. I bet there's more water hovering in the sky up there than in the ocean."

"PJ, rain doesn't hover. It only comes down and wets you and causes accidents."

She pointed at the window to the sky. "That's hovering. Look at that."

"Where are my clients? We can't make money with an empty office. I should be out there getting clients or solving cases."

"No, no. You don't need to get clients anymore. You're famous. The clients come to you."

"Clients? You mean a lot of crazy maniacs, sometimes crazier than the criminals."

"That's one time—NeuroDancer."

"Blade Gunner case?"

"She saved you."

"Her brother?"

"He tried to, but he didn't know it was you. Besides, you became buddies."

"Electric Sheep Massacre?"

"Okay, he was crazy, but you've had hundreds of clients. Those are only a few." We heard the front door buzzer. "I'm not going to allow you to infect me with your negativity. It's not even lunchtime, and that may be your client." She pointed at me. "No negativity with the clients."

Perspective

PJ: "You are too negative most of the time. People don't like to hire negative people. Speaking of clients, when am I getting more money?"

EXCERPT FROM: *Blade Gunner (Liquid Cool, Book Two)*

The office was closed, but most businesses were closed on Christmas Day. The doors were locked, and the "Closed for the Day, Please Call" neon sign was flashing, but PJ and I were there. I had turned my office into my own version of a television store, with flat screens on every inch of one wall, each on a different news channel.

Anything that happened, I wanted to see it live.

I didn't have to worry about Blinky. The crazy slider was in New Vegas DJ-ing a Christmas party. It wasn't that I thought he was still in danger, any more than Phishy. It was that I wanted everyone accounted for at all times.

Phishy was on Sidewalk Johnny Brigade duty—I had them on the streets. It was doubtful they'd see or hear anything relevant with the surveillance blanket of Metro Police, spacemen, and the Martians over the city, but that was how random chance worked. They couldn't be everywhere; neither could we, but one of us would be at the right time and place.

"What is it we're going to see on the TV?" she asked. "All this news is boring. Why don't you have any international news channels on?"

"I want the Metro news on. Not people babbling in languages I don't understand."

"English isn't the only language spoken in Metropolis. Haven't you heard your future parents-in-law speak?"

"Don't remind me."

"And the Martian speaks Martian."

I glanced at her. "There is no Martian language."

"Yes, there is. He spoke it to us."

"He was playing around."

"If you were to watch international news, you'd know there are a dozen off-world languages."

"Why would people make up new languages when there are already a thousand languages spoken on Earth?"

"Cruz, you are always a party pooper. Stop poopin' the party; let people make up languages and have fun."

Recap

While positivity empowers, negativity is a total energy drainer.

We have all encountered this in life. People gravitate to positive people and avoid the negative ones. That's another social certitude as old as humanity itself. Be one of those positive people whenever you can.

FIFTH MONTH
May
Classic Sci-Fi Actor Birthdays

CHARACTER (ACTOR) SHOW/Movie

May 5: Bishop (Lance Henriksen) Aliens

May 6: Cmdr. Jeffrey Sinclair (Michael O'Hare) Babylon 5

May 7: Newt (Carrie Henn) Aliens

May 7: Silik (John Fleck) Star Trek: Enterprise

May 7: Lt. Meeklo Braca (David Franklin) Farscape

May 8: Vir Cotto (Stephen Furst) Babylon 5

May 9: HAL 9000 (voice) (Douglas Rain) 2001: A Space Odyssey/2010: The Year We Make Contact

May 9: SAL 9000 (voice) (Candice Bergen as Olga Mallsnerd) 2010: The Year We Make Contact

May 12: Capt. John Sheridan (Bruce Boxleitner) Babylon 5

May 12: Donna Noble (Catherine Tate (Catherine Ford) Doctor Who

May 13: Dozer (Anthony Ray Parker) The Matrix

May 14: George Lucas 14 creator of Star Wars

May 16: Cassiopeia (Laurette Spang) Battlestar Galactica (Original Series)

May 17: Hudson (Bill Paxton) Aliens

May 18: G'Kar (Andreas Katsulas) Babylon 5

May 19: Chewbacca (Peter Mayhew) Star Wars: Original Movies

May 20: Dr. Phlox (John Billingsley) Star Trek: Enterprise

May 21: Captain Apollo (Richard Hatch) Battlestar Galactica (Original Series)

May 22: Captain Terrell (Paul Winfield) The Wrath of Khan (Star Trek)

May 25: Yoda (voice) (Frank Oz) Star Wars: Original Movies

May 26: Grand Moff Tarkin (Peter Cushing) Star Wars: Original Movies

May 27: Count Dooku (Christopher Lee) Star Wars: The Prequels

May 27: Capt. Christopher Pike (Jeffrey Hunter) Star Trek: The Original Series

May 29: Darth Vader (Sebastian Shaw) Star Wars: Original Movies

May 30: Miles Edward O'Brien (Colm Meaney) Star Trek: The Next Generation/Deep Space Nine

May 30: Dr. Dave Bowman (Keir Dullea) 2001: A Space Odyssey/2010: The Year We Make Contact

THE ENGAGEMENT MINDSET

About Engagement

"ENGAGE!" — CAPTAIN *Kirk, Star Trek: The Original Series*

We've covered the Action Mindset earlier, which often means "jumping in" and "getting started" with your goals. But there's more. You need to be engaged. If you're doing the work and mindlessly going through the motions and checking them off your planner, then that's almost as bad as not starting at all. Be engaged, involved, and "present" in what you're doing as you carry out your goals.

Excerpt From: *Liquid Cool: The Cyberpunk Detective Series (Book One)*

There were pockets in the city that had vortexes—that's what everyone called them. Wherever the rain came down between two heat vents, these spiraling circles of water would be created that were fun to look at. Kids loved to run through them, pretending to pass through dimensions or time, like in sci-fi movies.

Well, there was one right in front of Eye Candy. I came through the vortex with my new tan coat flapping, my new tan fedora pulled down just right on my head, and I could see Dot and the ladies had already seen me. Damn, I knew I looked cool. I opened the door and stepped inside. Dot, her boss Prima Donna, and her fellow fashionistas were standing there, like a pack, grinning at me.

The real reason for my swagger was the post-Phishy-shooting-me perception exercise, which was a secret I'd take to the grave when it came to Dot. I felt my chest was made of steel. Though, I wished I had a darker complexion like Run-Time or the Good Kosher Man because that area of my chest was still red and tender, but that was easy enough to hide.

"Well, look at you," Prima said. "We were starting to wonder if you had gone off-world and left your fiancée behind."

"I knew where he was," Dot interjected. "So, you're finished with the box?" she asked me.

"I'm finished," I answered.

"And?"

"And nothing. Other than…tonight is date night."

The women laughed.

"Date night?" Dot asked incredulously. "You lock yourself up in your place for over two weeks, show up at my job trying to look suave, and now it's date night all of a sudden."

"Well…yeah," I answered. "The hovercab is waiting."

Prima glanced at Dot.

"He's got spunk, China," Goat Girl said, half-laughing. "Gotta give him that."

"China Doll, you are excused for date night," Prima said to Dot.

"Are you sure? Because I'm not sure I'm sure."

"She's sure," I said. "Guess where we're going?" It wasn't just the ladies, but all the customers within earshot wanted to know. "The Booty Shaker."

Dot let out a yell, jumped up, and ran to the back room.

"Why doesn't my man take me to classy dance joints?" Pinkie asked aloud.

"I don't know," Cyan answered. "Mine doesn't either. I'm thinking we got the wrong kind of man. Hey, Cruz, you got any male friends of the hetero persuasion, like you, and single? Pinkie and I need to trade up."

"Me too," Goat Girl added.

"I'll put the word out," I said.

Dot reappeared with her purse, which, as always, matched her outfit exactly. "Let's go," she said to me.

Recap

Cruz is ready for action!

We've had the Positive Thinking. We've done the Planning. Now's the "good part." We're into the Action!

By this time, you should already have four months of progress under your belt. You see what's working. You've made adjustments in terms of possibly underestimating or overestimating what you can accomplish in a week. You may have already accomplished some things, too!

The Planners

BE (LIQUID) COOL/MONTHLY PLANNER

MONTH:

SUN	MON	TUE	WED	THU	FRI	SAT

TOP PRIORITIES / GOALS

PEOPLE TO SEE / PLACES TO GO / REMINDERS

NOTES

RATE / ASSESS THE MONTH:

BE (LIQUID) COOL
WEEKLY PLANNER

WEEK:

M T W H F S S

MONDAY

TUESDAY

WEDNESDAY

THURSDAY

FRIDAY

SATURDAY / SUNDAY

WEEK'S PRIORITIES / TO DO

NOTES

RATE / ASSESS THE WEEK:

BE (LIQUID) COOL
WEEKLY PLANNER

WEEK:

| M | T | W | H | F | S | S |

MONDAY

TUESDAY

WEDNESDAY

THURSDAY

FRIDAY

SATURDAY / SUNDAY

WEEK'S PRIORITIES / TO DO

NOTES

RATE / ASSESS THE WEEK:

BE (LIQUID) COOL
WEEKLY PLANNER

WEEK:

| M | T | W | H | F | S | S |

MONDAY

TUESDAY

WEDNESDAY

THURSDAY

FRIDAY

SATURDAY / SUNDAY

WEEK'S PRIORITIES / TO DO

NOTES

RATE / ASSESS THE WEEK:

BE (LIQUID) COOL
WEEKLY PLANNER

WEEK:

M T W H F S S

MONDAY

TUESDAY

WEDNESDAY

THURSDAY

FRIDAY

SATURDAY / SUNDAY

WEEK'S PRIORITIES / TO DO

NOTES

RATE / ASSESS THE WEEK:

BE (LIQUID) COOL
WEEKLY PLANNER

WEEK:

M T W H F S S

MONDAY

TUESDAY

WEDNESDAY

THURSDAY

FRIDAY

SATURDAY / SUNDAY

WEEK'S PRIORITIES / TO DO

NOTES

RATE / ASSESS THE WEEK:

Week 19: Hard Work

DON'T WISH FOR IT. Work For It!

EXCERPT FROM: *Liquid Cool: The Cyberpunk Detective Series (Book One)*

Today was my first shoe-leather day after almost a week of biz research. GW was my first real client—start to finish—and I had no one else since then, so I was on a mission, doing what all the business books tell you. Get off your butt and find your next client.

"I'm here to see Mr. Smalls," I said to the lobby receptionist.

"He's expecting you?" she asked.

"Yeah," I replied with a lie. "Here's my card."

She took the card from my hand, read it, and looked up at me.

"Detective?"

"Yes, private detective."

The woman almost seemed frightened. "I'll announce you immediately."

People-Droid had been the seventeenth company, or so I visited. I started at the first business tower on the corner and would work my way up each tower, then down the street. This was the first company on the third floor; I had 100 more floors to go, and each had six businesses, on average. I figured my shoe-leather soliciting would take me a few years to complete just this district.

"You can check, but I think you really should compare my presentation to the flunkies they're about to send you. But Mr. Smalls, I understand you need to make the best business decision for your company. Here's my business card—it has my mobile on it—and if you change your mind, I'll get myself back to your office. I want to establish a good clientele of corporate businesses, such as yours."

The man took my card and glanced at it.

"I'll let myself out, but thank you for the opportunity to present."

I left the office.

I didn't expect ever to hear from the man. I just consigned myself to a very, very long day of shoe-leather soliciting. That's all I could do. I had to make my own connections. No one would do it for me. Every business guy and gal I ever met said the same thing: Starting a business is brutal, but once you get your first client, number two is easier, and then comes number three, four, and five. Then you reach a critical mass where those first ones start sending you business automatically. But be prepared for the initial orgy of unfiltered, soul-crushing rejection. Well, this day was already that, except for the brief chat with Smalls.

Perspective

To be or not to be? Work harder or work smarter?

EXCERPT FROM: *Liquid Cool: The Cyberpunk Detective Series (Book One)*

GW's case was a missing person. Mr. Smalls' case was corporate espionage. When I returned, they escorted me all the way to the office at the end of the hall. Waiting for me were more people in suits, male and female than I had ever seen in one room in my entire life. Run-Time had three VPs. This company had like fifty, including Smalls. Probably one of the many reasons they were a second-tier company rather than a first.

"I'm going to make this brief, Mr. Cruz," Smalls' boss said from his seat at the head of the long conference table. He was a much larger man, in a black pinstripe suit and wearing blue-tinted shades. "I want you to find out who's stealing from our warehouse."

All the VPs were sitting at attention around the long conference table and turned from him to look at me in unison. It was funny to watch.

"Find them and then do what? Police?"

"No police. Notify our internal security," he answered.

I knew what that meant. It meant the internal security would be judge-jury-executioners. I heard all about the world of corporate espionage. Stealing was rampant between the megacorporations and if they used the phrases "internal security" and "espionage," as in the case of stealing, it meant the security were on-the-payroll gangsters who made people disappear permanently. The corporate world, government, the streets—they were all a bunch of criminals. But as long as they paid me, I had bills to pay.

I nodded. "All I need are the details, and I'll get on it today. If I can recover any of the products stolen, do you want them recovered for an additional fee?"

"Do you even know what products we make, Mr. Cruz?"

"You make cosmetic bionic parts—the best in Metropolis. My fiancée has one of your models—NS model."

"The neck and trapezoid replacement model," one of the female VPs said.

"Yeah. She was in a terrible accident as a teenager, and it saved her life."

It was like a giant arctic cloud had lifted from the room. Suddenly, they were interested in me. Suddenly, they liked me. I realized this is what business was all about. Connections. If you knew someone they knew, went to a school they went to, used their product, and had some human-interest story to go with it, you were "part of the team." It was so simple. Smalls was more interested in me, because I knew a fellow businessman. Smalls' boss and company were more interested that I knew someone who directly used their bionic (and very expensive) product. No one really seemed to care whether I was any good as a detective.

Smalls said as he glanced at his boss, "I'll get him fully briefed on the situation."

"Mr. Cruz," his boss interrupted. "You're not a mindless solicitor, then. You seem to know all about my company. Do you also know about our problem?"

"I do. And who's stealing from you."

Smalls and all the other VPs looked at me with surprised expressions.

I said, "The only way for someone like me—a new detective in the industry—to get new clients and beat out established detective firms, is if I'm willing and able to do a lot of work, the established firms won't. I have to be able to walk into a business, knowing all about their case before they tell me a thing—basically, have the case solved. That's the only way, because the expectation of performance is so much higher for us new guys than the established firms."

"You're a smart man, Mr. Cruz," Smalls' boss said. "Who stole my products?"

"Your neighbor."

"My neighbor?" Smalls' boss looked at the other VPs. They looked at me.

"The Tech-Human company across the hall?" he asked. "Those motherless sons-of-bitches, I knew it."

I leaned forward in my chair and rested my elbows on the table. I looked right into the eyes of Smalls' boss all the way across the table. "Your neighbor," I repeated.

Now he knew who I meant, and a look of disgust came over his face. The two of us were the only ones in the room who knew what I meant.

Small's boss stood from the table. "Cut Mr. Cruz a check for his retainer and have the second one ready for when he concludes the case and a third for a bonus."

"Yes, sir," Smalls said as he stood, too.

All the VPs around the table stood in unison.

"Anything else, Mr. Cruz?"

"If my work is to your satisfaction, I'd like to get a business review, too."

"Fine, fine." He turned to Smalls. "Handle that too."

Recap

It's not always about working harder. It's about working smarter and effectively.

Cruz was definitely working harder than most other detectives would have to establish himself. But he also did his homework to cleverly get his "foot in the door."

No matter how simple or mundane your own tasks may be, the principles are the same: work hard, work smart, stay the course, and get back on track if you fall off course.

Week 20: Don't Forget the Family

CRUZ: MY MA POINTED at my father and said in Spanish-accented English, "Kendo master."

EXCERPT FROM: *Liquid Cool: The Cyberpunk Detective Series (Book One)*

Meanwhile, at the Concrete Mama...

"Cruz, your parents are here!" Phishy peeked in the door to tell me.

"What? My parents? Where? Here or on the mobile?"

"Here!"

The notion that my parents would fly all the way to Metropolis made little sense to me, but it was them. My mother came in, holding her little purse in front of her like she always did. This one was dark brown; she had others. Both had matching black slicker coats and black boots over their pants instead of under. She smiled at me. She never wore much makeup but had a perfect complexion, and her black hair was always pulled back in a braided ponytail. They were practically the same height—shorter than me by an inch or so. My Pops came in, his graying mustache and beard, wearing a fedora that looked suspiciously like my own, but he hated hats. In his hand was a sheathed sword. Now, I knew it was really him. My father was a prime example of the negative effect of Japanese samurai culture on the general public. He carried that sword everywhere.

"Ma, what are you doing here?" I stopped myself, did the son thing, and gave her a hug and a kiss.

"Pops," I gave him a hug. "When did you get here? How did you get here? It's dangerous out there. You shouldn't have come here."

My mother smiled and spoke in Spanish.

"Yes, Ma, but it's even more dangerous out there than usual."

My Pops had unsheathed his sword and was swinging it around.

"And no sword is going to scare away any street punk or whoever it is after me. Put that away, Pops, before you put your eye out."

There was a bang at the door, and everyone jumped.

"Who's banging my door?" PJ yelled and pointed her rifle at it.

The Wans were poised with their weapons. My Pops was looking at the door, holding the samurai sword, as if it was a bat, and he was about to swing, and my Mom…

"Mom! Why is your hand in that little purse of yours?"

She looked at me sheepishly.

"I know you're reaching for a piece of that candy and not for some concealed weapon, right?"

She smiled at me and nodded.

I looked at Dot; we both shook our heads.

"I say we elope and leave the four of them, and everyone else, behind."

"I agree," she said and then yelled something at her parents in Chinese. They just smiled at her, and she threw up her hands.

There was a knock at the door. This time, PJ went to look at the door-cam. My Pops was swirling his sword around again with one hand.

"Pops! You're going to put your eye out. And what are you going to do with that? Someone shoots at you; you'll whack the bullet back at them?"

The door opened, and there was a bunch of sidewalk johnnies there. A man behind them pushed through.

"Cruz!"

He fired a gun at me!

My father swung at the laser blast and hit it back right at the gunman. The round hit the gunman in his face, and he yelled out as one of his eye sockets began to illuminate. Every sidewalk johnny in the hall jumped him and took him down to the floor. Phishy was in the hall, too, and reached to close the door, but PJ just kicked it closed.

"Why are strangers always trying to shoot me?" I yelled out. I looked at my Pops. "You whacked that laser bullet back at that guy."

He grinned and twirled the sword around.

"You've been tricking me all these years, Pops."

My Ma pointed at him and said in Spanish-accented English, "Kendo master."

Perspective

Family is part of the "show" whether you like it or not. So don't neglect them.

EXCERPT FROM: *Write Me a Murder on Jules Vernes' Island (Liquid Cool, Book Nine)*

On Jules Verne's Island with Cruz, his wife, Dot, Cruz Jr., and the newest member of the family, Kat.

"Where have you two been?"

Dot stood in the kitchen as Cruz Jr. and I came in through the door of our bungalow. I stopped.

"Dot, why are you wearing a Sherlock Holmes hat?"

"Just something I picked up."

I noticed on the couch that Kat was wearing a little Sherlock Holmes hat on her head, too.

"Dot, I am not Sherlock Holmes."

"I can be your deputy."

Dot had something in her hand as she walked over to Cruz. Jr. and took off his black fedora.

"Deputy?" I asked. "Are we gunfighters at the O.K. Corral? What's that on my son's head, Dot? You got a Sherlock Holmes hat for him, too?"

"Cruz, we have work to do."

"We?"

"Yes."

"Where did you get these hats, Dot? This is a sci-fi island. Why would they have Sherlock Holmes merchandise?"

"Because Sir Arthur Conan Doyle was also a sci-fi writer."

"He was?"

"Yes, he wrote Lost World."

"He wrote that? The island with dinosaurs."

"No, a secret region of South America with prehistoric animals and creature men."

I smiled. "Dot, how do you know this?"

"Cruz, I do know stuff, too."

"They sell this in the store?"

"The island has a full merchandise store of classic and contemporary sci-fi writers and, in Sir Doyle's case, a companion section of Sherlock Holmes merchandise."

"So why are you putting strange headgear on the heir to the Liquid Cool Detective empire?"

Dot laughed.

"What about Kat?" she asked.

"Firstborn is always the heir. She can be the VP."

"Or the co-heir?"

"Co-heir? There's no such word...or concept."

"You know...like in marriage. Husband and wife, you know."

"Oh, yes, I see. Yes, it's becoming clear to me now."

"Is it?" Dot said, with her arms folded.

"Yes. Co-heir. I remember that word now."

"I'm glad your memory is returning."

"Yes. So I am." I looked at Cruz. Jr. "Cruz Control, you, me, we men will talk privately offline."

Cruz Jr. giggled, clapping his hands and nodding.

"You two do know I'm still standing here?" Dot said.

Recap

Don't isolate yourself from family and friends as you work on personal growth or achieving great things unless you plan to be a hermit on a secluded island or on a cloaked planetoid. But wouldn't you want them to visit?

Week 21: Build Your Tribe

CRUZ: ...WITH MY ENTIRE *network of friends and associates. That was my ace in the hole.*

EXCERPT FROM: *Blade Gunner (Liquid Cool, Book Two)*

I had to give it to Phishy. The Sidewalk Johnny Brigade was his idea completely. All were wearing fedoras, and most were wearing Liquid Cool T-shirts under their clothes. PJ thought it was stupid, but she thought everything he did was stupid. I did, too, but they had turned out to be a legitimate resource for me and my business. Police had their network of confidential informants throughout Metropolis. I had my equivalent with the sidewalk johnnies.

The most impressive of all of them was Sidewalk Sid. I'd always thought of him as one of Phishy's main sidekicks, but he could do things on his own.

He filled me in on what he'd seen while on the streets of Whiskey Way. I didn't care why he was there—it was another one of the many seedy sections of the supercity. He had given me significant intel relevant to my case.

I shook his hand and gave him a few bucks for his trouble, though he didn't ask for it and hadn't expected it.

"Did it help, Mr. Cruz?"

"It sure did, Sid," I replied. "Have everyone keep their eyes and ears open."

"You got it, Mr. Cruz."

I opened my personal office door for him and followed him out.

"Stupid man called," PJ said.

"Phishy called?" I corrected.

"Yeah, him."

Perspective

Cruz: I pointed to the sky. "My friends are here."

EXCERPT FROM: *AI Confidential (Liquid Cool, Book Six)*

I first met Bite-Size in my NeuroDancer case; Phishy introduced us. He was a roly-poly of a kid with spectacles, and he smoked. He ran the Netsite Movie-Town Madness and knew more about movies than anybody. I didn't think I'd ever work with him on a case again since I planned to stay as far away from the movie industry as possible—I felt it had an overabundance of crazy maniacs. But I had been impressed with him, and his name was one of the first that popped into my mind when I was thinking about who I could hire to run my own secret project.

I told him not to, but he showed up in a Liquid Cool T-shirt. What was worse was that the hovercar he arrived in was driven by his parents! I watched from my hovervan as he wandered into the crowd of sidewalk johnnies outside. He waved to the parents as they flew away. I could already hear the laughter. My great contractor was a little kid being shuttled around by his parents.

He was led inside, so I waited. Wilford would give him the debrief, not to say my name out loud. One of the sidewalk johnnies waved to me from the main entrance. I wasn't looking forward to this part.

I got out of the hovervan, and immediately it started. The sidewalk johnnies at the main entrance were laughing. I came in, and all the people on the ground, chairs, and cots were laughing. In the center office, Wilford was red; he'd been laughing. Bite-Size stood there with arms folded—not laughing.

"Bite-Size!" I yelled. "How could you? You're old enough to drive. Why did you have your parents drive you?"

"I don't drive."

"What's wrong with hovertaxis?"

"Why am I going to pay for a hovertaxi when my parents can drive me? They were going the same way."

All this did was start the laughter again, with Wilford leading it.

"Is this your secret operator?" Wilford asked. "A toddler? When's Cruz, Jr. getting here?"

"If I'm going to be laughed at, I can go home," Bite-Size said with a huff.

"They're laughing at me!" I told him.

BE COOL

Bite-Size raised his hand in the air. That got my attention and everyone else's. We heard commotion outside, and then the door opened. Ten kids marched in, walking to him—they were all identical in every way. They stopped and turned to face out.

"Ladies and gentlemen," Bite-Size began. He put his cigarette in the corner of his mouth. "Which of these individuals are real? Which of them are evil killer androids ready to rip your guts from your belly? I know what you're going to say! Just shoot them, but that's too slow. Robots will always be able to move faster than a human, unless you're one of the few 90% cyborgs. No! You need—my Turing Glasses! You need the ability to know human from android at a glance. Look at them! Who's who?"

Bite-Size pulled a gun from his jacket and aimed at them. Of course, we were not able to tell who was who, but the real kids were ducking.

"Bite-Size!" I yelled. "Put that gun away, and the safety's on."

Wilford walked to Bite-Size's demonstration group and looked at him. "Turing Glasses?"

"Yes," Bite-Size said. He held out a pair of shades.

"How does it work?"

"I can show you."

"Where did these androids come from?"

"The movie studios, of course. People have no idea that the entire stunt performer industry is practically gone. No one says anything for political reasons—the whole robots taking people's jobs thing. I borrowed them. Not the actors, though. They're quintuplets I had to hire, which I expect a certain person to reimburse me fully with a bonus."

"Okay, Bite-Size," I said.

Wilford looked at the shades. "You made this?"

"Cruz designed it. He gave me the specs. I had some guys I know create them. I told them it was for a movie."

Wilford looked at me. No one was laughing now.

Recap

Earlier, we discussed how important it is to pick your key associates. However, it's not a one-time, do-it-and-done endeavor. You're always building your network for knowledge, connections, or socializing.

Building your tribe also doesn't mean you're running it or even have to be a major player. Simply being a member of a great tribe or team of colleagues is just as valuable.

Who's Compstat Connie

CRUZ'S ORIGINAL MENTOR

Random violence happened in Metropolis all too often. But this wasn't random. I couldn't prove it yet, but the bigger question was—why? I would learn everything possible and impossible there was to know about that night of the crime. So, before I went into the "box", I had to visit Compstat Connie. She was like the female version of Wilford G. Megacorporations had machines that knew all there was to know worth knowing. The City had Connie and, lucky for me, I first met her when I was a police intern kid in school. So that, not my business card, was my introduction to her.

City Hall looked different because of its white marble interior, flecks of embedded black paint, and huge columns from ceiling to ground throughout. But it was ruined by the video displays everywhere that showed the Mayor and City Hall meetings, department meetings, committee meetings, ad infinitum.

This was the second time I had business at the City in the space of a few days. Based on all the referrals the Government Guy gave me, I would be here a lot more often.

Downtown Metropolis was the nerve center of the city. I would never say the brain because that implies intelligence. The city was not that and never would be; it was what controlled the brain. Its monolith towers were no bigger or taller than any other in the city, but they always looked different when I flew by in my vehicle. Some said it was its historic architecture of lighter colored paint for its exterior in contrast to the dark hues of the surrounding towers. But really, in the dark, rainy skies, no one notices. It had to be a state of mind. You knew it was the center of power, so you intuitively saw that in its buildings when, in reality, it was the same as everywhere else.

While the City Clerk's office was in a prominent place in the main city towers, the Crime Information Center (CIC) of the Police Department was in what could only be called the basement levels. The Clerk's office had guards and other visible security; CIC had nothing.

Compstat Connie had to be in her late seventies, and she ran the multi-hundreds-of-millions-of-dollars division. But when I entered the subterranean offices, she was at the counter sorting through papers like she was an entry-level worker. It was the same with the Government Guy, who was at a counter doing his own work. It seemed in government, unlike the corporate world, you may get the title and the salary, but you did the same grunt work you did as when you were first hired.

It was still unbelievable because it was such an important office for the police higher-ups. CompStat (Computer Statistics) was all the crime data collected in the city. That was her division, and it drove everything that the police did—deployment, budgets, resources, and personnel. The stats made it into every government press conference, including all the way to the mayor.

Week 22: Mentors

THAT'S WHY I VISITED Compstat Connie. She was a true data Einstein.

EXCERPT FROM: *Liquid Cool: The Cyberpunk Detective Series (Book One)*

The book I found myself glued to was not the 1,000-page tomes of the first category or the 400-page page-turners of the second, but this 60-page book titled How to be a Great Detective with 100 Rules. It was written by a guy who had been a private eye for 70-plus years. In fact, he died only a few years ago at the age of 92 and had worked right up until the end. The book was brilliant. I had read it five times already and was reading it again. The rules seemed basic, but his one-paragraph explanation of each was packed with real insight and his own folksy, street-wise expertise. He was the real McCoy—not any fake movie-land detective. You could tell by the way he communicated. He must have led an amazing life. To live 92 years in Metropolis—the things he saw and experienced. It's too bad he didn't write a compilation of his life through his cases.

I put the book on the floor, sat there, and sighed. It was the only book I checked out from the library. Here, I was sitting alone in my legacy residence, reading the accounts of a man who lived a real life, a long life, and was quite content with it. I knew that because he kept at it until he died. Nothing stopped him—the mean streets, the meaner streets, uber-government agencies, megacorporations. He did his thing.

I wished I had met Mr. Wilford G., the 92-year-old private eye. He lived and had a lot less than I had. What was my excuse then?

Perspective

Cruz: I touched the tip of my hat as an acknowledgment to my posthumous mentor, Wilford G.

EXCERPT FROM: *Liquid Cool: The Cyberpunk Detective Series (Book One)*

"Why do you look familiar?" she said, watching me from the counter. It seemed like there was no one else in the office, with row after row of shelves to the ceiling filled with file boxes.

We were now sitting in her tiny office. I handed her the "graduation" picture from the last day of my police internship—students and police personnel.

"Well, look at that," she said, holding the picture. "Back when my hair had color other than white. Cruz, isn't it?"

I was amazed. "There's absolutely no way you'd remember me from all those years ago." I laughed. "I wasn't memorable, and there were like fifty other interns running around."

"No, I remember you. I may be old, but I have a great memory. You hung around my division."

"I interned for you."

"And the uniformed officers, too."

"You do remember me."

"I told you. What can I do for you?"

"I want to become the male version of you."

She laughed. "Meaning what?"

"It was the talk you gave to us."

"I remember people, but I can't remember one of all those silly presentations I gave back then. I couldn't remember it, even if it was yesterday. It's always off the cuff, spur of the moment, when I give presentations."

"You told us how everything is connected, and your division looks at all the data. And after it absorbs every data point, it can see the connections, trends, and patterns. That's the ultimate in crime-fighting tools—those connections."

"I said that?"

"You did."

"And you remember it?"

"I do."

"Why would a high school kid remember a speech like that? Were you going to be a cop?"

"No, but it helped me with other occupations. Seeing connections where other people didn't. That's why I'm visiting. I want to do that for one specific day."

"A specific day? What day?"

I knew the day and time like my own birthday.

Compstat Connie reached behind the counter for her mobile computer and started typing.

"What stands out to you about the day?" I asked.

There was a specific reason I asked the question, and if Compstat Connie was the same casual human computer she was before, she'd basically do my work for me—cutting off hours, maybe days, from me being in the "box."

She stared at her screen. "That was the night of the big shootout at Joe Blows." She read more. "And the kidnapping of a little girl at Alien Alley. All the rest of your standard car-jacks, armed robberies, rapes, office invasions, murders."

"But why did you mention those two specific incidents first?"

"They're anomalies. All the rest is normal fare in the city."

"That's what I mean," I said to her. "I need to be able to see anomalies and understand how your mind gets you there. How long will it take you to teach me?"

"Do you have five decades to spare?"

I laughed. "No, but I'll give the time I need to give. Think of me as your returning intern two decades later."

"I thought you were some kind of hovercar guy."

"I have a new occupation, but don't tell the Clerk's office."

She chuckled.

"I'm like a private detective."

"Now that intrigues me."

Recap

There are many benefits to finding the right mentor. Mentors can help you unlock your potential and guide you in your life goals. They can be advisors who help you gain knowledge and skills, empower and encourage your personal growth or career development, and help identify weaknesses or pitfalls.

Mentorships can be a one-time occurrence or an ongoing check-in relationship. You can also never have too many mentors.

Week 23: Be Cool

I DEFINITELY HAD A new look for what I mentally was calling the "new me."

EXCERPT FROM: *A.I. Confidential (Liquid Cool, Book Six)*

Cruz and Wilford G. are driving to an appointment.

"That's different. My memory goes way back to the dinosaurs in that area," G said, grinning. "Cruz, you're way too uptight for a youngster."

"Youngster?"

"You need to, to coin a common phrase, 'be cool.'"

"My agency is cool. I wear a cool hat. I have a cool vehicle. I am plenty cool already."

"Not act cool, Cruz, or have cool things. 'Be' cool. There's a big difference."

"I have no idea what we're even talking about. When are you going to see your family?"

Perspective

"We're all fine here now, thank you. How are you?" Han Solo, Star Wars: The Original Movies

---

EXCERPT FROM: *Liquid Cool: The Cyberpunk Detective Series (Book One)*

Dot took the day off to hang out with me in the office. It was a field trip of sorts, and she brought with her a group of high school fashionistas-in-training. It seemed like every kid in the city wanted to visit Liquid Cool.

I got back from my food run, and PJ yelled at me, "You just missed her! Run to the elevator, and you can catch her."

I dumped the bags of food in her arms and ran to the elevator. Who am I running after? I got a glimpse of Exe as the elevator doors closed. She managed to do a quick wave. I walked back to my office.

"What did she want?"

PJ handed me an envelope.

"What's with all these envelopes?" I tucked the envelope under my arm and focused on the food. We were all starving. PJ grabbed her nouveau-French-whatever and plopped it on her desk. Dot and I took our food into my office.

We set the food on the table in my sitting area.

"Are you going to open it?" Dot asked.

"Oh." I had already forgotten about the envelope.

I walked to my desk, grabbed a letter opener from my front desk drawer, and sliced open the top.

Dot joined me at the desk. I opened it and reached in.

It was an official Private Investigator License!

I stared at the document, speechless. It was affirmation that I was legal, and I no longer had to play games.

"Wow, look at the expiration date," Dot said.

The date was 100 years in the future. I had a private investigator license for life.

There was another document in the envelope. It was small, and I glanced at Dot. What could it be?

It was a reissue of my national ID card. Why would they do that? I had to stare at it before I noticed it. My title! It was listed as Private Investigator.

For all my adult life, I was a "laborer." In my eyes, that always meant the same as "human" or "mammal" or "Earthling". It was a constant reminder of failure. Everyone said otherwise, but I could never shake the feeling I was nothing. Laborer was the bare-bones basic occupation designation. You did nothing to get it. The computer assigned it to you automatically. You had to take an affirmative step to change your occupation designation, which I had never done.

No one cared about names in business. Titles! Metropolis was all about title status—the last prejudice.

The card said I had made it. My new vocation was real and had been rendered as such with the city government for all to see. There it was. I was crying. I didn't even have time to stop myself.

Dot was smiling and gave me a side hug.

"A better life is all I want for me and my girl."

I thought of when I was hiding in that new spot in that secret alley, days after my birthday. How far I had come in such a short time. Run-Time, Prima Donna, and so many others said my ticket would come, and now it had. I touched the tip of my hat as an acknowledgment to my posthumous mentor, Wilford G. I'd send copies of the license to Ma and Pops for framing.

There was a major storm brewing outside, but I said to myself that we'd take a half-day off from work to celebrate and stop by the Good Kosher man for a righteous rack of roses. Then I'd take Dot out dancing, and no storm would tell us different.

Recap

Let the successes happen. And be happy about it.

You've done the planning, you're prepared to win, you're doing the work and you are consistent about it. So when the wins happen, enjoy it. It doesn't matter if it's a small or huge win. It's still a win towards your goals.

As the book says, Be (Liquid) Cool.

SIXTH MONTH
June
Classic Sci-Fi Actor Birthdays

CHARACTER (ACTOR) SHOW/Movie

JUNE 1: Odo (Rene Auberjonois) Star Trek: Deep Space Nine

JUNE 2: Dr. Jennifer Keller (Jewel Staite) Stargate Atlantis

JUNE 2: Brandon (Justin Long) Galaxy Quest

JUNE 2: Ensign Travis Mayweather (Anthony Montgomery) Star Trek: Enterprise

JUNE 6: Ambassador Soval (Gary Graham) Star Trek: Enterprise

JUNE 6: Boba Fett (Daniel Logan) Star Wars: Episode II

JUNE 7: Ka D'Argo (Anthony Simcoe) Farscape

JUNE 7: Qui-Gon Jinn (Liam Neeson) Star Wars: The Prequels

JUNE 9: Padmé Amidala (Natalie Portman) Star Wars: The Prequels

JUNE 13: Jason Nesmith/Commander Peter Quincy Taggart (Tim Allen) Galaxy Quest

JUNE 17: Rory Williams (Arthur (Thomas Arthur) Doctor Who

JUNE 19: Pa'u Zotoh Zhaan (Virginia Hey)

JUNE 22: Tuvok (Tim Russ) Star Trek: Voyager

JUNE 28: Admiral Ackbar (Tim Rose) Star Wars: Original Movies

JUNE 28: Borg Queen (Alice Krige) Star Trek: First Contact

THE ADMIN MINDSET

About Admin

"LINE ONE." PJ'S VOICE came through my video-phone intercom. I thought it funny to hear PJ say "line one" when all I had was one line.

No one likes the "admin" work that has to be done in life. You might need to keep business receipts for reimbursement, check personal or work emails, or back up your files. We don't like it. We don't want to do it. But it has to be done.

However, we don't have to get bogged down by it either.

Excerpt: From Liquid Cool: The Cyberpunk Detective Series (Book One)

At the Liquid Cool offices...

It was Bugs. He reminded me a lot of the late 92-year-old Mr. Wilford G. The man came in wearing overalls over his purple suit, holding a contraption with one hand and a telescoping wand in the other. He was old-school, which was exactly why he was so much in demand. His services included listening device detection, motion detection security, intrusion defense security, video surveillance, door and wall defense security, door and lock augmentation, trap door, and panic rooms. He did everything that had to do with office security.

Even Run-Time used him, but Bugs wasn't considered an elite clientele operator. He wasn't listed in the Yellow Pages, but he was always working—all word-of-mouth. Those in the know knew he was the best, and everyone was content with keeping the secret amongst themselves. I knew about him because of Dot's boss, Prima Donna, so I felt comfortable talking to him. I didn't want all my legit referrals to come from Run-Time and not-legit referrals to come from Phishy. I had to build my own Rolodex on my own.

Bugs brought his crew—a two-man team. It would take them until early morning to finish installing all the equipment in the office, outside the office in the hallway, and all the other spots Bugs said were a must for me to take control of my total office security. I was never going to be sucker-shot at in my place of business, inside, coming, or going, ever again.

While the men worked, I kept my head buried in the books, studying my newfound vocation, specifically, private investigation and the law. I needed to know it as well, as criminals knew it when talking to law enforcement. I needed to know where the legal line was, so I could avoid it, or when needed, know when it was safe to step over. Technically, I was a borderline criminal anyway, operating as an unlicensed detective with illegal weapons and a cyborg secretary, barred legally from using her bionic arms to sort out any variety of low lives in her way.

My feet were up on my desk, books stacked up on my desk, and my mobile computer in my lap when PJ peeked in. Strangely, she was always on time.

"Who are all these men?" PJ never said good morning.

"They'll be finished soon. Have Bugs show you the controls for the buzzer, and your workstation has three video monitors now. One for outside the door, one showing the ground floor entrance, and the third shows our elevator."

"You won't have any money left after all this. You better get new clients so you can pay me."

"When I have legit clients coming up here, no punching. The police have us both flagged now. Things they let slide before, they won't now."

"What about metal detectors for the door? These men going to do that?"

"They did that already. Have Bugs show you that, too. And they installed some secret compartments, too, for weapons."

"I want to keep my rifle under the desk handy. It will do me no good hiding in a secret compartment. I need it next to my hand for quick-draw situations. I don't have that fancy pop-gun like you."

"Wear long sleeves, and you can have one too."

"I hate long sleeves. Long sleeves are for squares. I got nice arms, and they deserved to be shown off. If punks see the muscles, they won't be quick to cause any trouble."

"You want to show off fake arms with fake muscles?"

"Ah, you're just jealous. Go get someone to cut off your arms, and you can have cool arms, too."

"Have Bugs give you all the entry codes for the door and alarm system. And the bypass code for the metal detector arch. I don't want it going off every time you walk under it."

"What about your girlfriend? She'd set off the metal detector, too."

"I got that handled."

"What about cyborgs with that new fancy non-metal bionics?"

"The metal detector detects all metals and all alloys. They can't make bionics from wood or glass yet, so we're covered."

"What about plastic? That's what they use Up-Top. I don't expect higher-end clients and criminals to come into this dump, but you might as well get your money's worth."

"Nah, they say it's plastic, but it's an alloy. To be as strong as it has to be, it has to be an alloy, not any cheapie plastic they use for toys and average hovercars. And Up-Top doesn't use bionics; they use biotics. They grow body parts in hospitals."

"We don't have that down here, this cheapskate planet. But it's okay because bionics is better. Cyborgs are superheroes, not squares like Up-Top."

"Forget Up-Top. Just don't get caught illegally using those bionic arms, or you'll get thrown in jail again. You can't get paid a salary from jail."

It was an hour later when I realized the madness that was Punch Judy and I talking about nothing. Bugs was done, and he interrupted us. He led PJ back to her workstation first to show her all the modifications and controls. It took him about forty minutes to show her the full scope of her power over all things security before Bugs returned to my office.

"Punch!" I yelled as Bugs' eyebrows rose.

"What?" She popped into my office, and I threw the box to her.

"The business cards," I said.

She looked at the box, smiled, and disappeared.

"Sorry about that. We're a shouting office."

Bugs chuckled. "I noticed."

"How does it all look?" I asked.

"You'll be able to hold your own against even a full-scale office invasion."

"That's what I need."

"We're also taking care of all the wire maintenance. This building is centuries old, so we have to bury all the circuitry deep to keep it away from the bundled mess of every other floor and businesses that don't even exist anymore, but the wires are still there. So keep an eye on that. But only if you see issues with operating performance. You need not do anything else beyond that. You really are spending a lot of cash on all this."

"Don't remind me. Do you need me to walk through everything again?"

"I'll walk you through everything again, and you can tell me if I miss anything for you."

"That'll be fine."

He dug into his pocket and produced a small wooden box. "And I can't forget this."

He handed me the box, and I looked at him. "Do I open it?"

"All the systems I use are analog. I don't trust that Up-Top, digital, supposedly state-of-the-art technology. You want to rob me, then you will have to come right up to my place to do it. Not some hack with you in your underpants from a far, far away land. Do not bring any digital technology into this office. But if you do, use what's in the little box."

Recap

You already have the "right tools" to accomplish your objectives, but are you using them in the most efficient way possible? Are you even using the right tools to begin with?

When thinking of best practices, broaden your horizon. Is it more efficient for you to open up your laptop and log into some program on the Internet to manage your weekly planning goals and objectives? Or is it better to do all this on your mobile? Or is it better to have a simple notebook on your desk to write in?

Use the best system to increase your efficiency, not detract from it.

Also, "Admin" includes those little unexpected occurrences that pop up when they're least wanted, such as turning on a laptop and nothing happens! Or you go outside to be greeted with a flat tire.

Don't let any of it distract you. Deal with it and move forward.

The Planners

BE (LIQUID) COOL /MONTHLY PLANNER

MONTH:

SUN	MON	TUE	WED	THU	FRI	SAT

TOP PRIORITIES / GOALS

PEOPLE TO SEE / PLACES TO GO / REMINDERS

NOTES

_____

_____

_____

RATE / ASSESS THE MONTH:

BE (LIQUID) COOL
WEEKLY PLANNER

WEEK:

M T W H F S S

MONDAY

TUESDAY

WEDNESDAY

THURSDAY

FRIDAY

SATURDAY / SUNDAY

WEEK'S PRIORITIES / TO DO

NOTES

RATE / ASSESS THE WEEK:

BE (LIQUID) COOL
WEEKLY PLANNER

WEEK:

| M | T | W | H | F | S | S |

MONDAY

TUESDAY

WEDNESDAY

THURSDAY

FRIDAY

SATURDAY / SUNDAY

WEEK'S PRIORITIES / TO DO

NOTES

RATE / ASSESS THE WEEK:

BE (LIQUID) COOL
WEEKLY PLANNER

WEEK: M T W H F S S

MONDAY

TUESDAY

WEDNESDAY

THURSDAY

FRIDAY

SATURDAY / SUNDAY

WEEK'S PRIORITIES / TO DO

NOTES

RATE / ASSESS THE WEEK:

BE (LIQUID) COOL
WEEKLY PLANNER

WEEK:

| M | T | W | H | F | S | S |

MONDAY

TUESDAY

WEDNESDAY

THURSDAY

FRIDAY

SATURDAY / SUNDAY

WEEK'S PRIORITIES / TO DO

NOTES

RATE / ASSESS THE WEEK:

BE (LIQUID) COOL
WEEKLY PLANNER

WEEK:

M T W H F S S

MONDAY

TUESDAY

WEDNESDAY

THURSDAY

FRIDAY

SATURDAY / SUNDAY

WEEK'S PRIORITIES / TO DO

NOTES

RATE / ASSESS THE WEEK:

Week 24: Have A System

WHEN YOU HAVE A SYSTEM, You Never Waste Time Knowing What to Do Next

EXCERPT FROM: *Liquid Cool: The Cyberpunk Detective Series (Book One)*

The call came in when I was hunched over my desk, re-prioritizing my messages. I had the "hot" pile, the "hold" pile, the "hell no" pile, and a few other miscellaneous ones.

"Line one." PJ's voice came through my video-phone intercom.

I thought it funny to hear PJ say "line one" when all I had was one line.

Run-Time appeared on the video display with his trademark flat cap.

"How are you, sir?" I asked.

"I'm blessed, and I hear you've been too."

"I wouldn't go that far, but I've had a good start, aside from a few unpleasantries."

"Unpleasantries are a fact of life. Are you officially back from your vacation? The Box is what I was told you call it."

"I'm back with a new hat, new coat, and new attitude to make things happen. I'm back."

"Good. I have another client for you."

Perspective

Or You Can Just Wing It!

EXCERPT FROM: *Liquid Cool: The Cyberpunk Detective Series (Book One)*

It could have been reporters, but I was taking no chances. I stood at my desk, loading the bullets into my magazine. PJ was sitting on one of my inner office lounge area chairs, loading up her two shotguns.

I may have had guns now and had a natural aptitude for shooting, but I was no gun person. And PJ was an ex-posh gang member, so she definitely wasn't a gun person. You didn't take good ammo out of your weapon and then load up new ammo, just because new boxes of ammo came in. But we did it anyway because it's "fresh" ammo straight out of the box, right?

Phishy glanced back and forth between us as if he were watching a tennis match.

"Why don't you load up, too, Phishy?" PJ said to him.

"Oh no. Phishy is a lover, not a fighter." He smiled at her.

"A dead lover or a live fighter. Hmm. What is better for me and my life?" PJ said as she cocked one of her rifles.

"Phishy, I want more ammo," I said.

"Cruz, you're getting a bit obsessive about the safety."

"How many gun battles have I been in now? People trying to sucker shoot me all over the place. I had a major shootout before leaving to rescue the little girl and then another shootout trying to rescue the little girl. Phishy, this isn't a matter of perspective. We need more boxes of ammo."

"But isn't a detective supposed to think his way out of battles?" Phishy sincerely asked.

PJ burst out laughing.

"You stupid man," she snapped at him.

"More boxes of ammo, Phishy," I said. "The hovercar was flying right outside my window with a spotlight."

"Oh, okay. I'll get more. But Cruz, this isn't cheap stuff."

I walked to my desk and opened the front drawer. His eyes opened wide as he saw the wad of cash.

"If you even think of hiding this cash the way you did the last time, I'll ban you from my office."

"Where's my cash?" PJ said, standing from the couch.

I ignored her. "Did you hear me?" I asked Phishy.

"I'll do it outside."

I threw the cash at him, and he caught it with ease. "Get out of here and bring me more ammo."

Phishy ran out of my office, smiling. We heard the reception door close, and I just shook my head.

"Where's my cash?"

"Why would I give you any cash when you can't even prioritize my messages so I know what cases to take on? Maybe I should waste my time talking to more ladies with the gators in their bathtubs."

"That wouldn't be a good use of your time. You need to go out there and solve cases and bring back the money. You're famous now. How hard can that be?"

The voice of a man at my office doorway so startled us, I reflexively dropped my box of ammo to the ground to reach for my gun; the bullets bounced up and down on the hardwood floor. PJ had let go of her shotgun; it hit the rugged floor, and it discharged. The blast blew out my window (again) and sucked all the messages that were neatly stacked at the edge of my desk out into the sky.

Recap

As long as there is a method to your own "madness," it works and keeps you on track, then go with it.

Week 25: Set Aside Time to Plan, Assess, and Adjust

CRUZ: "PLANNED OUT my destiny to be the greatest detective in Metropolis."

EXCERPT FROM: *Liquid Cool: The Cyberpunk Detective Series (Book One)*

Two weeks ago, it began. I parked my Pony, went up to my place, and locked the door behind me.

I would put myself in the "box". It wasn't a real box and wasn't even a physical thing. It was what I called completely separating yourself from people and any possible distractions to get some major life task done. Like going off to a secluded island, but it could be anywhere, even your own place. The key was unplugging from everyone and everything to create your own "fortress of solitude" for an indefinite period.

When I walked back into my offices fifteen days later, I didn't quite know what to expect. Half a month was a long time for the principal of a new business to be absent. They say when you start a new company, you're a slave to it for at least ten years, with no time off and no vacations. Maybe so, but I did what I had to.

The door was open, and there was Punch Judy with her arms folded with a smile.

"Well, look what came in from the rain," she said. "Is that a new hat?"

"New hat, new coat," I answered.

"When you get new things, they're supposed to be different from the old ones."

"I like the colors I had. All I needed was some modifications."

I felt different, and it was more than the new clothes. PJ could manage the office without me for a while. I was impressed.

"You look rested, too," she said. "Was that the first time you ever slept? Did you ever leave your place?"

"Not even once. Defeats the purpose of the Box."

"Box? What is the Box? You locked yourself in your place for two weeks like a house mouse. All these fancy phrases and concepts for simple things. So when I sat on the steps of our building, was I in the Box?"

"No. You were sidewalk-sallying it. The Box is doing something specific without anyone to bother you."

"What did you do in your box?"

"Planned out my destiny to be the greatest detective in Metropolis."

"That's what I like to hear," PJ proclaimed. "You need to go into the Box more often. You are too negative most of the time. People don't like to hire negative people. Keep talking like that, and you'll have all the clients. Speaking of clients, when am I getting more money?"

Perspective

Cruz: My glasses allowed me to zoom in on his face and see into the shadows where he stood. He was grinning—so he had night-sight too.

EXCERPT FROM: *AI Confidential (Liquid Cool, Book Six)*

Cruz, G-Man, and Quix at an out-of-the-way eatery.

"Cruz, you're young, and you're new. That's not how this biz works. It's not a hovercar race where you can study every inch of the course and plan accordingly. You rarely, if ever, know what the whole course is until you get there. The detective biz is the business of reacting—reacting to the lie, the scam, the chase, someone trying to shoot you, something not turning out the way you expected, someone turning up dead who was not supposed to. Life can't be planned."

"Mr. Cruz, if I can add," Quix said. "I've been on many operations. You can plan a military op for years, and all those plans can go out the window in ten seconds when it's real, and something shows that no one anticipated."

"We still need the plan."

Recap

You've done your plan—it's a masterpiece. Unfortunately, it is only a working document, meaning you'll be assessing and adjusting as you go. But it's all good. Change is inevitable because life is often unpredictable, as a passing meteorite in space.

Week 26: Big Rocks versus Small Pebbles

RUN-TIME: *"THE BIG picture shouldn't trump little pictures, but the little pictures shouldn't destroy the big picture either."*

EXCERPT FROM: *Liquid Cool: The Cyberpunk Detective Series (Book One)*

Run-Time shook his head. "You don't know that."

"Is this one of those 'see the big picture' speeches? Run-Time, you've known me practically all my life. I don't care and never have cared about the 'big picture.' I'm a simple guy. Did you scratch my car or not? I don't care about the socio-economic forces that led to your father losing his job and your parents turning to a life of crime and beating you up and you becoming a bad person. I don't care. Did you scratch my car or not? Did you kill that old man or not? Did you run down that girl in your hovercar and flee the scene of the crime or not? If people spent more time with the 'little picture,' then the 'big picture' wouldn't be so screwed up."

Run-Time was always Mr. Optimism, even as a child. But the man who stood in front of me was so far from that, it scared me. He stayed quiet for a moment. I don't know if he was trying to think of the best response or was just plain tired.

"I'd like you to meet someone."

"Run-Time, they want me to meet some police widows and widowers."

"I know, but this is important. The big picture shouldn't trump little pictures, but the little pictures shouldn't destroy the big picture either. Where will we be if Metropolis goes up in flames? You and I live here, you know."

Recap

This is always a challenge. You have your big-picture goals but need those smaller steps to get there. There are the "big boulders" you have to maneuver through in life, but all the "small pebbles" on your path could easily make you trip and fall. That's why juggling these Big Rocks and Small Pebbles can sometimes get tricky. Never lose focus on the primary goal, but don't forget the rest.

Week 27: Priorities

"THAT BLAST CAME FROM the Death Star! That thing's operational!" — Lando Calrissian, Star Wars: The Empire Strikes Back

EXCERPT FROM: *The Moon Is a Good Place to Die (Liquid Cool, Book Eight)*

No introduction here. I've been arrested by Metro PD! I've been in Metropolis solving cases and surviving gun battles but have never been arrested once—until now. Sure, I came close. I'm a working street detective.

But never for real. So, no time for games, witty banter, or any gripping stories. I've been arrested, my vehicle has been impounded, and the police have their paws on my prized omega-gun. This is bad, very bad. I've been framed hard by a pro—all bases covered, planted evidence conveniently laid out for the police detectives, incriminating photos and vids, and worse still, phony witnesses. I've been wrapped up with a big red bow for the authorities. This bad guy must be smiling from ear to ear, thinking he's some kind of criminal mastermind genius. He's obviously never spoken to the Guy Who Scratched My Vehicle. He should have spoken to the lobotomized Red Rabbit, the late NeuroDancer, the later Mr. Viper, the late Mr. Vega, the later Ripper, the late Mr. Diagram, and plenty more. How does the saying go? "Don't make me angry. You won't like me when I'm angry." I know who you are, you skell bastard. The second I get out on bail, I'm coming for you, Mr. Three-Armed Man! Run, run. I don't care where you go; I'm going to get you. Leads or not, I'm going to get you. In fact, I may already know where you are.

Yes, The Moon Is a Good Place to Die! (The bad guys, not me!)

Recap

Sometimes, you don't have to figure out or decide on your primary goal. You don't have to juggle "Big Rocks" and "Small Pebbles." Your priority is crystal clear.

About Adaptability

There's more than one way to shoot a xenomorph. (Aliens)

However, you must always be able to adapt to changing circumstances, new realities, and new information. If you don't have the wisdom to know when to barrel forward or to adjust, then that's what your "associates" and mentors are for.

Week 28: Research

RESEARCH IS INVALUABLE

Cruz: When I was a kid, I used that same principle to get into hovercars. I spent time at hovercar repair shops and the salvage yards. I learned all about cars from the scraps. I learned how to build them from the ground up. Once I understood the basic concepts, I could build any car, from an old junker to a classic, like my Ford Pony.

EXCERPT FROM: *Liquid Cool: The Cyberpunk Detective Series (Book One)*

Yet, here I was, in the public library on 40 Winks Street. There were three left in the City. In the comfort of your own home, you could download any content you wanted to your digital book reader, but frankly, who had time for that? There were a gazillion books out there in cyberspace. Being a librarian was actually a serious profession with value; they had advanced degrees in data mining, sifting, and record compiling. Libraries sifted through all the data garbage, the clutter, the Trojan horse X-rated material, and sub-standard nonsense to present you with what you typed into your search and gave you the best of the best. Yes, libraries were also a major hang-out for the sidewalk johnnies, but they were clean and quiet. Here, I was reading book after book on…the private investigation industry.

There were only a few main categories. The first was the procedural detective books. They went into quite a lot of detail about surveillance, stake-outs, skip tracing, computer tapping, hard drive cloning, etc. Most of it was very dry or common sense, and I could see why the books didn't sell.

The second category was the best sellers—the Hollywood-style super detectives. These "true" stories were of gun battles with crime lords, beating up cops, sleeping with clients, secret consultative work with Up-Top multinationals, and more gun battles. Entertaining, but all stupid. None of it real.

The book I found myself glued to was not the 1,000-page tomes of the first category or the 400-page page-turners of the second, but this 60-page book titled How to be a Great Detective with 100 Rules. It was written by a guy who had been a private eye for 70-plus years. In fact, he died only a few years ago at the age of 92 and had worked right up until the end. The book was brilliant. I had read it five times already and was reading it again. The rules seemed basic, but his one-paragraph explanation of each was packed with real insight and his own folksy, street-wise expertise. He was the real McCoy—not any fake movie-land detective. You could tell by the way he communicated. He must have led an amazing life. To live 92 years in

Metropolis—the things he saw and experienced. It's too bad he didn't write a compilation of his life through his cases.

I put the book on the floor, sat there, and sighed. It was the only book I checked out from the library. Here, I was sitting alone in my legacy residence, reading the accounts of a man who lived a real life, a long life, and was quite content with it. I knew that because he kept at it until he died. Nothing stopped him—the mean streets, the meaner streets, uber-government agencies, megacorporations. He did his thing.

He had a metal heart, but back then, if you had heart disease in your genetic history, the doctors would automatically replace your regular heart with an artificial one to be on the safe side. He had bionic hips and fingers—a fall down stairs had caused the former; a nasty habit of smoking nasty cigarettes caused the latter. But again, he did his thing, his way.

I wished I had met Mr. Wilford G., the 92-year-old private eye. He lived and had a lot less than I had. What was my excuse then?

Perspective

"The best research you can do is talk to people" — Terry Pratchett, British science fiction and fantasy author known for The Hitch Hiker's Guide to the Galaxy and the Discworld series.

EXCERPT FROM: *Liquid Cool: The Cyberpunk Detective Series (Book One)*

Before I decorated my own offices, I did a tour of all the detective firms in the city. They all fell into two categories: the high-end, one-hundred-man firms that looked and smelled like a high-end legal practice and the bottom-end, small firms that always seemed to share space with some bail bonds outfit. There seemed to be no in-between, and I immediately planned to establish myself in that space, along with taking all kinds of clients—private persons, government, and corporate. Those two things were to make me unique, and

I desperately needed to be unique in this industry to have any chance of survival.

Box was a one-man outfit, nothing to stand out from any other in the Yellow Pages, but he had a reputation as a licensed private eye who'd do any job you wanted, as long as the price was right. "Any job" was code for illegal. Those who knew the detective biz called him a "scumbag." I had no reason to doubt them.

His offices were on the fifth floor of a business tower on Whiskey Way. Across the hall was a bail bonds office, and as a result, it was the smelliest, grungiest place with people hanging around. Since it was a common set-up for low-enders, it must have been a mutually beneficial situation for all involved.

I pushed open the front door to enter; the interior was dim and dank. Box's office was not even an office but a half-office. The other half he shared with some other detective firm. I could see a haze of cigarette smoke hanging near the ceiling.

"What do you want?" a male voice asked.

My eyes finally made out the figure of a man, standing at a file cabinet, who turned and was looking at me.

"Looking for Box," I answered.

"You got an appointment?"

"Do I need one?"

"That didn't answer my question."

"I'll go to another detective then, where the customer service is a bit more customer-friendly."

"Don't do that. Wait there."

The man closed the file cabinet and disappeared, or I couldn't see him anymore, as I stood there continuing to glance around.

"He'll see you." The man had returned.

I stepped forward, even though I had no clue where I was going; it was that dark.

"The office in the back with the light on," the man said.

This was some kind of office. It seemed the lack of light was to hide all the unsightly clutter. I walked back to the only place that had light. I stopped and peeked into the office. There, seated behind a desk, was Box.

"Box?" I asked, even though I knew it was him, but he didn't know I had been checking up on him.

"You know it's me, so why are you asking?"

I stepped inside and didn't ask as I took a seat.

He cracked his knuckles, then put one hand on his desk while the other hand was out of sight behind the desk. I put both of my hands on the desk.

"I came to hire you for information."

"Information? I'm a detective. I don't give information. Who are you?"

"I'm a detective," I said.

His unfriendly face turned into a solid frown.

"Why are you here?"

"I need a bunch of information from you, and I'm happy to pay for the information if I have to."

"What information?"

Recap

Research should be the most enjoyable endeavor in your Admin Mindset. You're an investigator, just like Cruz.

Research: The systematic investigation into and study of sources in order to establish facts and reach new conclusions.

In your quest to be something or do something, the research you do helps you to achieve that success. You're educated on the facts. It helps you answer what, when, how, and why questions. You discover pitfalls you may not have even thought of. It helps you become as much of an expert as you need to be.

SEVENTH MONTH
July
Classic Sci-Fi Actor Birthdays

CHARACTER (ACTOR) SHOW/Movie

JULY 1: Darth Vader (David Prowse) Star Wars: Original Movies

JULY 1: Dominic Keating (Lt. Malcolm Reed) Star Trek: Enterprise

JUL 2: Admiral Cartwright (Brock Peters) Star Trek: The Voyage Home/First Contact/The Undiscovered Country

JULY 8: Tank (Marcus Chong) The Matrix

JULY 9: Bail Organa (Jimmy Smits) Star Wars: The Prequels

JULY 9: Ensign Hoshi Sato (Linda Park) Star Trek: Enterprise

JULY 10: Darth Maul (voice) (Peter Sarafinowicz) Star Wars: The Prequels

JULY 12: Jabba the Hutt IV (Ben Burtt) Star Wars: Original Movies

JULY 13: Han Solo (Harrison Ford) Star Wars

JULY 13: Deckard (Harrison Ford) Blade Runner (Original Movie)

JULY 13: Capt. Jean-Luc Picard (Patrick Stewart) Star Trek: The Next Generation

JULY 14: Harry Dean Stanton Brett Jul 14 Alien

JULY 15: Tyrell (Joe Turkel) Blade Runner (Original Movie)

JULY 16: Michael Garibaldi (Jerry Doyle) Babylon 5

JULY 16: Tommy Webber/Lieutenant Laredo (Daryl Mitchell) Galaxy Quest

JULY 17: J. Michael Straczynski, creator of Babylon 5

JULY 22: Chancellor Valorum (Terence Stamp) Star Wars: The Prequels

JULY 26: Kira Nerys (Nana Visitor) Star Trek: Deep Space Nine

JULY 29: Gul Madred/Star Trek: The Next Generation; Chancellor Gorkon/Star Trek: The Undiscovered Country (David Warner)

JULY 29: Wesley Crusher (Wil Wheaton) Star Trek: The Next Generation

JULY 30: Mr. Homm (Carel Struycken) Star Trek: The Next Generation

JULY 30: The Terminator (Arnold Schwarzenegger) Terminator

JULY 30: Morpheus (Laurence Fishburne) The Matrix

JULY 31: Kyle Reese/The Terminator; Corporal Hicks/Aliens (Michael Biehn)

DON'T BE YOUR OWN ARCH-ENEMY

About Self-Sabotage

"FEAR IS THE MIND-KILLER. Fear is the little-death that brings total obliteration. I will face my fear. I will permit it to pass over me and through me."
— Frank Herbert's Dune

Self-sabotage is a very real thing. You'd think a person, more than anyone else, would root for their own success. Unfortunately, some people subconsciously or consciously destroy their own path to success.

The reasons are many: buried trauma they haven't dealt with, basic laziness, but more often, it's just plain fear. People are afraid they'll actually succeed in their life goals, ambitions, and dreams. The status quo is "what I know," it's safe. Success means something new, and for some, that's scary.

You have no chance of success if you are your own ultimate enemy.

Excerpt From: *The UFO Case (Liquid Cool: From the Crazy Maniac Files, Book Three)*

At the Blood Red Sea Hotel...

More monarchy corporate soldiers flew in through the window from the sky.

I knelt down above Jinn. He stared at me with no emotion.

"You were the chief of staff to the king of the monarchy. You had a royal position for most of your adult life. You had real power. You could have done so much good for your people. Instead, you remained driven by hate. You said the king couldn't recognize you from the real Jinn. Really? You were offended? All this because you were offended? Maybe he didn't recognize either of you because you were too common for him to notice. Or maybe, he didn't notice because he meets a hundred people every day and can't commit all those names and faces to instant memory recall. You really are a crazy maniac. You wasted your life for nothing. All you will be remembered for is this. Your failed terrorist plot. You'll never be remembered for what good you could have accomplished."

"We are what we are," Jinn managed to say.

"That's nonsense. I was a laborer and a hovercar racer on the amateur circuit. I wanted more, so I became more. A foreign private detective helped bring you down. I'm sure you'll have a long time to reflect on it."

Recap

Our sci-fi detective, Cruz, has encountered a vast array of criminals. However, many of them laid the foundation for their own demise long before crossing his path. Many of them had everything right in their lives, but they sabotaged themselves.

You, of course, are on the "good guy/gal" side of the universe, but the lesson to be learned is the same.

The Planners

BE (LIQUID) COOL / MONTHLY PLANNER

MONTH:

SUN	MON	TUE	WED	THU	FRI	SAT

TOP PRIORITIES / GOALS

PEOPLE TO SEE / PLACES TO GO / REMINDERS

NOTES

RATE / ASSESS THE MONTH:

BE (LIQUID) COOL
WEEKLY PLANNER

WEEK:

M T W H F S S

MONDAY

TUESDAY

WEDNESDAY

THURSDAY

FRIDAY

SATURDAY / SUNDAY

WEEK'S PRIORITIES / TO DO

NOTES

RATE / ASSESS THE WEEK:

BE (LIQUID) COOL
WEEKLY PLANNER

WEEK:

M T W H F S S

MONDAY

TUESDAY

WEDNESDAY

THURSDAY

FRIDAY

SATURDAY / SUNDAY

WEEK'S PRIORITIES / TO DO

NOTES

RATE / ASSESS THE WEEK:

BE (LIQUID) COOL
WEEKLY PLANNER

WEEK:

M T W H F S S

MONDAY

TUESDAY

WEDNESDAY

THURSDAY

FRIDAY

SATURDAY / SUNDAY

WEEK'S PRIORITIES / TO DO

NOTES

RATE / ASSESS THE WEEK:

BE (LIQUID) COOL
WEEKLY PLANNER

WEEK:

M T W H F S S

MONDAY

TUESDAY

WEDNESDAY

THURSDAY

FRIDAY

SATURDAY / SUNDAY

WEEK'S PRIORITIES / TO DO

NOTES

RATE / ASSESS THE WEEK:

BE (LIQUID) COOL
WEEKLY PLANNER

WEEK: M T W H F S S

MONDAY

TUESDAY

WEDNESDAY

THURSDAY

FRIDAY

SATURDAY / SUNDAY

WEEK'S PRIORITIES / TO DO

NOTES

RATE / ASSESS THE WEEK:

Week 29: Keep Your Ego In Check

CRUZ: *"I WAS THE CAUSE of the chaos. All because of ego."*

EXCERPT FROM: *Liquid Cool: The Cyberpunk Detective Series (Book One)*

Like clockwork, a video-call was routed to our police cruiser, and we postponed my visit with the widows and widower of the fallen police officers who wanted to meet me. We flew to Let It Ride Enterprises, where Run-Time was waiting for me. On the way, I caught up on the news I had tried to avoid. I wanted to hurt the Mayor and the Chief but set in motion a chain of events that no one could predict. Who knew how many people had been and would be victims of criminal punks, because there were no police on the streets because of me? Within an hour of my "performance" on Holly Live's news interview show, the Police Chief's inner circle confronted him in a private meeting. During that meeting, the Police Chief was grievously shot, and two other captains were shot. That same day, police officers walked off the job, taking their police cruisers and weapons with them. By nightfall, all 500,000 had quit and had surrounded Metro Police One.

In the old days, you could set a building on fire. But it was a world of monolith towers that couldn't burn, so the police dumped enough trash around the building and set it ablaze. They also barricaded the Mayor and staff in City Hall. The Mayor called a state of emergency, which was unprecedented, but went a step further. He called in Interpol, who agreed to take control of the City and arrest the police. That started a war, and now, there was a stalemate with five Interpol spaceships hovering above City Hall to protect the buildings and the Mayor, who had not been out of the tower in five days. The City was holding its breath.

Run-Time looked like he hadn't slept in five days. "Let me ask you," he began, "do you understand what has been set in motion?"

"You mean what I started."

"You said it."

Run-Time warned me, but I didn't listen. I acknowledged that he understood the politics of things better than I ever would. However, I knew that fact profoundly now. I was the cause of the chaos. All because of ego. Would I ever be able to sleep if people died because of my ego?

Perspective

Don't let excess pride create more problems for yourself.

EXCERPT FROM: *Liquid Cool: The Cyberpunk Detective Series (Book One)*

At the Liquid Cool office...

I never expected to see them ever again, but there was the Guy Who Scratched My Vehicle and the same girlfriend standing in my new detective's office, staring at me with smirks.

"Well, well," he said. "A detective. I should have known."

I had just gotten a basic desk and three chairs for my new office. Basic furniture and delivery was quick and easy. I could feel my blood boiling. Why were they here? How did they find me? I wasn't even looking at them anymore. I sat behind my desk and looked up, and they both were sitting down in front of me, smirking.

"You probably thought you'd never see us again," GW said.

"I kinda thought that's how we left things."

"Were we surprised to hear that you were a detective."

Was this more of Phishy's doing? "Who told you that?"

He smiled. "Yeah, I was told that, too. You're a confidential detective."

This had to be Phishy!

"Well," he continued, "the wife and I need a detective. We did some looking in the Yellow Pages, and there are so many in there that it makes your head spin. And when you have no one to recommend someone, you're just playing Russian roulette with your wallet. Then we heard about you. We said we got personal experience with that psycho. He locks his sights on you, and you're done. He'll never stop till he gets what he wants. Don't ever be on the opposite end of his sights when he locks on you. The perfect detective. Surprised you didn't do it sooner."

"What makes you think I'd ever take you as a client?"

"People beating down the door to hire you, are they?" his girlfriend-wife quipped.

"You can't still be sore about the incident? I paid you your money. So we're even steven."

"Any man who hurts a man's woman, his kids, his family, his pets, his vehicle...you damage a man's vehicle and...he needs to be put down. You scratched my vehicle. I would never work for someone so venal. No way. No how."

The smirks on their faces were gone. They realized I was not over it.

"You really are psycho. Hold a grudge for this long. It was over five years ago. Yeah, you're the right psycho for this, and as the wife said, no one else is beating down the door to hire you."

"Listen here, I have integrity. I have standards. I'm going to pick the clients I work for. That's what I'm going to do. I'm going to have solid clients with integrity."

His wife burst out with a laugh.

"Good luck with that, psycho," he said and turned to his wife. "Watch this."

He threw a bag on my desk and leaned back. The smirks had returned to their faces.

I looked at the bag—slightly open, filled with small bills. I looked at them, looked at the bag, stared at it. This was a critical junction in my life—what kind of detective would I be? Principled or just some ratty PI for hire. Starve or have money for bills and food.

I grabbed the bag of cash.

Recap

In one instance, Cruz didn't keep his ego in check, and bad things happened. In the next, he swallowed his pride, kept his cool, and got himself one of his first clients in his new vocation.

There's nothing wrong with a bit of ego. A healthy dose of ego drives determination, assertiveness, and focus. Ego can also help you stay the course when things go off course, overcome obstacles or setbacks, and ultimately succeed.

But with all human traits, too much is always a bad thing, which is why you need to keep it under control.

Week 30: Avoid Drama

"STAY OUT OF TROUBLE." — RoboCop, original movie

(Okay, maybe using Cruz isn't the best example for this chapter.)

EXCERPT FROM: *Digital Samurai (Liquid Cool: From the Crazy Maniac Files, Book Two)*

My right hand was fine. My Pony was fine. The Liquid Cool office and my Concrete Mama home were fine. As a recovering germophobe, my mind had conjured up the possibility I was infested by microscopic, self-replicated nano-robots on my skin. When I was given a clean bill of health, as were all my possessions, workplace, and home, I felt stupid.

"What did you think happened?" Bugs asked.

"Honestly, I don't know."

Bugs was a "sweeper" and security tech guru. He reminded me a lot of my posthumous mentor, Wilford G. Bugs was old-school but the best. Listening device detection, motion detection security, intrusion defense security, video surveillance, door and wall defense security, door and lock augmentation, trap door, and panic rooms were his business. My best friend, Run-Time, had introduced us when I first got into the detective business.

I don't think I'd ever seen him wearing anything other than his standard uniform—dark overalls over his purple suit, holding his custom-built contraption with one hand and a long telescoping wand with the other. He arrived at the Concrete Mama with his team of two college-kid-looking workers. He'd cleared me, my Pony, and they finished my apartment.

"Did you think your hand was going to fall off, or she infected you with nanites?"

"Nanites?"

"Microscopic robots—"

"Bugs, I know what nanites are. I'm anti-robot, no matter the size, and my family is anti-humanoid robot too."

"Android."

"What?"

"Your anti-humanoid robots. Those are androids."

"Them too."

Bugs laughed. "I still want to know what you thought shaking someone's hand would do to you."

"I don't know. It's how he described her. Then, when I saw them shut down the headquarters and the bio-suits land..."

"Nothing more than precautionary," Bugs told me.

"Ever heard of cyber-assassins?"

"Yeah."

I'd washed my hands like twelve times using all my decon gels I bought from my CDC supplier.

"What can you tell me?"

Bugs joined me in the kitchen. "You don't want to meet one."

"Too late."

"Serious?"

"A client."

"Client? Why would they hire you?"

"It's complicated."

"You'd better stay away from them."

"A paying client."

Bugs chuckled, shaking his head. "What do you want to know?"

"How do you beat them?"

"You can't."

"So if I ever did battle with them—"

"You'd be dead. Even running away might not save you."

"Let's rephrase the question. If I were to encounter a hostile one, what would I do to ensure I escaped unharmed, knowing there's no way I could beat them?"

"That's the main thing. You can't beat them. Only the best samurai soldiers could challenge them offensively. Your strategy would have to be defensive and evasive. Defend and run away, fast."

"How do you know about them?"

"We tangled with one—once."

"Run-Time?"

"Not Run-Time directly, but security at Let It Ride. This was many years ago. Run-Time was new to the world of expansion in the corporate sphere. A megacorp didn't like it. His company had dealt with corporate and samurai soldiers, every kind of gangster and thug imaginable, every kind of cyborg enforcer, digital samurai, but then we tangled with a cyber-assassin from Up-Top."

"Up-Top?"

"Yeah. But we had some weapons from Up-Top. Kind of like you with your Up-Top gun. We learned a lot about cyber-assassins that day, that long day. We locked down the tower, but he got in still. Got in, even with the lockdown. He was invisible to video surveillance, motion sensors, and infrared sensors. Digital samurai were scary when Earth was digital, not so much when new analog came in. Cyber-assassins remained scary because they could manipulate machinery."

"How?"

"Don't know how. They did it."

"Can you walk me through the encounter and how you defeated him?"

"We didn't defeat him. We escaped from him."

"You were there."

"I was head of security back then. We escaped. He ran off. Run-Time found the people who could track him down. We blew his hoverplane out of the sky as it left its rooftop landing pad. He wasn't able to beam himself out of that."

"The Council guy called them walking, fighting, killing computers in human form."

"He was downplaying them. Long time ago, they used the word transhumanism. Transforming the human being with sophisticated technologies to enhance human intellect and physiology."

"Is that when they thought you could download the human mind into a computer?"

"Yeah. Early cyberpunks and the rest weren't too bright. Like most things, the idea came before the ability to do it for real. But the reality never matched that original idea. Evolving the human race beyond its current physical and mental limitations through technology. Evolving, no. Creating test-tube slaves, yes."

"Cyber-assassins are cyborgs or bio-gens? And slaves?"

"Both. The property of the megacorp that created them."

Property was the same word D.G. used.

"Don't you want me to sweep your office, too?" Bugs asked me.

"Yes. I'll drive you, and you can walk me through how you escaped that cyber-assassin."

"Your client."

"I'm not worried about my client. I'm worried about the other one."

"Two of them! Cruz, you're involved with two of these things?"

"We'll talk on the way."

Perspective

Cruz: It was way too much excitement for me. I ran away as fast as I could.

EXCERPT FROM: *Liquid Cool: The Cyberpunk Detective Series (Book One)*

At the diner...

Then it began again. The girl was standing and cursing again, and the mother, as if by levitation, moved back across to her and was screaming at her with full intensity. I was paying attention, but I still had no idea what they were saying—kind of like Dot and her mother, but they were yelling in another language. This was English, but it wasn't. My brain wasn't comprehending a word of their yelling. Then I saw it. The girl punched her mother in the face KO-style. The mother fell to the floor like a rock. GW and father rushed at her like the dogs.

"I'm out of here," I said to myself and exited the Cafe.

"Hey, you!"

I turned to see the Cafe's owner glaring at me.

"Why did you bring these crazy people into my business?" He barely finished his sentence when he spit at me.

I was out of range, but I gave him a dismissive gesture as he ran back into the Cafe. I turned to walk away again.

"Hey, you!"

I turned and reflexively ducked as a bowl of rice barely missed my face. The owner ran back into the Cafe.

I would not wait to see what else he had planned.

"Hey you!"

I was quarter way across the street, but turned. The owner was preparing a wind-up throw, like those silly cricket players, and this time, he threw an egg at me. It barely missed as I lurched forward. Were we little children in kindergarten? A grown man was throwing eggs at me.

He prepared another of his winding-up throws for me. Since we were in kindergarten, I stood on my tippy toes as if it was dodgeball—I was ready for him. He threw it, but it went wrong. The egg went high up in the air and smashed on the windshield of a passing hovercar that was descending to park. It slammed on its air-brakes, hanging twelve feet in the air. Its passenger door lifted up, and a kid crawled from the driver's side to the passenger seat.

"I'm going to kill you!" the kid yelled at him.

I didn't know if it was a full moon or not, but the hovercar driver jumped! I expected he had bionic legs and would land effortlessly, but all I heard was a sickening crack, and the expression on the kid's face was that of someone who had been hit in the face with a sledgehammer. The kid was lying on the ground, screaming and crying, while the Cafe owner was laughing and pointing at him.

Then there was a spark from the kid's hovercar, hanging in the air, as something disengaged the air-brake. The hovercar descended diagonally, straight for the cafe owner. The man ran through the doors as the hovercar crashed through the doors after him! All I heard was things breaking, people screaming, and smashing sounds. Then, a crash that seemed to shake the ground.

That was it. It was way too much excitement for me. I ran away as fast as I could.

Recap

Yes, a Metropolis street detective like Cruz is definitely the wrong person to give any life lessons with this chapter. So do the opposite of Cruz—avoid drama wherever and whenever possible.

Week 31: Resist the Urge to Be Stupid

CRUZ: THE CORPORATE ads wanted you to buy something, and the government ads wanted you to do something. The average citizen, on a normal day, was supposedly bombarded by no less than fifty thousand messages in the city. No wonder people were stupid. All those subliminal messages were taking up all the free space in a person's brain—the universe's ultimate disk hardware.

EXCERPT FROM: *Liquid Cool: The Cyberpunk Detective Series (Book One)*

At the Liquid Cool offices...

I looked, and PJ had a laser rifle in each arm.

"PJ, stop that nonsense. You can't shoot a different weapon in each hand, even with bionic arms. This isn't the movies. You don't have two heads and four eyes. You use two hands to shoot one weapon, so you don't shoot something or someone you're not supposed to."

"But we did that all the time when I was a gang member."

"And how did that work out for you?"

"Okay, Cruz, I'll give one away. You're always a party pooper, poopin' the party."

Perspective

"Mr. Cruz, that's a stupid story."

EXCERPT FROM: *Classic Cyborg (Liquid Cool: From the Crazy Maniac Files, Book One)*

The main office door opened, and there she was—The Electric Lady. That's what everyone called her. Her first name was Justyna. She was in standard yellow jumpsuit and red hard hat attire, but she had some fashionable heels and orange-tinted shades on.

"You," she said.

I stood to shake her hand, but she folded her arms.

"My father hired you?"

"Yes."

"You go tell my father that I'm a grown woman, and I can see whoever I want."

"Oh, the boyfriend," I said.

"He told you."

"No. I saw him leave in the silver hovercar."

"Yes, the boyfriend. You tell him to stay out of my life."

"Do you always date criminal cyborg maniacs?"

That was a mistake. She snatched me and literally threw me through the front doorway. The only lucky part for me was that the door didn't break as I flew out and landed hard on the ground outside. I was immediately overcome by the noise and the sight of flying hoverbots everywhere. Yep, Electric Lady was a cyborg, too, I said to myself.

I decided the best approach was to stay on the ground. She stood over me as I lay there as if I were relaxing.

"Comfortable?"

"I am, actually."

"Get up off my ground and get out of my factory now. I won't throw you the next time. I'll kick you and shatter your ribcage."

I reached over and tapped each leg under her jumpsuit—the sound of metal.

"I promise to leave after I talk to you for five minutes. Your father hired me, but he didn't hire me about your boyfriend."

"Why then?"

"Because someone is trying to kill him, and—please don't kick me—your boyfriend is on the suspect list."

She reached down and picked me up like a rag doll.

"What are you talking about? That's a lie. My father is spreading lies."

"Miss, I don't want to get in the middle of a family dispute. Can we talk for ten minutes?"

"You said five minutes."

"I lied."

"Follow me," she commanded and marched off.

I had to return my crushed fedora-hard hat combo to my head as I followed her along the outer perimeter of the factory wall to another set of doors. As I walked, I looked at the activity of the robots—large and small robot arms everywhere.

"I've never been to a glass factory. What type of glass?" I asked. I had to do something to keep her from even thinking of throwing or kicking me.

"Piorun Glass is a leader in the industry. Optical glass for Up-Top spaceships and satellites, fiberglass for Metropolis and around the world, glass steel for law enforcement and the military, structural glass for construction, and much more. Here."

She had led me down a hall to another office, but this time, it was high-class all the way, one fit for a megacorp president. Every piece of furniture was made of some kind of colored glass. Her office colors were blue and white.

"Tell me about these lies from my father," she snapped as soon as she sat down.

I sat in the single chair in front of her desk. "Your father feels his life is in danger."

"From my boyfriend? A lie!"

"Not from your boyfriend. From a small list of people that includes your boyfriend."

"He wouldn't dare."

"Your boyfriend? Why?"

"I'd kill him."

"Would you? Kill your boyfriend, go to prison for a few decades, and lose all this? That's tough talk from someone not involved in the crime world. Prison actually isn't fun, in case that's what you heard. How long have you been seeing your boyfriend?"

"None of your business."

"You want me to rule out your boyfriend as a suspect? Then answer me."

"A year."

"Has he ever talked about your father, ever?"

"I pursued him. He didn't even know who my father was."

"And why would you do that?"

"Do what?"

"Pursue him."

"Because—"

"Because of what? Because he's a gangster? It's kids like you who give kids like you a bad name. That's just plain stupid. There are other ways to annoy your father besides dating a gangster killer, or didn't they teach you that in private school?"

"What's your name?"

"Cruz."

"Mr. Cruz, I have a growing impulse to knock your head off."

"Who's Pink Machete?"

"What?"

"Who's Pink Machete?"

"What is that?"

"Who's Franken-borg?"

This time, she said nothing.

"Oh, so you know that one. You're a gangster groupie, is that it? Like your mother."

She jumped up from her chair. "Your ten minutes are up. Tell my father to stay out of my life."

"Miss. If your father wants to poke into your life, I don't think there is anything you, with your fancy bionics, or me, with my fancy guns, is going to do to stop him."

I stood from my chair but stopped at the door.

"Miss, you need to dump the boyfriend and stay away from all of them. I look around and see a twenty-five-year-old running her own successful company. You'd risk all that and your life just to spite your father. That's not just stupid; that's psychotic. You better seek counseling. These people will get you killed, and daddy won't be there to save you."

Recap

Some of us are better at resisting this urge than others. Supposedly, it gets easier as you get older. However, it's sometimes tricky to know whether it's stupid or smart until after the fact. Don't worry; you'll be too busy with your Witty, Pithy, and Profound Sci-Fi-Based Inspiration to be anything but smart.

At least, that's the plan.

Week 32: Do the Right Thing

"IF WE SACRIFICE OUR code, even for victory, we may lose that which is most important: our honor." — *Obi-Wan Kenobi: The Clone Wars*

EXCERPT FROM: *Liquid Cool: The Cyberpunk Detective Series (Book One)*

I raced out the main doors of the office tower into the street. People were already encircling the mess that used to be a human being. Besides my germophobia, I had no tolerance for anything disgusting or nasty, which a splattered body definitely was. I pushed through the crowd and held my hand in front of my eyes to shield my delicate sensibilities from the mess. The rain had stopped. Now, when it needed to rain, it wasn't.

The man used to be a large man. I couldn't believe I was kneeling in front of the mess, but I had to get his ID. My hand went for his pants pockets, and, lucky for me, my fingers found the wallet. I pulled it out and quickly opened it. There was the ID card of my sucker shooter. I pretended my eyes were a camera, and I memorized the name, address, phone, and stats.

I paused and felt a wave of panic. The crowd surrounding the body and congregating on the streets was gone. It was like a bad movie where the guy realized he was the only one on the street and wondered why as he looked up to see Godzilla stomping him with his left foot. I looked around, and my gaze stopped at the reason. Two big street cops were watching my every move. I never even saw or heard their hovercruiser.

Perspective

"I'm living in a world of crazy maniacs." — Cruz

EXCERPT FROM: *Classic Cyborg (Liquid Cool: From the Crazy Maniac Files, Book One)*

The boy pest had gotten up from his spot and marched over to me again. "I demand to know how many guns you have!"

When I pulled my omega-gun from my jacket, his face went white, and he ran away faster than a cyborg with supersonic bionic legs. The weapon was literally not of this Earth, illegally acquired on the Up-Top black market from an associate named Phishy, but the silver weapon could be modified to shoot any kind of solid or laser round. I had seen him. I fired clear across to the other side of the roof as I ran. One of the joggers in a blacker slicker was hit in the back. When I finally reached the person, I turned him on his back so I could clearly see his face.

"You shot me!" he yelled at me, shaking from the pain. "Why did you shoot me? Is that legal?"

I was surrounded by residents, parents, and kids as I knelt down near him and dug into his pockets.

"Oh, look at this," I said and handed a picture of my client's daughter to her father. Both parents were standing behind me. "Here's more." I pulled out more pictures. "Are you a fan of this girl?"

"It's not against the law to carry pictures of children."

I stood up from the ground. "I spotted you outside the building when I arrived. I'm sorry, did you think you were invited to the birthday party? Well, you weren't, and you're not a resident of this building. I bet trespassing isn't your only crime. I bet you have a police record a mile long. Stalking is a crime, and stalking a child is a bigger crime."

"I'm not stalking anyone." He sat up slowly.

"Keep your hands where I can see them," I said.

From the corner of my eye, I saw the client's daughter come out of the crowd with a gun in her hand. "You're dead, you old, dirty bastard!"

I snatched it from her. "Give me that! And watch the language."

She kicked me in the leg. "Ouch!" I cried out. "Behave yourself!" I yelled at her.

I happened to glance back and saw the father aiming another gun at the stalker! I snatched it. "Stop it! What's wrong with all of you? There are cameras on this roof. We've made a legal citizen's arrest, but if you shot him, he can call the police on you."

My eye immediately switched to the mother. If father and daughter were crazy maniacs, then she was probably one, too. Her hands were empty, but she watched me with a smirk. Her eyes and mouth widened. "Gun!" she yelled.

I jerked my body to the side as I fired into the stalker's chest. I jumped up and quickly looked at the object in his hand. It was only a pair of dark shades. I turned to look behind me. The mother was smiling. The father was smiling, and the daughter was smiling. In fact, everyone on the roof was smiling—except me.

"I'm living in a world of crazy maniacs. Call the police, ambulance, whatever. I'm outta here." I pointed at the parents. "Don't think that setting aside half that yummy chocolate birthday cake for me and my family is a bonus. I want the real bonus you promised, meaning cash."

Police hated police shows and police "reality" shows even more for good reason. They gave the general public lots of ideas, but usually all the wrong ones. Yelling out "gun" was a public favorite to get the police to shoot someone for you. I was a licensed private detective with a carry and conceal permit for any legal weapon on Earth, and I was always armed. That made me a pseudo-cop, and everyone knew it. I didn't like being manipulated by anyone, even if I was well-paid for it.

The stalker wasn't dead, but he wouldn't be leaving his future hospital room anytime soon. Police found his hovercar, and there were a lot more than just pictures inside—lots of illegal weapons, which he didn't have permits for. So, his future hospital recovery room was going to be Metro Prison.

The life of a street detective in Metropolis was one of keeping one eye on the bad guy, another on the victim, and another on the client. You never knew which one of them would do something stupid, including trying to shoot you. I didn't like getting shot.

Recap

The best definition of character I have ever heard and still use to this day is, "Character is doing the right thing, even when no one is looking." Brilliant!

Week 33: Manage the Negative Emotions

"PHISHY IS A LOVER, not a fighter." — Phishy

EXCERPT FROM: *Blade Gunner (Liquid Cool, Book Two)*

We marched through everyone and out the front entrance into a torrent of rain.

"Phishy, if you don't tell me what this is all about, I'll be leaving you right here. I have a warm, dry apartment waiting for me."

"I need you to go with me on a job as my bodyguard—to make sure everything stays proper."

"I'm not doing a bodyguard job."

"Don't worry. It's not dangerous at all. You take us there and wait in the car; we'll go in to get our stuff, then we'll come back out. You don't even have to use your vehicle."

"That's not a bodyguard job. That's a lookout job for criminal activity."

Phishy laughed. "I'm not a criminal, Cruz. I'm as straight as you are. Oh, he's here!"

A large red hovercar descended to the ground. It looked like an old hoverfiretruck, though only half the length.

"Phishy, I'm not going anywhere."

"Ten bills," he yelled at me and looked back up, waving to the hovertruck.

Ten bills. Hmm? That would make a big dent in the balance of my omega-gun.

"Cruz, my man!"

A look of shock gripped my face, and my mouth hung open. Before me was a dark mustached, bearded stick of a man, wearing a red slicker jacket and Christmas hat, both covered with flashing indicator lights. He had his arms outstretched as if he expected me to run into them for a hug.

Blinky!

What's the one thing that any classic hovercar collector or restorer fears above all? Your vehicle getting stolen! It was a delicate balance of keeping your precious vehicle in mint condition and deciding to fill it to the brim with the latest anti-theft technology on the market. There was no right answer. It often came down to where you lived and if you had access to a private garage. I never did, but I had all kinds of secrets in protecting my

Pony. I pretended not to care about hovercar security at all, when I was actually as obsessive about it as I was about my vehicle not getting scratched.

However, there was one time in a classic hovervehicle's life when it was completely vulnerable—at hovercar shows!

There I was, as a kid, entering my Ford Pony into one vintage hovercar show after another. That's how you built your rep, especially if you wanted to get into the classic hovercar restoring business. If you couldn't restore your own vehicle, no one was going to hire you to touch theirs. Right from the start, I impressed the OG "original gangsters" of classic hovercars. The old-timers inspected my vehicle from top to bottom, sat in the driver's seat, and revved the engine. They looked at each other and nodded. Getting their thumbs-up seal of approval meant to everyone who was anything in the classic hovercar biz that I was legit, and operating at the top of the craft.

At a hovercar show, your vehicle was there for people to see. The doors were open, the keys were in the ignition, and the engines were purring. No one stole at a show. People had gotten executed for less. Well, that's what I'd thought.

One fateful day, I was chatting it up with the OGs about their vehicles, each centuries-old model worth millions, with hulky bodyguards standing next to them at all times. Then I heard it. Every classic hovercar driver knows the sound of their own vehicle's engine. We dream about it. I turned around to see a laughing guy in a Santa suit slam my doors shut from within the vehicle!

By the time I bolted to my Pony, it was in the air. However, the guy was not driving it away. He was doing a complete aerial donut. The spinning didn't stop, and now everyone at the car show was watching, some laughing, some surprised, others in shock, as I was. Then he stopped, and the hovercar dropped. People dived for cover, thinking it was crashing to the ground, but the man braked inches above the ground. The door opened, and all I heard was laughter as the man got out. He was thin but much taller than me.

I was on fire, and it didn't matter whether he was five times my size. I was going to kill him. He saw my face and took off like a gazelle. I ran after him.

"You're dead!" I yelled.

The man in the Santa suit never stopped running. He never looked back and never slipped on the wet ground (I slipped several times). Thirty minutes of running through the city streets became an hour. I swore with every OCD fiber of my being that I was never going to stop until I caught him and beat him ugly.

Two hours later, my legs simply gave out, and I collapsed to the ground. I wasn't out of energy, but my legs had their own mind. I sat on the ground, watching the Santa man disappear into the distance and into the rain.

I was no less enraged, but I literally couldn't walk anymore. Luckily for me, more than one attendee from the hovercar show had followed me while I was chasing the Santa man. They got me into a hovertaxi, and back to the show, where the OGs had loaned me a couple of their bodyguards to watch my Pony.

"Does anyone know that thief's name?" I angrily asked.

"Yeah," said a guy with long, flowing white hair. "His name is Blinky. He's a small-time hustler in the city."

I looked for him but never caught up with him again. I heard about him from time to time. No other fool wore a blinking Santa suit all year round—but that was a long time ago. I had been a kid in high school. As you get older and move on with life, you forget about all that silliness. But I never did forget his name.

I gave Phishy a dirty look, gave Blinky a disgusted look, and spun around to go back into my building.

"No, Cruz, we need you." Phishy ran after me.

"Why are you with him?" I pointed at Santa man.

"Blinky? He's an associate. He brought me the job."

"What job? I still don't know what any of this is about."

"I'll tell you all about it, man," Blinky interjected.

"Man? I'm not talking to you."

"Man, where's all this hostility coming from? Why you hatin' on Santa?"

"You are not Santa!"

"What'd I do to you, man?"

"You don't remember, do you?"

"Remember what, man?"

"A younger Blinky jumps into a classic red Ford Pony at a major classic hovercar show and does endless donuts with said vehicle."

Blinky started giggling. "I remember that. Man, that was, like, fifty years ago."

"Try not even twenty years ago."

"Man, some kid chased me. Was that your kid?"

"No, man, that was me."

Blinky burst out laughing, and then Phishy started laughing with him.

"That was you, man? Where was your hat? You weren't wearing your hat."

"My hat came later."

"Phishy, man. This cat chased me for hours. If I didn't have my stimulants, he would have caught me for sure. He was going to run the entire length of Metropolis to get me, but his legs must have given out on him." He looked at me, laughing. "You were that kid, man. Glad to see you've bulked up a bit. A wet kitten had more mass than you did back then."

"Drugs. I should have guessed it." I said to Phishy, "You and your man, Blinky, can do this job without me."

"We need you, Cruz."

"Phishy, the man asked a legit question." Blinky moved closer to me. I should have punched him. "Cruz, my man, Phishy and I are picking up an item for resale. That's it. You get to drive my vehicle. You can even do some donuts if that makes you feel good. We pick up the item while you wait in the truck. When we come out, you drive away."

"Yeah, Cruz," added Phishy.

"Why do you need a getaway driver?"

They laughed.

"Getaway driver, man? It's nothing like that."

"Phishy, you said something about a bodyguard."

"Yeah, a car bodyguard."

"What's the item?"

"Cruz, we'll pick it up and show it to you," Phishy said. "You know I don't do any crimes above misdemeanors, and this one is not even that. There's nothing to worry about. Your second best man wouldn't do that to you."

"You're getting married, man?" Blinky asked.

"No, you can't come to my wedding," I said. "We don't believe in Santa."

Perspective

Cruz: I could feel my own fumes of anger radiating from my body.

EXCERPT FROM: *Liquid Cool: The Cyberpunk Detective Series (Book One)*

It was only the next day. I lay on the floor on my back, thinking about all the potential names I had come up with for my soon-to-be-real, one-man detective agency. I got the emergency work blanket from my vehicle's trunk, which was for use if I ever broke down and needed to do work on the Pony—which would never happen. I lay on it on the floor, which was littered with crumbled wads of paper. I had been doing this for the last three hours. The only sound for the longest time was the rain against the tall windows, and then I heard it.

The door opened, and I sat up quickly, looking into the reception area. I realized the door must have been unlocked all this time, which was completely out of character for me. I was the OCD guy, who checked the front door to make sure it was locked five separate times before I went to bed. Who could it be? Did the Realtor guy return? Was it some street punk? Two people appeared at my open office door.

It was him! The guy who scratched my vehicle!

When you were kids in elementary school, stepping on and scuffing a man's pair of kicks (sneakers) was a fighting offense. But boys grew out of that childishness. They grew to be men when scratching their hovercar was a fighting offense.

That was easily five years ago, but I had not forgotten his face. Though I never expected to see his ugly mug ever again in my life, I remember the day he scratched my vehicle, almost like it was yesterday.

There were people who drove, and then there were drivers. For us real drivers, there was no such thing as an accident that wasn't your fault. It was the core of the defensive driving mindset. You must anticipate any contingency, and if a bad thing happened, the blame resided with you. But I had safely parked my vehicle and was just about to turn it over to my mobile security guy—actually, it was Flash—and go about my day.

This maniac came out of nowhere, going against traffic, dove, turned in a semi-circle, hovered above the road, dipped closer to the ground, and stopped, scratching my car and slamming into a concrete parking stall divider.

My mouth hung open in shock.

The guy got out and surveyed the damage to his car but could not care less about what he had done to mine. My spotless, perfect, immaculate, heavenly red Ford Pony was gouged by a deep blue-gray scratch straight through to the metal. My eyes were bulging with rage.

"Get over here!" I yelled. "You scratched my vehicle!"

The guy was on his mobile and completely ignored me, carrying on a conversation.

I looked at Flash, who probably saw the growing agitation on my face.

"Just call your insurance and get away from me, you plonker," he said.

I lost any bit of composure remaining and ran at the guy. I was going to punch him, push him, whatever. As I neared him, he turned and dropped his mobile to the ground to brace for my attack. Suddenly, someone grabbed me from behind—it was Flash.

"He's not worth it," Flash said. "No, Mr. Cruz. You can't assault him. He'd be able to call the cops, and they'd haul you away."

"You scratched my vehicle!" I yelled again.

"So what?" he yelled back.

"You're going to pay every dime it takes to fix it!"

"All it needs is a paint job with a spray can!"

I went ballistic, and Flash really had to hold me back.

"It's a classic hovervehicle, and they're going to have to strip off all the paint and redo it paint coat by paint coat—fifty at least. You don't touch up a classic hovercar with a spray can!"

"Screw you! My insurance is not paying for that. Get a spray can from the local market. One coat. I may even have a can in the trunk for you."

I desperately tried to reach for his face and claw it off, but Flash restrained me.

"You touch me, and I'll sue you and take that pile of junk from you!"

My head was throbbing; I was so enraged. It took Flash fifteen minutes, at least, to calm me down, but I did, eventually.

His insurance paid, but it was a bargain basement one. All I got was ten percent of the damages. I sued him in small claims court. He never showed up, and I won my judgment, but the clerk said good luck getting him to pay. There would be an arrest warrant filed, but no police would ever act on it with murderers, rapists, and gang members to deal with.

I did all I could do, so I did all that I shouldn't do, channeling all my OCD negative energies at him. I found out where he lived, where he worked, his girlfriend's house, his favorite market, and every place he went. I stalked him. I stalked him twenty-four hours a day. And I made sure he saw me.

At the beginning, he laughed at me, throwing a curse or two at me and an occasional obscene gesture. Then he got angry, especially when I followed him to his girlfriend's or when they went to a restaurant for dinner.

The girlfriend was never amused by me, and one time, she came out to go somewhere—he was still in the residence—and saw me and ran back inside. Soon after, I could see she was getting scared—and so was he.

There was a massive rainstorm, so much so the hovercars were staying out of the sky. But not me. I staked out a spot right across from his place, and I could see their silhouettes watching me from the third story. If they were on a higher floor, they would have ignored me, but people who live close to the ground look out their windows at the ground. It's just what you did. And there I was.

They thought they were clever one day and sneaked out of their residence the back way to their hovercar and had gone to another neighborhood, clear across the city. I illegally bugged their car, and I set it to ring my mobile if their hovercar started up.

The looks on their faces when they came out of the restaurant and saw me were priceless. They were really scared and bolted away from me. I realized I had reached into my jacket for something, and they thought it was for a gun.

The next day, the Guy Who Scratched My Vehicle came out of his residence, his girlfriend standing behind him and watching, and he threw a brown paper bag at me.

"Take it psycho," he said. "You got your money. Count it."

I picked up the bag from the wet ground and opened it. I knew they expected me to just take it and go, but I walked a few feet, sat right on the sidewalk, and counted every bill. They watched me with utter contempt.

When I finished, I got up and left, glancing back one last time to glare at them. I actually gained nothing in my episode of madness. I got every dime to fix my car, but the expense in time and money of following them and doing the surveillance on them was all on me. But I felt good, as most fools do.

Perspective

"Be mindful of your feelings" — Mace Windu, Jedi Master, *Star Wars: The Prequels*

(Okay, this one is just funny!)

EXCERPT FROM: *Write Me a Murder on Jules Verne's Island (Liquid Cool, Book Nine)*

We were in the balloon for so long that the kids had fallen asleep on the glass floor of the basket. They wanted to stay awake and see, but their eyes wouldn't let them. We'd also lost track of the time with the sun. It was actually nighttime, and if we didn't return, we'd miss dinner.

The hot-air balloon may have looked vintage, but it was equipped with a backup hoverengine in case of emergencies. The regular motor was quite advanced, but simple to use. I'd planned to let Cruz Jr. land us but he was asleep. We sat down softly on the landing pad of the main hotel, where Ms. Modula and Mr. Runner waited.

"How did you enjoy it?" she asked.

"We loved it," Dot replied.

I carried Cruz Jr., and Dot had Kat in her arms. The kids got their bearings, but they had that sleepy-eyed look.

"Dinner still being served?" I asked.

"Oh yes, Mr. Cruz. The kitchen was waiting for your return."

As we stepped out of the basket, Ms. Modula led the way while Runner attended to the balloon.

"What's on the menu tonight?" Dot asked.

"It's banquet style, Mrs. Cruz."

I stopped myself from convulsing. My wife shot me a disapproving look.

"I'm fine."

"Cruz, behave yourself," she said. "You're not a germophobe anymore."

"How can I be with two kids touching everything? I had no choice."

"Cruz, I'm about to start ignoring you."

Sure enough, we entered the dining area, and it was buffet-style. Then it happened. I heard someone sneeze. Not a little sneeze. The kind of sneeze that was like when you were driving and the hovercar ahead of you cleans its windshield. The water sprays over their windshield, yours behind them, and anyone else around.

It was bungalow prowler Rich Maxima. My eyes locked on him like a guided missile. With the same hand he used to cover his sneezing mouth hole, he wiped the front of his tank top. My mouth dropped open. Was that his version of properly washing and scrubbing his nasty hands? At this point, I had set Cruz Jr. on the ground beside me.

"Daddy, what's wrong?"

"I'm on stakeout," I reflexively answered.

Maxima grabbed a clean plate from the stack with the same nasty hand, and I almost swallowed my tongue. He took a fork and chopsticks from the utensils table with the same nasty hand. Then he approached the food. The man was going to contaminate the entire island's food supply for the night! Food my family was going to eat!

"Cruz!" I heard my wife scream.

I ran and tackled the man before he could spread his pestilence. How I got from where I was standing to where he was, I couldn't remember. But I did. The man was on the ground where he belonged. His plate and utensils were on the floor around him.

Maxima rolled onto his back, beet-red, gritted teeth, and he slowly got to his feet with a growing menace and clenched fists.

"Please, gentlemen." Runner appeared between us.

"Why did you do that?" Maxima yelled at me.

"Go wash your hands!" I yelled.

"What?" Maxima was genuinely confused.

"You sneezed on your hands, and you transferred that nastiness to the plates, the utensils, and were about to contaminate all the food. If I want to feed my family your germ spit nastiness, I'll have you spit in a cup and feed them from there. Go wash your hands, you dirty animal!"

I heard commotion behind me and turned. Cruz Jr. was laughing, my wife was laughing, Kat was giggling, Runner lost his battle to keep from laughing, and I realized that all the other writers were already seated with their food, laughing. Maxima was even redder than before and blew past me for the restrooms.

"I want fresh plates and utensils," I told Runner.

"Yes, sir. Right away," Runner replied.

"You tell him," Jean Code said aloud, lifting her glass in a toast to me. "Hear, hear."

Special Note

There are, of course, legitimate times when negative emotions can be very much appropriate.

EXCERPT FROM: *I, Alien Hunter (Liquid Cool, Book Five)*

From the beginning of the corridor to the Nostradamus, the airlock entrance was not far at all, but it seemed as if we were marching to Outer Mongolia. We may not have been thinking about space aliens burying into our eardrums anymore, but there was something very ominous about the Nostradamus when we reached it. I had never believed in inanimate objects having the stench of death, but that's what I felt. Even I had a difficult time moving forward, but I did.

Sometimes, automation can be demonic. The door automatically opened, and both Flash and I almost had heartaches. Our delicate minds thought "the alien" opened it from the inside and not the automatic programming of the craft.

"I can't take much more of this," Flash said.

We collected ourselves and began the walk forward. I took a deep breath and found some bravery within because I knew what we might see very soon—Flash didn't.

The craft's bridge was where we were going. We reached it, and everything was on as normal, but there wasn't a soul around. Flash was an excellent mechanic, and I, of course, had been the hovercar restorer, so we both could figure out the controls on any spacecraft—even Martian. We both thought the same thing and walked to the communication stations.

"Cruz, what's that?"

The captain's comm panel and the separate communications post were covered in amber gel. The controls looked like they were corroded.

"Forget it. We need to find the people." I was already exiting the bridge when I noticed I was alone. I turned around. "Flash, what are you doing?"

"There's acid spit on the comms."

"That isn't acid spit. Don't let your imagination control you."

"What is it then? It's burned out the circuits."

"There is no such thing as alien acid spit. Flash, pull yourself together. We're the only two on board."

"Cruz, maybe you were right—"

"No, Flash, you're not backing out now. We're here now."

We continued down a corridor with me in the lead. As a freighter, the Nostradamus wasn't only a huge craft, but there were so many places to hide; there was no way only two people could do a proper search.

"We're going back," I said to Flash.

"Why?"

"We're going to secure the bridge and let robots do the searching for us. We don't need the comms because we have our mobiles."

For the first time, I saw the real Flash. He smiled. "Good plan, Cruz."

We returned to the bridge, and I walked to the captain's station. First, I secured all the doors, including the airlock. No one else could get on or off the craft.

"Robots or cams?" I asked.

"Robots," Flash answered.

Flash tried to find any robots on the craft that we could activate. I tried to do the same with the craft's cameras. We found them listed in the Nostradamus's equipment directory, but none could be activated.

"Do you hear something?" Flash asked.

We listened for a while, and it was clear there were voices coming from somewhere in the freighter. Flash had a deer-in-the-headlights look.

"We have no choice, Flash."

"No! I'm not leaving this room. It's a trap."

"Whether it is or isn't, we're going. You're armed, and I'm armed."

"But can we spit acid?"

"Stop that. There's no such thing. You're going to give me and you a heart attack. We're men! We're strong! We're brave!"

Flash wasn't happy. He wanted to run again—and I wanted to follow.

Recap

Classic Cyborg: "I needed something to replace all that anger at my core. Always thought of martial arts as a way to kill a man. Never knew it could be used for anything else, but that's what I've done all these years. Replaced the anger with the serenity of purpose."

NEGATIVE EMOTIONS CAN be so destructive and sideline any forward progress.

Anger, worry, fear, depression, self-doubt.

Any of these negative emotions can self-sabotage any self-improvement. Too many people are stuck in a repetitive loop of negative thoughts about themselves and their chances for success in anything.

Some people are better than others in pushing aside those negative emotions. People like Phishy never seem to have them at all and are always in good spirits, which is the mindset we want to have.

Whether negative emotions are a constant companion or rarely bother you, don't let them be the hard obstacle or nagging distraction to your success. Life may already throw enough curve balls at you to keep you from achieving your goals.

Master your emotions with self-control and discipline. Learn the techniques to help you manage them on your own or get sincere help from others.

EIGHTH MONTH
August
Classic Sci-Fi Actor Birthdays

CHARACTER (ACTOR) SHOW/Movie

AUGUST 1: Ronon Dex (Jason Momoa) Stargate Atlantis

AUGUST 2: John Connor (Edward Furlong) Terminator 2: Judgment Day

AUGUST 2: Zhora (Joanna Cassidy) Blade Runner (Original Movie)

AUGUST 3: Merovingian (Lambert Wilson) Matrix Reloaded

AUGUST 4: General George Hammond (Don S. Davis) Stargate SG-1

AUGUST 6: Gillian (Catherine Hicks) Star Trek: The Voyage Home

AUGUST 7: Jake Sisko (Cirroc Lofton) Star Trek: Deep Space Nine

AUGUST 10: Commander Susan Ivanova (Claudia Christian) Babylon 5

AUGUST 11: Darth Sidious (Ian McDiarmid) Star Wars

AUGUST 12: Amanda (Spock's mother) (Jane Wyatt) Star Trek: The Original Series/The Voyage Home

AUGUST 15: General Grievous (Matthew Wood) Star Wars prequels

AUGUST 16: Director James Cameron: Terminator, Aliens, and many more

AUGUST 16: Dr. R. Chandra (Bob Balaban) 2010: The Year We Make Contact

AUGUST 19: Gene Roddenberry Creator/Exec. Producer Star Trek: The Original Series/Star Trek: The Next Generation

AUGUST 19: Dr. Daystrom (William Marshall) Star Trek: The Original Series

AUGUST 19: Dr. Kate Pulaski (Diana Muldaur) Star Trek: The Next Generation

AUGUST 19: Commander William Riker (Jonathan Frakes) Star Trek: The Next Generation

AUGUST 21: Trinity (Carrie-Anne Moss) Matrix movies

AUGUST 21: Lt. Valeris (Kim Cattrall) Star Trek: The Undiscovered Country

AUGUST 23: Darth Maul (Ray Park) Star Wars prequels

AUGUST 24: R2-D2 (Kenny Baker) Star Wars: Original Movies

AUGUST 24: Kes (Jennifer Lien) Star Trek: Voyager

AUGUST 24: Bra'tac (Tony Amedola) Stargate SG-1

AUGUST 25: Dallas (Tom Skerritt) Alien

AUGUST 28: Samantha Carter (Amanda Tapping) Stargate SG-1

AUGUST 28: Dr. Beverly Crusher (Gates McFadden) Star Trek: The Next Generation

DON'T PANIC. LIFE'S SUPPOSED TO BE UNEXPECTED

About the Unexpected

YES, WE MAY NOT LIKE surprises, but they are an irresistible, capricious force in the universe.

Most chapters in the book focus on mindset because you may not be able to change the unpredictable. However, you can absolutely control how you respond to it.

Excerpt From: *I, Alien Hunter (Liquid Cool, Book Five)*

"I'm not flying a flying saucer!" I protested.

We were in the cockpit. Merlin was flipping buttons all over the place. "Mr. Cruz, you don't have a choice."

"Why can't you fly it? It's your spaceship."

"Because I have to tell you my story, and you're going to be my means of escape."

"Escape?"

"Mr. Cruz, you're going to fly the craft while I jam their tracking means. You can do the former but don't have the technical expertise specific to this craft for the latter."

I was looking back at the exit, but the doors had already closed. The main monitors had turned on, and the police were flying down into the cavern, and all I heard was the barrage of gunfire against the hull. The police had far more powerful weapons, and they'd be opening up with those any second. I felt like a trapped rat on the Titanic.

"Mr. Cruz, sit here!" I did what he said. "I'll start us off, but pay close attention to all that I'm doing." He hit the ignition button, and the entire craft shook, and I immediately felt it jump up. We were hovering. He pushed the throttle forward, and if I hadn't been accustomed to rocket-like launches before, I would have thrown up, passed out, or passed out while throwing up—that's how fast we flew forward. All I saw was blackness; then we punched through. It was a fake wall, and we rocketed upward into the sky.

"Mr. Cruz, take the throttle. You have to get used to the controls."

"I can't fly a spaceship!"

"I'm letting go in 3-2-"

I grabbed the throttle. "I bet you staged all of this. You knew the police were tailing me."

"I don't have time to allay your paranoia. I'm paranoid enough all by myself. I'm going to begin my story. When I'm done, there will at least be two people in the universe who will know."

"Know what?" I couldn't believe it. We were heading out to space. "Where am I going?" I can't fly into space."

"When you pass the stratosphere, you'll level off." A warning siren was going off.

"What's that?"

"Slow down just a tad."

A massive space jet ripped past us, and I almost let go of the throttle. "You're going to get us killed!"

Recap

Cruz's detective life is probably a bit more excitement-filled than any of ours, but if he can "go with the flow" with all that's thrown at him, we can, too, in our lives.

The Planners

BE (LIQUID) COOL / MONTHLY PLANNER

MONTH:

SUN	MON	TUE	WED	THU	FRI	SAT

TOP PRIORITIES / GOALS

PEOPLE TO SEE / PLACES TO GO / REMINDERS

NOTES

RATE / ASSESS THE MONTH:

BE (LIQUID) COOL
WEEKLY PLANNER

WEEK:

M T W H F S S

MONDAY

TUESDAY

WEDNESDAY

THURSDAY

FRIDAY

SATURDAY / SUNDAY

WEEK'S PRIORITIES / TO DO

NOTES

RATE / ASSESS THE WEEK:

BE (LIQUID) COOL
WEEKLY PLANNER

WEEK:

M T W H F S S

MONDAY

TUESDAY

WEDNESDAY

THURSDAY

FRIDAY

SATURDAY / SUNDAY

WEEK'S PRIORITIES / TO DO

NOTES

RATE / ASSESS THE WEEK:

BE (LIQUID) COOL
WEEKLY PLANNER

WEEK:

M T W H F S S

MONDAY

TUESDAY

WEDNESDAY

THURSDAY

FRIDAY

SATURDAY / SUNDAY

WEEK'S PRIORITIES / TO DO

NOTES

RATE / ASSESS THE WEEK:

BE (LIQUID) COOL
WEEKLY PLANNER

WEEK:

M T W H F S S

MONDAY

TUESDAY

WEDNESDAY

THURSDAY

FRIDAY

SATURDAY / SUNDAY

WEEK'S PRIORITIES / TO DO

NOTES

RATE / ASSESS THE WEEK:

Week 34: The Unexpected

"BOBA FETT? BOBA FETT? Where?" Han Solo, Star Wars: The Original Movies

EXCERPT FROM: *Liquid Cool: The Cyberpunk Detective Series (Book One)*

CRUZ GETS A SURPRISE visit from his girlfriend, Dot, at his new main 100th floor office in Buzz Town ...

"Very good, Mr. Cruz. How did you Sherlock Holmes all that? Are you that good?"

"I am, Mrs. Cruz. Oh, let me get my cup." I jumped up to grab my cup from my main desk. "What can I get you? I even have my own mini stash in my office."

The door to my office smashed in as a large man flew past me, knocking the cup from my hand. The thug slammed into the window.

We heard the pulse blast sound from under his jacket. After a second delay, the window shattered as the thug rose from the floor with such a look of menace that I knew that no good was about to come next. The thug glared at me, reached into his jacket, and raised his arm towards me. I didn't consciously notice the gun until after I already reacted.

Pop!

My pop-gun popped out and the pulse bullet blew through his neck with a cloud of smoke and blood. His face, with a shocked look, fell forward off his body, and then his entire body fell back out the window.

Perspective

"That is me. I am Ichi Jumper."

EXCERPT FROM: *The Electric Sheep Massacre (Liquid Cool, Book Four)*

When I'd left my Liquid Cool office with the Surf Brothers, it wasn't even lunchtime yet, but here I was walking out of Metropolis Police Central, and it was almost 9 pm. I was told that they'd let the Surf Brothers go at around 6 pm, so the extra hours they kept me was for spite.

I tried to find out who the body was, but they weren't talking. Officers Break and Caps weren't even the primary interrogators. They dropped me off, and then I never saw them again for the rest of the time I was there. It was a marathon of questions, waiting, eating snacks, and watching TV while waiting. This was how it was done: now, centuries before I was born, and would be done centuries after I was dust, so there was no reason to get upset over it.

Since I'd hitched a ride with the Surf Brothers, it meant my Pony was still at the office parking bay, which was not acceptable. The officers did allow me to make a few calls at around 5 pm, and I had PJ call Let It Ride Enterprises to get a mobile security guard to watch it; my normal guy was on vacation. I walked outside from a side entrance to the public area, where I could catch public transportation (Hell no!) or get a hovercab.

"Hey, hey!" I heard shouting and someone approaching me.

It was an Asian man coming towards me, wearing a yellow jacket over a black turtleneck. He had blond hair, but I was almost positive it was a wig. He seemed to have no facial hair at all, including no eyebrows.

"Are you Mr. Cruz?" he asked in his Japanese accent.

"Who wants to know?" I asked.

He stopped in front of me, pulled his silver business card holder from his jacket, and pulled out a card. When he handed it over, he waited until I started to read it when he said, "Ichi Jumper."

"Ichi Jumper?"

"Yes."

"What's that?"

"That is me. I am Ichi Jumper."

"What do you want?"

"You were at the River with the police and the dead men."

First, he knew where I'd been and who I'd been with. Second, he knew there was more than one person dead.

"Who are you? I've got your name, but who are you?" I asked.

He had a mean expression on his face, and he poked his index finger into my chest as he talked. "Stay out of this, Mr. Cruz. It does not concern you."

"Stop that." I attempted to slap his hand away, but he'd already pulled back. "What doesn't concern me?"

"Stay away. Ichi Jumper has warned you. There will be most severe consequences next time."

"Don't you threaten me, you blond-wigged mutt!"

He wasn't even listening to me.

"Ichi Jumper has spoken!"

He jumped into a waiting hovercab and it flew away.

Perspective

"Wait a minute, Doc. Are you telling me you built a time machine... out of a DeLorean?" — Marty McFly, Back to the Future

---

EXCERPT FROM: *I, Alien Hunter (Liquid Cool, Book Five)*

At the Liquid Cool offices...

"We found out from contacts there on Mars that he booked a passage on the Nostradamus—a commercial Martian freighter bound for Earth," Mrs. Cosmos said. "That's all of it, all that we know. That's why we need a detective."

"What do you want me to do? This isn't a missing persons case. You're alleging some kind of government conspiracy."

"It is a missing persons case, Mr. Cruz. My brother went on that space freighter and disappeared. We can't reach him, and no one else can. The freighter has been out of contact for its entire 13-month journey. All you have to do to solve this case is get a communication channel open to that freighter. Regardless, we plan to personally be there when it lands at the spaceport in two weeks."

"This seems like a stretch. I'm a detective, not a communications tech or spaceship greeter."

"You solve missing person cases, and that's what this is. It's just a bit different." Mrs. Cosmos stood from her chair and walked to the common desk in the room. She walked back to me and handed me a disk. "We already downloaded all the files. All my brother's vid-messages for you."

"We even were able to record some of the government messages," Mr. Cosmos added.

"Government messages?"

"Mr. Cruz, whatever happened to my brother is their doing. Neil suspected this was going to happen."

"Why would the government care if your brother found or didn't find extraterrestrials?"

"Mr. Cruz, extraterrestrials have been coming and going to Earth for centuries," Mrs. Cosmos said. "They work in the government and all the top megacorps."

I had been thrown down the rabbit hole. "Them?"

"Yes, Them," Mrs. Cosmos said, nodding. "Them is not the government. Them is the extraterrestrials working in the government."

"They don't want the public to know they're here," Mr. Cosmos said. "They'll do anything to prevent that."

I put a hand on my forehead. I hadn't been thrown into the rabbit hole. I had always been there. "Are you telling me your brother was made to disappear by extraterrestrials working in the government?"

"Yes!"

"Mr. and Mrs. Cosmos, what exactly do you expect me to do then? I'm a private street detective. I'm not a galactic James Bond with my own personal spaceship."

"You're resourceful. You can use your contacts to find out what happened to him. We know he is on that space freighter bound for Earth. We've been tracking it. But we need you. No one will tell us anything. We've even tried normal channels and illegal methods to contact the freighter. Nothing! It like it's a—dead freighter."

Mr. Cosmos huffed, "Mr. Cruz, the freighter has been incommunicado for 13 months. If they know we've hired you, the government will cooperate to make you go away."

"Or," I added, "they'll stonewall even more. So the government or Them did what? A freighter has a full crew. What are you alleging is the conspiracy? What happened to the crew? I'll play."

Alarms screeched, and I jumped so high in my chair that I thought my head would knock the ceiling. The alarms were that loud. "What is that?" I yelled.

"It's the warning alarms," Mrs. Cosmos answered.

"For what? What are those sirens for?" I could barely hear myself yell.

"Something's falling to us from above," Mr. Cosmos answered.

"What?"

People burst into the room, and the Cosmos ignored me as they all ran. I followed them into the express elevator back up to the surface, then outside. I saw a name on the side of one of their hovertruck plow-pickers, but the words completely emptied from my mind when I looked up to the sky.

I stopped in my tracks, looking up like everyone else. I must have still had rats on the brain because as I stared up at the massive object falling from the sky, all I thought was that it looked like a giant turd. However, there was nothing funny about the situation. I realized that this was a real rock, a real meteor, and it was much larger than I originally judged. It was heading straight for us!

"What are you standing here for? Run!" I yelled to everyone.

Suddenly, the panic was unleashed, and everyone ran, most screaming. I had always been told that meteors burnt up in the Earth's atmosphere. Then why was this humongous rock almost on top of us?

I greatly misjudged—we all did. All I remembered was running, but the ground collapsing beneath me followed almost immediately by being blown up into the air. The sound was deafening, and a wave of heat and dirt covered me.

I was a simply a private street detective. Was I about to be killed by some random meteor from space? The wife was not going to be pleased. Didn't this space rock know I was "famous"?

Recap

The unexpected and the ridiculous. You can't plan for them. But be on the lookout, and don't let them take you off course. You must focus on your goals like a laser beam.

Week 35: The Ridiculous

"AM I DANCING, DOCTOR?" Data to Dr. Crusher, Star Trek: The Next Generation, Episode: "Data's Day"

EXCERPT FROM: *Digital Samurai (Liquid Cool: From the Crazy Maniac Files, Book Two)*

"Cruz," PJ called out.

She didn't yell, but her tone was a bit off.

"What is it?" I walked back out into the main office area.

Near the main door stood a middle-aged Asian man, in an expensive silk suit staring at us.

"How did you get in here?" I asked.

"You speak like children. Westerners banter much but say little," he said, not looking at me but gazing around the office.

"I think I read that in a fortune cookie once," I said.

He locked his eyes on mine. "I will walk from where I stand into your office. In your office I will slice your desk and every piece of furniture into pieces. I will leave, and you will not see me again."

"Why would you come to my office to cut it into pieces?"

"I come to see if you can stop me, Cruz-san."

"If I do?"

"Then we can talk further. We must see if you are worthy to be hired by the Hiero Corporation. Worthy to be in the company of neo-samurai."

We never saw the sheath. He pulled his samurai sword from his right sleeve. It was a real sword, and it could do more than slice a wooden desk to pieces. Depending on the material, it might have been able to slice PJ's bionic arms to pieces, too.

"This is a mistake," I said.

"For you?" he asked as he took a side stance, sword held with both hands and angled pointed to the ground. The man was wearing slippers, which meant he was a real samurai soldier.

"I'm not going to let you come into my office and slice up my furniture."

"Cruz, don't joke with him," PJ said.

"Then stop me," he said to me. "Maybe your woman can after I cut off her arms."

He shouldn't have said that.

"Only one man ever cut off my arms," PJ yelled.

"You found him and killed him?" the samurai asked.

"No," PJ said. "He's standing right next to me."

I could draw a gun faster than most people, but a real samurai, even a mediocre one, could move faster than I ever could. But that wasn't my aim. I fired my omega-gun at him as soon as I could pull it from my shoulder holster. He swatted both laser blasts with his samurai sword like they were nothing. That told PJ that the material of the sword might very well be able to slice off her bionic arms. She wasn't having any of that.

She punched the metal barrier that made up her receptionist desk at him. He jumped up, knees up to about his eye level, nearly touching the ceiling as the barrier smashed into the wall behind him. I fired three more shots at him as he was jumping. Again, he swatted all my blasts away.

PJ grabbed and flicked her chair at him with maximum bionic force. It flew at him at sonic speed, but he sliced it in half; both pieces went around him. I switched my omega-gun to machine-fire. He seemed to know I'd done so and threw something at me. I never saw it because it moved too fast. I heard the shuriken hit the wall behind me with a tremendous thud. My reflexes couldn't have moved me out of the way in time. He intentionally missed me but likely cut off a piece of my ear or something just to show me who was master. I realized my hat was gone.

PJ was doing her own throwing. Anything her hand grabbed, she threw at him faster than my eyes could follow. Vases, scissors, cups, pens—all turned into deadly projectiles.

I pretended to stumble, dropping my omega-gun. I could see the surprise in his face. I grabbed a handful of beans from my jacket and desperately threw them at him. He laughed, catching one in his hand, looking at it, and tossing it—while he was swatting PJ's projectiles.

He thought they were peanuts, I'm sure. My Mexican jumping beans began to explode, making sounds like loud firecrackers. He was startled, but before he could stop his own reaction, I shot him point-blank with my pop-gun, hidden under my left sleeve. He crashed into the wall.

PJ had already grabbed her electric shotgun and shot him again. I aimed my omega-gun and fired an explosive round. There was an explosion, but also an explosion of black smoke. I dove at PJ, pushing her to the ground. Shurikens embedded themselves into the wall around us.

We couldn't see him, and that was bad news. I fired, machine-gun style, around PJ's desk. She fired her shotgun; then she opened the bottom drawer of her desk. I had no idea, until then, that she kept grenades—a lot of them.

As I heard my office being blown up, the phone rang. I grabbed PJ's hand to keep her from throwing another grenade. She looked at me.

"It's okay," I said.

She was surprised to see me stand. She jumped up from the floor, too, to look around. The office was black and blown up. The door was closed, but the samurai soldier was nowhere to be seen.

I leaned over and answered the vid-phone. His face appeared on the display screen. He wasn't in the hallway. He stared at us from our parking lot surveillance cameras. PJ and I were so angry we could explode. We looked around the office again. The walls in front of us were riddled with bullet and laser blasts, the waiting area furniture and the magazines were blown to pieces, and the paint was all black and burnt. The office looked like it had been hit by artillery fire. We turned around, and the wall was covered with deeply embedded shurikens, including my Liquid Cool neon sign.

We looked back at the monitor. He watched us. We were shaking with anger. He showed no emotion.

"Your skills are poor," he said, "but you did demonstrate misdirection, though rudimentary, and an element of surprise. It is only because of that last action we are talking. We can talk. You may be suitable."

He moved away from the camera and disappeared, hanging up. We looked up at what had been my beautiful office. We wanted to kill that samurai soldier real bad. And he was on his way back up.

We had enough firepower in the office to fend off an army, but PJ and I were nervous. Our eyes were glued to the monitor of our surveillance cameras. I had a completely illegal laser machine gun in my hands; PJ had a heavy pulse rifle.

I glanced to the side. My tan fedora rested on the floor. One of those throwing stars knocked my hat right off my head. That hat could stay on my head in a gale-force wind, but there it sat. It looked undamaged, but my nerves weren't.

We heard the elevator beep.

A petite Asian woman in a black suit and white blouse underneath exited. She was followed by a young Asian man, then another. They filed out of the elevator in a column. The door opened, and they entered. She saw us and smiled, then did a Japanese bow and continued inside. All those who followed stepped in, smiled, bowed, and entered. PJ and I didn't know what to make of them. They didn't look like corporate soldiers.

The elevator beeped again, and we watched a paint crew, then laborers in overalls arrive. Another group arrived and set up a hover-platform. They arranged three chairs and a table on it. The young Asian woman gestured for us to have a seat, sitting across from each other. The samurai master entered with three large men, definitely corporate samurai soldiers. I'd seen their type before. Our attacker sat at the head of the table on the hover-platform as it rose about six feet in the air. He handed me his business card: ECHO. There were Japanese letters underneath, then a phone number. More people arrived, male and female.

Sometimes in life, you have no idea what the hell is going on. That's how PJ and I felt sitting on the hover-platform with Japanese waitresses serving us tea and crackers. The man blew up my office, and now his people were serving me tea. All around us, his crews were restoring the office—buffing then repainting the walls, repairing the bullet holes and laser blasts. They replaced the carpets, swept, and then buffed the floor. My Liquid Cool neon sign was replaced. They repaired PJ's workstation. They replaced our waiting area for clients. One of the men gave my fedora a professional spray wash and brush in front of me and placed it back on my head perfectly. As each crew finished, they faced us, bowed, and left the office. Moments later, all the crews were gone. The first Asian woman stepped out of the office, followed by the three large men, who closed the door. It was now just the samurai man, PJ, and me.

"How do I address you?" I asked the man.

"EE-KO," he said.

I looked at the card: Echo. Good thing I asked him. I didn't want to make him mad and have him blow up my office again.

I said his name, heavily stressing the "E" as he did. "Well, Mr. Echo. You have my attention. Though, you could have accomplished that in a less dramatic way."

"It was a test."

"Yes, you weren't trying to kill me. However, we were trying to kill you."

He smiled. "I was never in any danger."

"My little son is practicing to be a ninja himself. But to meet one in real life. I really liked the throwing stars. I didn't know they were still used."

"I am a samurai master. No ninja. We have many tools, many weapons, many you do not know of."

"How did you sneak into my office without being seen? PJ and I were right here."

"Your eyes were open, but you were not seeing."

"Tell me, did you really hear me switch settings on the gun? You couldn't have."

"I did. Your weapon is from off-world. I know of it."

"You withstood our weapons fire. Skintight body armor? Did you get that from off-world?"

"Our body armor is made here on Earth. It's better than any off-world."

"So, Mr. Echo, what may I be suitable for?"

"To assist me in my task."

"You don't look like a man who needs assistance from anyone, let alone me."

Perspective

"You know," said Arthur, "it's at times like this, when I'm trapped in a Vogon airlock with a man from Betelgeuse, and about to die of asphyxiation in deep space that I really wish I'd listened to what my mother told me when I was young."

"Why, what did she tell you?"

"I don't know, I didn't listen."

Douglas Adams' The Hitchhiker's Guide to the Galaxy

EXCERPT FROM: *The Moon is a Good Place to Die (Liquid Cool, Book Eight)*

For some reason, I was a kid whisperer. I don't know what it was about me that attracted crazy maniac children. Though I seemed to also attract crazy situations, that was different and I was sure that all Metropolitans encountered the same thing.

I parked my Pony in the megatower's secure parking bay and made my way to the elevators. Lucky me, they lived only a few levels up. Unlucky for me, adolescent kids were everywhere in the halls hanging around.

"Why aren't you all in school?" I asked a group of them clustered together, all on their devices.

They ignored me, and I looked at their devices. They were having a group chat.

"Is there some reason you can't talk to each other like normal people? Maybe if you were in school, you'd learn how to do that."

"We're not your kid, old man," one said.

"I am not old."

"Today's a holiday," another said, but I didn't believe him.

"See. That's all you had to tell me. I was concerned about your well-being. It's what we adults do when it comes to the youth of our city. Now, all you have to do is talk to each other instead of texting."

"Hey, old man, when you mouth-talk, you can't send cool images or change the fonts."

"Mouth-talk?"

I was going to have a long conversation with the wife tonight. We had to keep Cruz Jr. and Kat far, far away from the youth of today.

The door of my potential client was close to the elevators. I rang the bell and stood to the side—a habit I picked up from the police. You don't want to be standing in front of the door in case someone decides to shoot you through it.

Cruz, do people shoot you through the door often?

Shut up, Dent. I'm telling my story.

The door opened, and instead of preteens, an army of children stood there, all dressed in animal suits, which was very appropriate. Hyperactive didn't even begin to describe these kids. They literally couldn't keep still, and their eyes and mouths opened wide with glee at the sight of a new adult to torment.

"Who are you?" a couple of them asked in unison.

"Cruz."

"The detective!" one of them yelled and almost fell over.

"Do you want to see a magic trick?" one of the kids asked me.

I attempted a method of communication that I often used with little children, including Cruz Jr., and was equally as unsuccessful.

"No," I replied forcibly.

"I'll show you."

"No."

"Pull my finger." The kids started laughing like hyenas. I think one of them was in a hyena costume.

"No."

"I will!" another kid said.

He pulled the other kid's finger. The "pull-ee" vomited out fake green slime. Then the puller vomited out fake yellow slime. How cute.

The kids were on the ground, laughing hysterically. A puddle of green and yellow slime around them.

I wondered how long I'd have to wait until the adults showed up. A woman appeared, wearing an apron, and she yelled at them at the top of her lungs. The laughing kids jumped up and scattered like they were street criminals running from arriving police cruisers. They were gone.

The contrast between teens and preteens was a tremendous gulf. The former didn't want to move; the latter couldn't stay still. The former were like doped-out human lampposts; the latter were like doped-up human ferrets. Was this what I had to look forward to with Cruz Jr. and Kat? Pick your poison. I think I preferred the hyperactivity. Just keep them in a padded room without any breakables, and since they were so noisy, you'd always know what they were up to. With the tragically "too cool for school" teenagers who didn't like mouth-talking, you'd never know if they were even in your place or out on the street doing crimes. Maybe I'd chip them like my Pony.

The woman had raccoon-eye makeup—way too much. My wife and her fashion police colleagues would give her a ticket.

"You Cruz?" she asked.

"Yes."

"Come in and close the door before something runs out or something runs in. There are animals on this floor."

I closed the door quickly. The woman walked back around the corner. I didn't like when people disappeared, but the TV was on. When I came down the hallway, there was an open living room on one side and a woman cooking in the kitchen on the other. Someone else stood up from a chair in the living room and walked to me.

"Hello, Mr. Cruz," the man said, extending a hand.

Before I could greet him, something whipped behind me at incredible speed. I spun around, but whatever it was was gone.

"Don't mind him," the man said, shaking my hand. "Have a seat."

"Can you tell me who 'him' is?" I asked.

"Man-eater is harmless." The woman appeared in the living room without her apron.

The two adults sat on their couch. I sat across from them. In the other rooms, I heard the army of kids. I also heard something running around. My eyes scanned the room, and I noticed that the walls of the entire apartment looked like rock, including handholds for climbing.

"Good exercise, rock climbing is," the man said.

"Yes, it is. My office said you have a possible case."

My mind was focused on how quickly I could get out of there. The army of kids was bad enough, but these people had some kind of wild animal running around their place. I didn't want to know what it was. The pair worked for an animal preservation park and apparently bred like animals themselves, dressed their kids like animals, and also had wild animals running about.

"How can I help?" I asked.

The man reached over and handed me a photo. It was of some monkey.

"Captain Fantastic," he said.

"A monkey."

"Captain Fantastic isn't a monkey. He's a lemur."

"Big eyes, striped tail, ears. A monkey."

"Lemurs are marsupials, not monkeys."

"I'm not a pet detective."

"He was kidnapped," the man said. "We know who did it. We know where he is. The police won't do a thing, so we want to hire you."

"All you have to do is rescue him," the woman said. "We don't care how."

Whenever clients used phrases like that, it meant the case would inevitably involve some kind of illegality.

"I appreciate—"

Whatever animal was in the apartment ran behind me faster than light-speed again. The couple saw the nervousness on my face.

"Man-eater is harmless," the woman said again.

People don't name harmless animals "man-eater."

"I lost my train of thought. Yes. I'd only be taking your money."

"Money is no object," the man said. "Captain Fantastic is very important to our family. He must be rescued. Money is no object."

"No object at all," the woman said.

All detectives liked easy money. I was no different.

"Where is he?" I asked.

"A private collector," the man answered.

There it was. The illegality. It meant I'd have to break into someplace.

"If that's the case, the police are the ones to call."

"We have no proof to give the police."

"Then how do you know he's there?"

The husband and wife looked at each other.

"We know," he said.

"I bet you do," I said. "Give me all the details. If you can prove Captain Fantastic is yours, I can check on my own who the—"

"Kidnapper," the woman interjected.

"Who the kidnapper is. I may take the case. I need to study it."

The animal whipped past me again at light speed. I leaped up to catch a glimpse of it, but it was too fast. I missed it again. I looked at the couple again with a stern look.

"I know what you're going to say: Man-eater is harmless."

"But he is," she said to me.

"All the animals in the apartment are human-friendly."

"All? Animals? There's more?" I began looking around. "Okay, well, give me all those details on the lemur."

"Captain Fantastic," she corrected.

"Yes, the captain."

"Mr. Cruz, I believe you are our man," the man said as he stood. He shook my hand again.

We walked toward the door—finally! But then I heard something rush up behind me and stop. The couple looked at what was behind me, smiling. I felt like that little kid in a horror movie: full moon, pitch black, alone, with the creature or psycho standing behind me. I slowly and nervously turned around. Behind me was some cute, hornless, spotted deer. It stared at me with big black eyes, its entire body trembling as if it were using great energy to even stand still, and running around was actually its natural state.

"Say hello to Man-eater, Mr. Cruz," she said. "As you can see, her name is a bit of a joke since deer don't have teeth and don't eat meat."

"I'm safe then."

"Harmless."

At that moment, I heard the army of kids running around the corner to me. Man-eater was gone in a blink of an eye, and I wished I could've run away too.

The same kid ran to me and said, "Pull my finger this time." He was giggling.

Another kid did the honors. The kids started sniffing the air, then laughing again.

"Eww!" "What's that smell?"

The kid fell to the floor laughing.

"Stop it, children. It's a natural bodily function," the man said to them.

"Don't mind Amphi, Mr. Cruz," the woman said.

"Yes, he's harmless." I pointed at the giggling kid on the ground. "It's bad enough I have to be subjected to Cruz Jr., but I will not be skunked by you."

That only made the kid laugh louder.

Then, some kind of rainbow-colored pelican thing flew past my face, making me jump back and almost fall. Now, all the kids were on the floor laughing.

"What was that?!"

"That was Professor Seuss."

"Okay, I'm out of here!"

I ran for the door. I was literally in a zoo and had to escape immediately.

Cruz, the pet detective. Not if I could help it.

Recap

Just laugh and go with it. What else is there to do?

Week 36: Don't Be Afraid to Ask For Help

CRUZ: ISOPODS! I HAD to fight my growing flight instinct.

EXCERPT FROM: *A.I. Confidential (Liquid Cool, Book Six)*

Wilford reached down, picked him up, and threw him against the wall, shattering one of those crate covers. Brackets began to scream. I knew Wilford was still strong for a man a nickel away from the big 1-0-0, but he didn't throw him so hard against the wall to cause Brackets bodily injury.

I saw them!

Wilford turned, and I was nothing but a distant figure in the distance.

"Help me!" Brackets yelled. His body was crawling with isopods!

Superman had Kryptonite. I had isopods. Every hero has a weakness; that's part of the contract. Clinically, I was a recovering germophobe. To go from almost having to be sent to a bubble colony on the Moon, to being able to live and thrive in Metropolis was real progress, but I was still "recovering." That meant certain things could trigger an attack. Even if I wasn't a germophobe or recovering one, I could not and would not deal with isopods. Jumbo roaches, rats, and isopods were my own personal trinity of terror.

"Isopods are the most terrifying. People always say that science fiction can never create something scarier than what already exists in nature. Biologists say isopods are crustaceans—part of the same family as shrimp and crabs. I'd say that those biologists are big fat liars. Shrimp and crabs are cute animals that deserve to crawl around on the sea floor or grace a person's dinner plate. Isopods are space alien creatures deposited on our planet and deserve nothing less than total extermination. Some biologists are at least trying to be honest in saying they're related to woodlice! That means they're blood suckers. But Metropolis doesn't have any real wood anymore, so that means the blood-sucking would be an invasion of the body snatcher, vampiric kind. To this very day, I remember a documentary where an isopod infested a fish and literally took the place of the poor fish's tongue. That meant the isopod would eat the fish's food before the fish could eat it, before it could even get to its stomach. What a way to live. The alien parasite takes over your own body part. That's what isopod infestation is, and there is no science fiction scarier than that—because they're real. The very whisper of these alien creatures could bring me to the edge of an attack. But seeing a live one, or a horde of them, means a full relapse.

"Their bodies protected by a rigid, exoskeleton comprised of overlapping segments, their bodies segmented—fused from head to tail, large beady eyes, not one but two pairs of antennae, thoracic legs arranged in seven pairs, multiple sets of jaws, ability to breathe underwater as easily as on land. The

Alienists were right! We have been invaded by space aliens! It's Them! It's the isopods!"

"Mr. Cruz!" one of the CDC orderlies yelled.

I started to run again. "I'm infested!"

The orderlies tackled me to the ground as another ran to me and jabbed me with a needleless injector to sedate me.

Perspective

"I see you." — Mac, Predator played by Bill Duke

EXCERPT FROM: *Liquid Cool: The Cyberpunk Detective Series (Book One)*

"I'd like to start this month's evening meeting of the Metropolis Soldier of Fortune Meet-Up Club with everyone going around the room and giving us your name and a little something about yourself. It's customary that first-time visitors go first. Any volunteers?" he asked. The man looked like his skin had been cooked over an open flame. Survivor of a war? Or the victim of a bad plastic skin job?

I raised my hand.

"Thank you, young man. Tell us about yourself."

I stood from my chair. "My name is Cruz, and I'm a detective, new to the biz, in fact. I didn't know where else to go, so I came here. I'm going into Mad Heights, and as many of you know, it's not the nicest part of the city. But I have a real case that forces me to go there and track down members of a particular and particularly deranged animal gang. But you don't go into Mad Heights without bodyguard protection. I bet with all the law enforcement, military, and mercenary experience in this room, there's got to be at least one person who could help a young guy, like me, starting out. I'm so inexperienced at this that I don't even know people who know criminals or anything about that world."

"Then you're in the wrong business, sonny," one man said, and the room erupted in laughter.

"Probably true, but it's too late now. I already have my business cards." My quip got additional laughter.

"You can hire them, you know," a man said in the back on the other side of the room.

"Hire who?" I asked.

"You can hire animal gang members as bodyguards. Anybody can."

"How do you do that?"

"Call 'em."

"Where?"

"They advertise in the Club's cybernet magazine, along with every other criminal in the city. Between body armor and bombs—bodyguards," the man said.

Recap

Asking for help.

For some, it's not as easy as it should be. We make excuses like: they're too busy or I might sound stupid. Some people worry they might be viewed as weak or incompetent. Nonsense. The worst thing that can happen is they say "no." And if they do, that's fine. Look elsewhere for help.

The culture of help is an integral part of society and humanity. Yes, we want to be "self-reliant" but there's nothing wrong with valuable help when it's available either.

Week 37: You'll Have Setbacks, Just Keep Moving Forward

"GAME OVER, MAN! GAME Over!" — *Private Hudson, Aliens, played by Bill Paxton*

EXCERPT FROM: *Liquid Cool: The Cyberpunk Detective Series (Book One)*

There was something satisfying about going into the office. I always hated the prospect of being chained to a cubicle or tiny office at some government or corporate job, like ninety percent of the people. I knew, even as a kid, I wouldn't do that, but I had little to show for it with my high principles. And with virtually every last human in the city in legacy housing, it meant people were devolving to the lowest possible denominator. Not having to worry about housing meant I could subsist on very little per month. But that meant all you were doing was existing. That's not really living, but that's what most people were doing. That's why so many people got themselves in trouble on the crime scene. But it was also why this detective thing was so exhilarating for me.

I stood in my office with my mobile computer on my sole office desk, marveling at the screen. I had reviews!

Trusted Reviews was the bible in customer service. Businesses did everything and anything for solid (good) reviews about their products and services. I think some little old lady started it many years ago, and every Average Joe and Jane went to it first when deciding what service or item to buy. There were all kinds of rackets and scams involved with companies trying to rig the system, but they were always found out, which was worse because then companies could get banned. Major players in an industry could brag about having thousands or even millions of reviews. The bottom line was, if you didn't have any reviews, then your company didn't exist, no matter how impressive your physical or virtual storefront on the Net.

I now had three. I couldn't believe it. GW gave me such a glowing review that I couldn't believe it was the same person. Then, there were those from his mother and father. All were lengthy (very good), detailed about finding the sister/daughter (even better), and mentioned me solving the case in a day when local authorities couldn't close the case in many months (the best).

I couldn't stop reading it and smiling. Maybe I could make this detective thing work. I liked that it gave me purpose. Human beings needed purpose, and it was fun, too.

There was some big commotion going on outside the front door of the reception waiting area.

Did I forget to lock it again?

I got up and walked to check, but just as I approached, the door swung open, and a punk, with his back to me, stood there with a gun. My body jumped as the man was shot once. He yelled, was shot a second time, and then his gun dropped from his hand as he fell. A third shot rang out, and he crashed to the ground. I had frozen in place, but now, my brain engaged, and I dove back into my office.

I heard one or more people running away.

I lay on the ground, watching the dead man on the ground. My eyes were tearing up. My new career was about to be taken away from me, before it could even get started.

Perspective

[After narrowly escaping the destruction of the International Space Station] "I hate space." — Dr. Ryan Stone, Gravity, the movie played by Sandra Bullock

---

EXCERPT FROM: *Biopunk Blues (Liquid Cool, Book Seven)*

I had parked the Pony in a secure parking lot, then had to ride an elevator capsule from the one hundred and twentieth floor to ground level into the rain, which started up again. I was not one to mind the rain, even in my bad mood, but I did mind the crowds of people all around me in their gray or black slickers and big ugly umbrellas in my face. I was wrapped up snuggly in my tan jacket, with my gloved hands in my pockets, wearing my snazzy aqua shoes so I'd never fall on my butt. It was a habit to reach up and give my tan fedora a pull.

A violent gust of wind blew my hat off my head!

I ran as fast as I could to catch it while it was in the air. I jumped. I missed. My hat landed in a big puddle on the pedestrian walkway. An optimist would have said, "Oh, what a beautiful puddle with the beautiful colors." I was not that person! Any kind of rainbow display in any groundwater was evidence of the chemical residue nastiness that existed on the streets of Metropolis or any big city.

"It's ruined!" I yelled as I snatched my hat up from the ground. Since it touched the ground, I was not putting it back on my head. It would never, ever go back on my head. No hat, no umbrella. I saw more than a few people laughing or smiling at me. Yeah, funny.

The important thing was that my hat had never been blown off my head before in my life, and I had been in some serious storms before. I actually had my fedora fitted with an invisible band that I could use and wrapped under my chin. The band was broken. This was an omen. I should have stopped then and there and immediately gone home. But I looked up, and I was standing in front of the apartment complex where my deadbeat client lived. I was there, so I decided I might as well get my money and go.

I was so tempted to toss my fedora in the big trash bin in the lobby of the apartment complex. It was not luxurious, but it wasn't a dump like in Free City—orderly and trash-free. No doorkeep in the lobby or signs of any automation. No one was to be seen as I walked to the elevators.

My inner voice told me to go home, but I was already in the elevator and on my way up to the two hundredth floor.

Recap

After a while, you won't miss a beat when it comes to obstacles and misfortune. The key is not to mind them because they are a part of life. Deal with them or ignore them as long as you keep moving forward.

NINTH MONTH
September
Classic Sci-Fi Actor Birthdays

CHARACTER (ACTOR) SHOW/Movie

SEPTEMBER 2: Neo (Keanu Reeves) The Matrix movies

SEPTEMBER 3: Dr. David Marcus (Merritt Butrick) Star Trek: The Wrath of Khan

SEPTEMBER 4: Lyta Alexander (Patricia Tallman) Babylon 5

SEPTEMBER 7: Delenn (Mira Furlan) Babylon 5

SEPTEMBER 9: Cmdr. Shran (Jeffrey Combs) Star Trek: Enterprise

SEPTEMBER 11: B'Ellana Torres (Roxann Biggs-Dawson) Star Trek: Voyager

SEPTEMBER 12: Ash (Ian Holm) Alien

SEPTEMBER 12: Cypher (Joe Pantoliano) The Matrix

SEPTEMBER 12: Na'Toth (Mary Kay Adams) Babylon 5

SEPTEMBER 14: Pavel Chekov (Walter Marvin Koenig) Star Trek: The Original Series

SEPTEMBER 14: Alfred Bester (Walter Marvin Koenig) Babylon 5

SEPTEMBER 20: Dominar Rygel XVI (Jonathan Hardy) Farscape

SEPTEMBER 22: Rose Tyler (Billie Piper) Doctor Who

SEPTEMBER 23: Lieutenant Athena (Maren Jensen) Battle Star Galactica (Original Series)

SEPTEMBER 23: Marcus Cole (Jason Carter) Babylon 5

SEPTEMBER 23: Keiko O'Brien (Rosalind Chao) Star Trek: The Next Generation/Deep Space Nine

SEPTEMBER 24: The Keymaker (Randall Duk Kim) Matrix Reloaded

SEPTEMBER 25: Luke Skywalker (Mark Hamill) Star Wars

SEPTEMBER 26: Sarah Connor (Linda Hamilton) The Terminator/Terminator 2: Judgment Day

SEPTEMBER 26: The Architect (Helmut Bakaitis) Matrix Reloaded

SEPTEMBER 28: Lieutenant Boomer (Herbert Jefferson Jr.) Battle Star Galactica (Original Series)

SEPTEMBER 30: Persephone (Monica Bellucci) Matrix Reloaded

DON'T OVERTHINK IT

About the Simple Things

"WHEN I FIRST LOOKED back at the Earth, standing on the Moon, I cried." — Alan Shepard, American astronaut, second person and the first American to travel into space

No need to make life more complicated. It can be quite simple when we prioritize, focus on, and appreciate the right things.

The Planners

BE (LIQUID) COOL/MONTHLY PLANNER

MONTH:

SUN	MON	TUE	WED	THU	FRI	SAT

TOP PRIORITIES / GOALS

PEOPLE TO SEE / PLACES TO GO / REMINDERS

NOTES

RATE / ASSESS THE MONTH:

BE (LIQUID) COOL
WEEKLY PLANNER

WEEK:

M T W H F S S

MONDAY

TUESDAY

WEDNESDAY

THURSDAY

FRIDAY

SATURDAY / SUNDAY

WEEK'S PRIORITIES / TO DO

NOTES

RATE / ASSESS THE WEEK:

BE (LIQUID) COOL
WEEKLY PLANNER

WEEK:

M T W H F S S

MONDAY

TUESDAY

WEDNESDAY

THURSDAY

FRIDAY

SATURDAY / SUNDAY

WEEK'S PRIORITIES / TO DO

NOTES

RATE / ASSESS THE WEEK:

BE (LIQUID) COOL
WEEKLY PLANNER

WEEK: M T W H F S S

MONDAY

TUESDAY

WEDNESDAY

THURSDAY

FRIDAY

SATURDAY / SUNDAY

WEEK'S PRIORITIES / TO DO

NOTES

RATE / ASSESS THE WEEK:

BE (LIQUID) COOL
WEEKLY PLANNER

WEEK:

M T W H F S S

MONDAY

TUESDAY

WEDNESDAY

THURSDAY

FRIDAY

SATURDAY / SUNDAY

WEEK'S PRIORITIES / TO DO

NOTES

RATE / ASSESS THE WEEK:

Week 38: A Purpose-Driven Life

"I'M JUST HERE FOR THE gasoline." — Mad Max (Mel Gibson), 1979

EXCERPT FROM: *Classic Cyborg (Liquid Cool: From the Crazy Maniac Files, Book One)*

Liquid Cool was a fortress of an office, especially since I was a "famous" detective and had already put down quite a few bad guys. We had all kinds of security cameras, sensors, and measures, including lasers and pulse shot-guns. If the man was sitting in my office, it meant that PJ had already scanned him thoroughly to determine the kind of cyborg he was. The amount of illegal street modifications available to the criminal cyborg class was endless, but if PJ allowed him in, it meant he had none of those.

However, I was apprehensive at this part. "Mr. Cruz," he said as he extended his arm. Even a "normal" cyborg could do tremendous bodily harm to a normal like me.

I shook his bionic hand. "Mr. Classic." I gestured for him to take a seat in one of the two plush chairs in front of my desk.

"Thank you." Though he walked around with no shirt under his jacket, he moved with class. He unfastened the button of his suit jacket as he sat. I noticed his neon tattoos had disappeared. So, he could turn them off, too.

"I notice an accent," I remarked.

"Yes, Polish," he answered. "My old country. Yours is Puerto Rico I understand."

"Yes, but no cool accent. Only boring Metropolis-ese, if I can make up a word."

"My father was very strict. He wanted all his children to speak the mother tongue and as many others as they could learn. Why learn to speak one language when you can learn ten, he'd tell us."

"I'm surrounded by family and friends who can all speak more than my one."

Classic smiled. "You do speak more than one language, Mr. Cruz. The most important one of them all. You speak the language of the streets. That's why you're the boss and not them."

"I've done okay."

"You're too modest, Mr. Cruz. People like us don't need to be modest. We can let others do that for us. We both started from humble beginnings. Some would say we started out at a great disadvantage from everyone else in our class, but here we sit—at the top."

"Am I at the top?"

"Yes. 'The top' doesn't mean money or power, necessarily. If you wanted that, you'd have that too. 'The top' means the best at whatever you set your mind to."

"What are you at the top of, Mr. Classic?"

"My former life or the current one? I also had a former life, like you. My previous life was more along the lines of the previous one of your French operations manager out there."

"Operations manager?" I laughed. "Thanks for letting me know. I hired her for one job, but she's been unilaterally promoting herself ever since."

He smiled. "She's like us—creating her way. Not allowing it to be created for her. I was a criminal, Mr. Cruz. I started out as muscle-for-hire, contracted by all the major crime gangs a long time ago. Classic Cyborg became my street name. I was a very scary person back then, but I soon grew tired of taking orders. The people I worked for—no one was scared of them. Everyone was scared of me, so why shouldn't I be running the big show? I formed my own gang, involved in all the criminal vice that there was, but did it better than anyone else. When I started, there were over two dozen cyborg gangs working in our territories. When I was done instilling a new order to our corner of the mean streets, there was only one—mine."

"Police never got you?"

"When you're the boss of a successful criminal gang, you better get used to being in court, in jail, or on the way in or out of both. I was no different, but nothing that I'd call serious. In or out of jail, I ran my empire."

"What happened to make you leave that life behind?"

Classic reached into his jacket and produced a digital plastic photo. "She happened." I looked at the picture of a young woman in his twenties. "All she had to do was be born. Classic Cyborg the Sadist became Daddy Classic the Softy."

"How can I help you, Mr. Classic?"

Perspective

"Who are you? What do you want? Why are you here? Where are you going?"
— Lorien, from a race called the First Born, Babylon 5

EXCERPT FROM: *Liquid Cool: The Cyberpunk Detective Series (Book One)*

I wondered if my fixation on the whole detective thing was because, for too long, I had nothing at all to fixate on. Idle people got excited at the most mundane. I was a laborer, a gig-worker. No permanent job, just odd job to odd job. I hated it, complained about it, but accepted it because I did nothing to change my situation. Millions of us sat around in our legacy housing all day, and I was one of them. We were our version of the leisure class, but when you're rich, it's acceptable; when you're not, it's pathetic. Aimless was aimless, no matter how much or how little cash you had in the bank. I never saw social class; I saw people who had a purpose. That's why Phishy didn't annoy me and Punch Judy did. He had purpose with his crazy self, and she didn't. I didn't like her, really, because she was kind of like me.

But I had to get serious. Being a detective was to be a one-time deal. I had no money for a license, no office, and honestly, the job was dangerous. I couldn't play games—I was getting married, assuming my future parents-in-law didn't off me before then.

Recap

It's important to remind yourself of core motivations to avoid drifting off-course. Keep yourself motivated, and move forward with purpose!

Week 39: An Enjoyed Life

WE SHOOK HANDS AND spent almost an hour small-talking about absolutely nothing, which was what friends do.

EXCERPT FROM: *Liquid Cool: The Cyberpunk Detective Series (Book One)*

Cruz and Run-Time...

I got Fat Nat to promise me to come clean with Run-Time and tell him the whole story with Easy Chair Charlie. I knew Run-Time would want to keep even further away from this whole situation than before. But the worst we could do was keep him in the dark about something this politically explosive; he'd never do that to us. Friendships are hard enough to come by in this city, so never blow one intentionally.

I was now in a foul mood. The least of which was the fact that a lifelong friendship was on the verge of dissolution. Friends were hard to come by in Metropolis, and friends you could count on were even more rare. Losing Run-Time's friendship would be a serious blow.

"What do you think, Private Investigator, Cruz? At the beginning of this, I bet you never thought it would all unfold as it did."

"I was betting I wasn't even going to get to the end."

"You did. We all did."

"Sometimes, I'll get quiet at my office desk or on the home sofa and wonder what the hell I'd gotten myself into. Then, I'd realize I had a big grin on my face."

Run-Time laughed. "Then life is good. Keep it that way."

"You gave me my first case."

"I gave you your first investigation gig. You got your case on your own. You made the case. No one else would have or could have done what you did. I'm glad I was there to help. Don't forget your friends when you get to the top."

I laughed. "You're the one at the top."

"You're right there with me," he said.

We shook hands and spent almost an hour small-talking about absolutely nothing, which was what friends do.

Perspective

"We are an impossibility in an impossible universe." — Ray Bradbury, American author and screenwriter

---

EXCERPT FROM: *Digital Samurai (Liquid Cool: From the Crazy Maniac Files, Book Two)*

I was never so happy to see that beautiful, ugly granite block of a building called the Concrete Mama—home! My no-frills monolith tower of legacy housing, which could withstand a planetary shockwave from a nuclear blast or an asteroid crash, was home to the Cruz family. I thanked my police drivers and couldn't get inside fast enough. The building doorman, Mr. Post, yelled "hello" from his station. He'd done such a great job getting rid of the lobby johnnies that used to hang out in the lobby before. My feet kept me moving to the elevators.

Out I came on the 150th floor and straight to room number 9732. The door was open, and there she was—China Doll. She was called China by women, and men called her Doll, but my family and I called her by her real name—Dot. I hugged my wife and gave her a long kiss.

My wife, always the consummate fashionista, was in a sparkling pink body-hugging dress, though she told me that it was called a cheongsam. Her hair was tied back, with the ponytail carefully resting on one shoulder, and her colored neck scarf of the day was a matching pink. Every finger had a colored ring, and each wrist had multiple bracelets. Yep, my wife looked like a movie star. I'm not going to lie.

"Look who's here," I said and picked him up in my arms. "What have you been up to all these days, Cruzie?" I gave him a kiss on the cheek, and he laughed.

I was home and wasn't leaving the apartment for days. I wasn't even going to leave to check my Ford Pony in the parking bay. That would wait. We had brunch, and we talked and played catch with Cruz Jr. I'd forgotten that I was exhausted and wanted to sleep. I'd sleep, and when I did it would probably be for twenty-four hours.

Recap

Yes, you want to "stop and smell the roses." But it's not a one-time, once-in-in-a-lifetime thing. You should do it regularly.

Week 40: Use Time Wisely

"THE ONLY REASON FOR time is so that everything doesn't happen at once." — Albert Einstein, German-born theoretical physicist, widely held to be one of the greatest and most influential scientists of all time

EXCERPT FROM: *Liquid Cool: The Cyberpunk Detective Series (Book One)*

I had been a busy bee. Besides being in Mad Heights, there was one other place I had been that they didn't know about. Before I went to the Soldier of Fortune Meet-Up meeting, I had made one other stop—back to the Free City apartment of Mrs. Easy Chair Charlie.

My day may have ended with gangster punks (Mad Heights), but it began with them, too. I strolled into Free City, and I knew the Free City gangs would try to jack me up again, and no business card would stop them this time. As I approached the tower of Easy Chair's widow, they appeared. It was the same kids; one after another, they walked to me.

"It's the detective again," one said.

"I didn't think he was dumb enough to come back a second time," said another.

I was in no mood.

"Get away from me," I said.

"That's it, Mr. Detective? You got no more fake business cards to show us?"

I really was in no mood for this.

"Guess where I'm going after this?" I asked.

"Why?" one of the punks responded.

"Mad Heights."

They all laughed. "You're not going to no Mad City, you square."

"When you go to a place like that, you have to be prepared to do what needs to be done. I should practice."

Instantly, the expressions changed on their faces. They knew where I was going.

Perspective

"I spent three days a week for 10 years educating myself in the public library, and it's better than college. People should educate themselves - you can get a complete

education for no money. At the end of 10 years, I had read every book in the library and I'd written a thousand stories." — Ray Bradbury, American author and screenwriter

---

EXCERPT FROM: *I, Alien Hunter (Liquid Cool, Book Five)*

Distractions were normal in the private detective business, but one had to push through it and get back to the solid work. Thanks to the PJ system of organizing my client messages, all I had to do was walk into the main office, into my private office, and grab the hot pile from the desk—all potential cases that were likely to be solved quickly and pay fast. That's what I needed. I could deal with sleazy and unethical clients, but I couldn't waste my limited time with crazy.

Recap

Regarding time: 365 new days, 365 new chances!

Week 41: Accept The Gift

I STOOD IN THE MAIN office, still in a daze.

EXCERPT FROM: *Liquid Cool: The Cyberpunk Detective Series (Book One)*

I drove to the business district of Buzz Town just before the lunch hour to meet the Realtor man. It wasn't Peacock Hills or Paisley Parish, but it wasn't Free City either. Buzz Town was not the best of areas, but it wasn't the worst—it was one of those in-between places, like Rabbit City, where I lived.

I met him on the 100th floor of the tower on Circuit Circle—some people called it the Circuit; others, the Circle. The Realtor definitely seemed like an Eye Candy client. Not a piece of clothing or hair out of place. Nice suit, matching slicker, nice boots, horn-rimmed glasses. He watched me as I toured the empty office space. The office was very spacious and was as large as the combination reception area and waiting area outside its doors.

"I asked, who's this from?" I repeated.

"The landlord is adamant about remaining anonymous, and it's futile to continue asking. My firm takes such requests extremely seriously. The only question is: Do you want it?"

"I'm not accustomed to accepting gifts without knowing who the gift giver is."

"I suspect you'll get over it."

I looked around again. Was this all a dream? I had been having an internal battle within myself about the whole "detective thing." First, I wanted to punch Phishy for spreading rumors. Now, I searched the Net for all the requirements to be a licensed private investigator in the City. The cost of the license fees was outrageous and far beyond my means, but I was also searching for ways to legally scam my way into it, like calling myself a "consultant" rather than a "detective."

"This is quite a lot to take in all at once."

"I suspect you'll get over that, too. If you take the offer, I can have you sign the paperwork right here, and you'll have the keys in hand as I leave."

I walked to look at the reception waiting area again.

"Is it a yes?" he asked.

"I could go down to the City and look up who the office belongs to."

"And you would see that my firm is listed as the landlord by proxy."

"Free?"

"You would be responsible for utilities and any furniture, of course."

"What are the terms? Is this a lifetime thing?"

"Hardly, but it is a legacy space, and the landlord-of-record would need to give you at least 90 days' notice for you to vacate. That's more than generous."

Who could it be? I asked myself. Run-Time wouldn't be anonymous. Dot didn't have this kind of money. Who?

"How old is the legacy?"

"Three hundred years."

The mortgage was paid off over 300 years ago and had been exempt from any government taxes ever since.

"Yeah, I'll do it."

"Good." The Realtor lifted his briefcase and opened it.

We used the briefcase as a desk as he had me "sign my life away" on a stack of documents.

"Do you know who the landlord-of-record is?"

"I do." He pointed to another line for me to sign my signature.

"They're not criminals, are they?"

"Do you know many criminals, Mr. Cruz?"

"I don't."

"Then it would be unlikely that my client is one. Please don't overthink this, Mr. Cruz. Someone gave you access to free office space for an indefinite period. Based on your surprise from our initial video-call, it is a person who is, at least tangentially, acquainted with your affairs. Since you're not a person of financial means, you can infer that the gesture is a benevolent one. If I were you, I'd count my blessings, furnish it, and start my business. I would not think about the who ever again. Last signature here, please."

He pointed, and I signed on the last dotted line of the last page of the documents. The Realtor took the pen and the documents from me and then returned them to the briefcase. He reached into his jacket pocket and then handed me a folded document and a set of keys.

"Your signed business tenant authorization and three sets of keys. Your official copies of the documents you signed will be delivered tomorrow."

"You knew I was going to accept the offer?"

"Why wouldn't you? The keys are copy-prohibited. If you need new keys, then you have to get a whole new door system. Very expensive."

"Tell him, thank you."

The Realtor smiled. "I never indicated what gender my client is, Mr. Cruz, but nice try."

He left me in the office space, walking out the way we came in. I stood in the main office, still in a daze.

I had a business office!

Perspective

The electric roller coaster of life was about to snatch me.

EXCERPT FROM: *Liquid Cool: The Cyberpunk Detective Series (Book One)*

Cruz at sleep at home...

"Yeah?"

I had answered the phone with the video off and was talking, but my conscious mind had not yet engaged. My eyes were still closed, and I could have been dreaming, actually.

"Cruz," Run-Time's voice continued. "I need a favor."

"Yeah."

"I need someone to kick around a bit and do some investigating."

"Investigating?"

"Technically, anyone can do it, but I want a third party. Someone reliable with street smarts who can do things discreetly. I thought of you. You're not on any gigs now, right?"

"Yeah."

"Come on down to the office tomorrow morning."

"Yeah."

"And Cruz."

"Yeah?"

"Take a look at the newspapers before you come in. The story about an Easy Chair Charlie and his ill-advised shootout with the police."

"Yeah."

I was a true vocabulary virtuoso when I was half asleep.

The electric roller coaster of life was about to snatch me.

Recap

Allow good things to happen to you. It's amazing how many people don't. Whether through hard work or just plain luck, grab those gifts of life thrown on your path.

TENTH MONTH
October
Classic Sci-Fi Actor Birthdays

CHARACTER (ACTOR) SHOW/Movie

October 2: Jabba the Hutt VI / Greedo (Larry Ward) Star Wars: Original Movies

October 5: Zack Allan (Jeff Conaway) Babylon 5

October 8: Sigourney Weaver October 8, Gwen DeMarco/Lieutenant Tawny Madison/Galaxy Quest; Ripley/Alien movies (Sigourney Weaver)

October 9: Capt. Jonathan Archer (Scott Bakula) Star Trek: Enterprise

October 9: Kwan/Tech Sergeant Chen (Tony Shalhoub) Galaxy Quest

October 11: Officer Aeryn Sun/Farscape; Vala Mal Doran/Stargate SG-1 (Claudia Black)

October 11: Zathras (Tim Choate) Babylon 5

October 13: Teal'c (Christopher Judge) Stargate SG-1

October 13: Scorpius (Wayne Pygram) Farscape

October 18: Stark/Farscape; Agent Brown/The Matrix (Paul Goddard)

October 18: Miles Dyson (Joe Morton) Terminator 2: Judgment Day

October 21: Leia Organa (Carrie Fisher) Star Wars: Original Movies

October 24: Sikozu Svala Shanti Sugaysi Shanu (Raelee Hill) Farscape

October 26: Quellek (Patrick Breen) Galaxy Quest

October 27: Richard Woolsey/Stargate SG-1/Stargate Atlantis; Holographic Doctor/Star Trek: Voyager (Robert Picardo)

October 27: Selmak/Jacob Carter (Carmen Argenziano) Stargate SG-1

October 28: The 11th Doctor (Matt Smith) Doctor Who

GIVING BACK (WHEN YOU CAN)

About Giving Back

"WE ALL HAVE OUR TIME machines, don't we? Those that take us back are memories... and those that carry us forward, are dreams." — G'Kar, Babylon 5

Now, the shoe is on the other foot. You're the one inspiring, helping and guiding others when you can.

Excerpt From: I, *Alien Hunter (Liquid Cool, Book Five)*

"Why did you hire another detective to do your investigating?" PJ asked me from her desk. I had returned to my office to be interrogated by my own employee.

"Because I didn't want to investigate the meteor."

"Why are you avoiding a key part of the case? Now you have to."

"Now, I have two things to investigate: the meteor and what unknown persons snatched up my detective who was investigating it."

"That's what you get for not doing your own work."

"Well, that means I have a job for you because I can't be everywhere, and I'm not hiring more staff."

"We need more staff."

"No. But—I will have you hire temp employees to report to you until this project is done."

PJ was now interested and grabbed her electric steno pad. "Now we're talking. I can be a boss too."

"I want you and your team to pull the pictures of every bystander at the crater and around Free Earth. Everyone. Then run those faces through the facial recog databases."

She smiled again. "I know what you're doing."

"What am I doing?"

"Whenever a bad thing happens, the bad guy comes back to the scene and mingles in with the crowd to watch for himself. Very smart. You're being very smart right now."

"Glad you approve. It's going to be a huge project because there were a lot of people there, so a lot of people talking pics and vids."

"But all on the Net. Got it. Identify all the people so we can find the bad guy."

"Or bad guys."

"Got it."

"But—be careful. Remember, my detective guy was snatched up."

"Because he wasn't working here. Liquid Cool can be a fortress when we need it to be. Besides, I got my laser rifle under the desk handy and more weapons too in the drawers. Can I arm the temps?"

"No, you cannot arm the temps! You, yes. You're an ex-felon, so you know how to handle weapons. There's no reason for any temps we hire to become felons, too. Just you."

"Anyone comes snooping around, I'll punch them through the building to splat on the ground." PJ flexed her bionic arms.

"Punching is okay, but let's avoid sending bodies to the ground 100 floors below. Hire your team."

"Yes, boss, so I can be a boss too."

Recap

There are many ways to "give back" in society. Of course, more broadly, there's charity and volunteering. There's also giving simple encouragement and being a good role model or mentor to others.

The Planners

BE (LIQUID) COOL/MONTHLY PLANNER

MONTH:

SUN	MON	TUE	WED	THU	FRI	SAT

TOP PRIORITIES / GOALS

PEOPLE TO SEE / PLACES TO GO / REMINDERS

NOTES

RATE / ASSESS THE MONTH:

BE (LIQUID) COOL
WEEKLY PLANNER

WEEK:

| M | T | W | H | F | S | S |

MONDAY

TUESDAY

WEDNESDAY

THURSDAY

FRIDAY

SATURDAY / SUNDAY

WEEK'S PRIORITIES / TO DO

NOTES

RATE / ASSESS THE WEEK:

BE (LIQUID) COOL
WEEKLY PLANNER

WEEK: M T W H F S S

MONDAY

TUESDAY

WEDNESDAY

THURSDAY

FRIDAY

SATURDAY / SUNDAY

WEEK'S PRIORITIES / TO DO

NOTES

RATE / ASSESS THE WEEK:

BE (LIQUID) COOL
WEEKLY PLANNER

WEEK:

| M | T | W | H | F | S | S |

MONDAY

TUESDAY

WEDNESDAY

THURSDAY

FRIDAY

SATURDAY / SUNDAY

WEEK'S PRIORITIES / TO DO

NOTES

RATE / ASSESS THE WEEK:

BE (LIQUID) COOL
WEEKLY PLANNER

WEEK:

M T W H F S S

MONDAY

TUESDAY

WEDNESDAY

THURSDAY

FRIDAY

SATURDAY / SUNDAY

WEEK'S PRIORITIES / TO DO

NOTES

RATE / ASSESS THE WEEK:

Week 42: Encourage Others

BE SOMEONE AWESOME today!

EXCERPT FROM: *Liquid Cool: The Cyberpunk Detective Series (Book One)*

Run-Time and Cruz…

"I don't know a thing about being a detective."

"What's to know? It was like asking me what's to know about being a company CEO. You do it, and you do it long enough, you become it. And it would seem you already have a head start on the promotion front."

"What do you mean?"

"Who's this guy called Phishy?"

"That Phishy!"

Run-Time laughed. "He could be your marketing genius, so be nice to him."

Run-Time was all about encouraging people to do more in their lives. I had seen him do so a million times, so this was my turn. As a legacy baby, I did have more free time than I knew what to do with.

"I'll give it a whirl and see what happens."

Perspective

G: "Well, look at you. I never heard of a Metro street detective who's also a fed profiler. You got that Up-Top weaponry. Connie told me you're memorizing the faces of all the criminals in Metropolis, and she didn't think you were crazy. Cruz, you're going to be quite dangerous soon."

EXCERPT FROM: *Liquid Cool: The Cyberpunk Detective Series (Book One)*

I sat at my desk, staring out the droplet-covered window with my cup of silk coffee in hand. There was no view but the line of monolith office tower buildings across the street with their tinted windows. However, I had a deep sense of satisfaction. It was almost like a dream I prayed would never end. I was just some laborer, a legacy baby one moment. Now, I was a self-employed business owner with an employee.

"Surprise!"

I was startled, but the smile never left my face as I turned around to see Dot peeking into the office from the door. She waltzed right in.

"Look at this," she said, looking around my space. "This is cool. You have a real place of business."

I set down my cup as she rushed me, threw her arms around me, and planted a kiss.

"Very impressive, Mr. Cruz," she said as she looked around again, then back at me. "You are a detective now. How do you like it? Wait."

She ran over to my door and closed it.

"I don't want to hear no animal sounds in there!" PJ yelled.

Dot laughed, and I held my laughter in.

"Well, Mr. Cruz?" she asked.

I picked up my cup as I bobbed my head up and down. "Love it."

She was back next to me. "Is it dangerous?"

"Not at all," I replied. "Lot of variety, which I like."

"Oh. Tell me about the corporate case."

"The Case of the Nighttime Bionic Parts Thieves."

"Cruz, that's a stupid name. Your agency is named Liquid Cool. How can you come up with a cool name for your business but give your cases such pathetic names? What was the name of the case before this one?"

"The Case of the Guy Who Scratched My Vehicle."

We both burst out laughing.

"That's what I mean," she managed to say while still laughing. "Enough! Cool names for all cases going forward."

"Gotcha."

"Tell me what happened."

I had two chairs in front of my desk, but I did like I saw so many other business guys do, like Run-Time and others. In the corner, I had my own arrangement of plush chairs around a glass table, the whole set up on another neon dark blue rug. Dot and I sat on adjacent chairs.

"It was some case," I started. "This company makes all these high-end bionic parts, but almost monthly, thieves were ripping off their warehouse. They had tons of security, but all their internal security guys couldn't figure out how it was possible. They fired a bunch of security heads over it. It was going on for months."

"How did you solve it then, Mr. Cruz?"

"Well...Mrs. Cruz...since it was the megacorporate world, I knew it had to be an inside job, but I knew they would have checked that right away. So how can a theft be an inside job without being an inside job? Answer. The boss is playing nighttime footsy with his neighbor, who happens to be the VP of his main rival. He thinks he's scammin' her for corporate secrets, while in actuality, she's swiping and copying his access cards while he's sleeping."

"Ohhhh," Dot said.

"Fake trucks, fake uniforms, and all they had to do is drive in and out with a cloned access card."

"Very good, Mr. Cruz. How did you Sherlock Holmes all that? Are you that good?"

"I am, Mrs. Cruz. Oh, let me get my cup." I jumped up to grab my cup from my main desk. "What can I get you? I even have my own mini stash in my office."

Recap

"Pay it forward" was a common phrase not too long ago. It meant for every act of kindness, do something in kind for that person or, even better, someone else altogether.

Week 43: Be Classy

CRUZ: THAT'S WHAT I said to myself when I first admired my new look in the full-length mirror at home.

EXCERPT FROM: *Liquid Cool: The Cyberpunk Detective Series (Book One)*

At the Liquid Cool offices...

"I've killed people with these boots!" was what I heard as I came out of the elevator. It was Dot's voice, and I knew it was the tone of a highly pissed-off China Doll. I didn't need to be a detective to figure out why.

She went by China Doll, but women who knew her called her China; men called her Doll. Only her family and Cruz called her by her real name—Dot.

She was the consummate fashionista, with every piece of clothing, every accessory, and every piece of jewelry being the trendiest and the most stylish. Leaving all that aside, they made her look "film quality." Today, she was adorned in a luminescent halter top under a glossy leather jacket, a sapphire blue pearl belt wrapped around her waist, black skin-tight pants, and topped off with black heels adorned with faux-diamond glitter. Her hair was tied back, with the ponytail carefully resting on one shoulder, always a colored neck scarf—today in basic black—and her makeup was always perfect and never overdone. Every finger had a colored ring, and each wrist had multiple bracelets.

Perspective

Damn, I knew I looked cool.

EXCERPT FROM: *Classic Cyborg (Liquid Cool: From the Crazy Maniac Files, Book One)*

"It's going to be bad!" PJ yelled from her desk.

The Storm of the Century was on its way, and we were busy (not really) at work in my Liquid Cool office in Buzz Town. As far as districts went in Metropolis, it wasn't the best of areas, but it wasn't the worst either. I liked to think that my presence as a new detective classed up the neighborhood a bit.

I started the Liquid Cool Detective Agency not even three years ago, leaving my previous line as a classic hovervehicle restorer and sometime illegal hovercar racer behind. All I had done was a simple favor for a friend, but it led to me being a full-fledged licensed private detective in the largest supercity on the planet. Already, I had solved some of the biggest and most dangerous cases that not even the big, fancy detective firms with a thousand agents could boast. Besides myself, PJ was my only full-time employee.

My office was on the hundredth floor of one of many office mega-towers on Circuit Circle. From my private office, I sat at my desk, staring out at the window with a cup of silk coffee in hand. PJ was right. A storm was coming, and it was going to be bad. I had a rare, clear view of the line of monolith office towers through the tinted windows. There was no rain yet, but the cloud cover above was so dark and dank that it seemed all the water on the planet was building up to crash down upon Metropolis any minute.

I swiveled around in my chair to see PJ appear at my open doorway. She was hired as a secretary, though I had no idea what she had promoted herself to these days. We started out as frenemies, but now she was my second in command. She had short, crimson hair, a simulated mole—a dot above her lips, today, matching her crimson lipstick-covered lips. Hip, female business suits were what she wore nowadays—sleeveless, knee-high skirts. The only reminder of her previous life was her heeled leather boots. In that previous life, she was a soldier in the punk-posh gang Les Enfantes Terribles in Neo-Paris, France. She loved her sleeveless tops to show off her buff, bionic arms. PJ's street name was Punch Judy because she liked to punch people and could, in fact, punch a three-hundred-pound cyborg through a steel and concrete wall.

But PJ wasn't just about the violence. Like me, that was only when needed. She had become the master…mistress…of customer service and "client acquisition." She had turned the main office area into a shrine to all my high-profile cases. There were framed pictures covering practically every inch of the reception area. Pictures of me at press conferences, at police scenes, with megacorporation senior executives, with the Council of Corporation president, me shaking hands with the Mayor…but my favorites were those with just the Average Joes and Janes of the supercity, including the client from my very first major case, Carol Num, after I successfully rescued her kidnapped daughter. These were the cases that made it all worthwhile, despite all the crazy maniacs I had to deal with and getting shot. I didn't like getting shot.

"Don't I have a client?" I asked.

"He's late, but look at the weather. We're lucky anyone is leaving their home."

"But nothing's happened, and it's barely raining."

"But it's going to be bad. I bet there's more water hovering in the sky up there than in the ocean."

"PJ, rain doesn't hover. It only comes down and wets you and causes accidents."

She pointed at the window to the sky. "That's hovering. Look at that."

"Where are my clients? We can't make money with an empty office. I should be out there getting clients or solving cases."

"No, no. You don't need to get clients anymore. You're famous. The clients come to you."

"Clients? You mean a lot of crazy maniacs, sometimes crazier than the criminals."

"That's one time—NeuroDancer."

"Blade Gunner case?"

"She saved you."

"Her brother?"

"He tried to, but he didn't know it was you. Besides, you became buddies."

"Electric Sheep Massacre?"

"Okay, he was crazy, but you've had hundreds of clients. Those are only a few." We heard the front door buzzer. "I'm not going to allow you to infect me with your negativity. It's not even lunchtime, and that may be your client." She pointed at me. "No negativity with the clients."

"Yeah, yeah. Until we get paid. I know that. But if it isn't the client, I'm outta here to find some non-crazy maniac clients."

"Let me see if a Monsieur Mania Fou is out there."

"No French allowed so early in the morning," I said as she disappeared from my private office.

<u>Recap</u>

Being classy isn't always about how you look. It can also be how you act. Whether dressed in a suit, t-shirt or jeans, isn't it cool to just radiance class?

Week 44: Help Others

"YAHOO!" HAN SOLO YELLS.

Han and Chewbacca grin from ear to ear in the Millennium Falcon, arriving to save the day.

Vader's wingman panics at the sight of the oncoming pirate starship and veers radically to one side, colliding with Vader's TIE fighter in the process. Vader's wingman crashes into the side wall of the trench and explodes. Vader's damaged ship spins out of the trench with a damaged wing...spins out of control with a bent solar fin, heading for deep space.

Star Wars: Original Movie

EXCERPT FROM: *Classic Cyborg (Liquid Cool: From the Crazy Maniac Files, Book One)*

Cruz with a new client at the office...

I opened the top drawer of my desk and took out my notepad. "I'll jot down any notes if I have to. Give me all the particulars. What is your livelihood?"

"Cyber-psychosis. Have you heard of it?"

"I've known people who've suffered from it," I replied.

"People think that everyone is a cyborg on Earth these days, but outside the criminal class, we're still rare. People have a bionic part here and there, but that's not the same thing. For the real cyborg, a significant percentage suffer from mental issues: depression is the most common, but there's the more serious, like a specific kind of REM behavior disorder where the cyborg tries to claw or rip off their cybernetic part or parts.

"That's my business. I help cyborgs. I'm a seventy-percenter myself, so I have credibility within the community. I started with retired criminals like myself, then expanded to the general cyborg community."

"How do you help them?" I asked.

"I'm a cyborg counselor. I help those with mental problems associated with being a cyborg live normal lives. It could be anything from a simple talk to full psychotherapy sessions. It could even be helping change their bionic part to make them less cyborg-looking. I'm very good at my new vocation. I was a high school dropout and a felon, but I now have multiple PhDs and am a certified counselor for the city of Metropolis—only in this country could such a ridiculous thing occur."

"You're Dr. Classic, then."

"Doctor. Yes, I suppose."

"What happened to make you come here today?"

I could tell that Classic was a smoker. He did that thing with his index finger and thumb, rubbing them together, then including the middle finger. I could see because of the look of his faux-manicured nails.

"It's a non-smoking office," I said before he could even ask.

He laughed. "But you wear that old-style gangster hat. You should smoke, too. It adds character to a person."

"Some other time."

Perspective

[Delenn's fleet arrives after Earth Alliance attacks Babylon 5]

Delenn: This is Ambassador Delenn of the Minbari. Babylon 5 is under our protection. Withdraw or be destroyed!

Earth Force Officer: Negative! We have authority here. Do not force us to engage your ship.

Delenn: Why not? Only one human captain has ever survived battle with a Minbari Fleet. He is behind me. You are in front of me. If you value your lives, be somewhere else!

Babylon 5, the TV series, Episode: "Severed Dreams"

EXCERPT FROM: *AI Confidential (Liquid Cool, Book Six)*

Outside the main lobby entrance was a group of Asian men standing around, smoking glowing cigarettes and wearing glowing yellow or blue shades under a large awning. Some of them had dark hair, some blond, and all in the same white shirts, rolled-up sleeves, and black pants—they were building employees. No one was talking, just enjoying their smokes outside.

"Hello," I said as I walked to them. They looked at me with complete indifference. "I'm looking for this man." I showed them Wil's picture on my mobile display, passing it by each of their faces. "I'm a legitimate detective, and I'm trying to find this guy." I put my mobile back in my pocket. "Who wants cigarette money?" I held some plastic currency in my hand.

One man put his cigarette in his mouth and held out his hand. "56th floor. Room D." I gave him the money.

The memories of those who worked the room rental business of any kind bordered on the freakish. He probably knew Wil's full name, when he checked in, as well as what he had for breakfast, lunch, and dinner. Two hundred floors, and they probably knew everyone on them.

When I exited the elevator capsules, I pulled down my hood and walked to the door. It was already open. There was Wil Jr. seated at a desk on the room's vid-phone. He was Caucasian, tall, slim but very muscular, and dark hair.

"Yeah, he's here now," he said. "No, you don't have to call the police. I know him. Thanks."

I chuckled. "They take my money down there and then call you up here to tell you I'm coming."

"What did you think they'd do, Cruz? Come in and close the door."

The desk was filled with paper, files, and disks, but the room was neat. Wil obviously hadn't shaved in days, but he didn't look distressed. He leaned back in his chair.

"Mary, was it?"

I walked to the open balcony and looked out at the view. "She's a police officer's wife."

"I knew I was stupid the second I hung up using the private mobile."

"What's going on, Wil? At least I didn't find you up here with another woman or something."

He looked at me. "Tell Mary you found me, and I'm fine. I'm simply working a case on my own time."

"Calling in sick—two days in a row."

"I needed more time to wrap things up."

"Mary used the words paranoid and obsessed."

"Mary over-exaggerates. I'm fine."

"Wil, unless you tell me what's going on, I'm not going anywhere."

"Did my wife hire you for that?"

"Yes, she did."

"No, she didn't. She asked you to find me, which you did."

"What's going on, Wil? You know your wife won't leave you alone until she knows what's going on. And Mary is not the over-exaggerating kind."

I glanced around the room.

"What are you looking for?" Wil asked, nervous.

"I'm looking for a clean place to set myself down since I'll be here awhile."

"You have to go. I came here to work, not be bothered by anyone."

"Get away from the wife, kids, and the world."

"Yes. Surely, you can relate to that these days."

"Oh yes, I can. Cruz Jr. is quite the menace to society in his hoverchair now. He's discovered a new principle of physics—speed."

Wil laughed. "Cruz, go away."

"I'll compromise with you. You go home to see Mary and tell her yourself that you're fine, and I'll hold the fort here for you since you don't need my help. I can watch all your secret files until you get back."

"Maybe I do need help." Wil looked distressed and placed his hand on his forehead.

"Are you going to tell me what's going on then?"

"How much do you charge for services?"

"Wil, just tell me, and I might not charge you anything."

"No, you know I can't get any services or work for free because of my position. I'd have to hire you."

"Hire me to do what?"

"It's an identity theft thing."

"Okay, but why would you get involved in something like that?"

"The identity they've stolen is Dad's."

Recap

You always generously help people, expecting nothing back in return.

Week 45: Be a Mentor

(NOT THE SITH KIND, though)

"When I left you, I was but the learner. Now I am the master." — Darth Vader to Obi-Wan Kenobi, Star Wars: The Original Movies

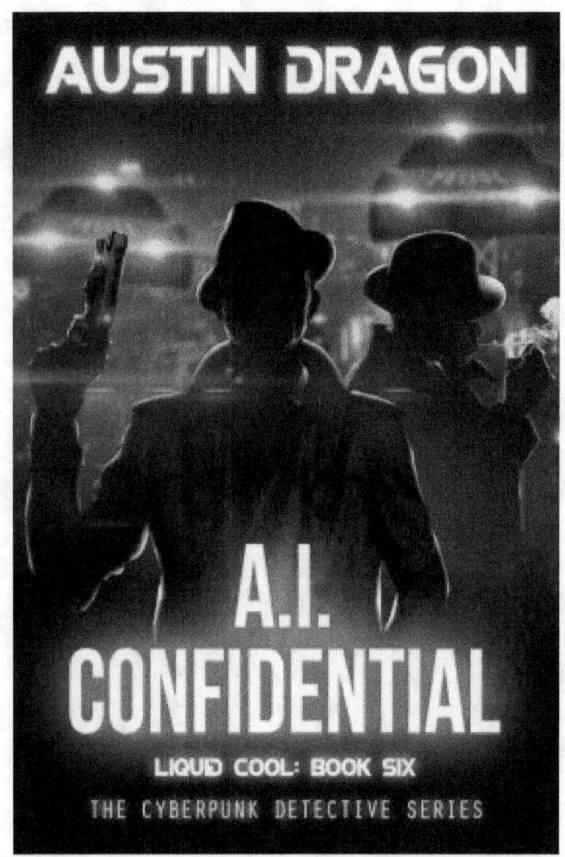

EXCERPT FROM: *A.I. Confidential (Liquid Cool, Book Six)*

An android with no synthetic human skin covering jumped from some debris to attack. PJ punched its head off with one blow, then with another, sent the rest of the body into the air away from us. The android wasn't alone.

I got to see for myself the modifications (illegal) to her bionic arms. She had some kind of strobe lights added to them. The flashing was disorientating to me, but for the robots, it was blinding. They didn't know what to do as PJ punched and pummeled her way through them.

The men looked at her, smiling. Not one of us had to fire a round. But then more came. We shot and bombed our way forward when Tiki raised his hand and pointed. I looked and noticed the hovertank. Quix was waiting for us at a semi-open rear door.

We ran to it, and Tiki and I both froze at the same time. On the ground was—me! The android copy was riddled with bullets. I looked up at Quix, and he had a saddened face.

"No!" I dropped my heavy rifle to the ground and ran in.

Immediately near the front door was one dead man and then a second. I ran to the front, where there was one very badly wounded, bloodied man, and then G.

"Hey, youngster," he whispered.

I leaned over him. They had him on the ground and had tried to dress his chest wounds as best as possible.

"G., you have to make it. That was the deal. We get Venn together."

"You'll get him for me."

"No, but you're supposed to be my mentor. Where will I get my inspiration? Your book only has 100 rules. I need the rest from you."

He smiled. "Cruz, you don't need me to be inspired. Bad people don't need incentives to be bad. They find excuses to do what they were always going to do anyway. Good people are no different. I was a P.I. for 70 years. No one was inspired by me until you. But you were always going to be a great P.I., with or without me. The city had me for a while; I pass the torch onto you. That's how life is, Cruz. In real life, someone always dies. No one can stop that. I was never going to live another 20 years anyway. 95 years is more than enough in Metropolis. You're the man, now."

In G.'s shoulder was one of those adrenaline pens. G. was literally pumped with stimulants to stay alive, but it was a street remedy that wouldn't last long. The ambulance had to get here in time.

"I already made the arrangements. Since I was dead and came back, that messed up some legal stuff, so I'll have my attorney make it all official and public with your office."

"My office? You're my secret benefactor?"

"It was Connie who called me back then and asked if there was anything I could do to help this kid who was starting out as a private detective. She said G., 'I know you got a spare office somewhere.' So, I gave you the one I had in Buzz Town. Looks like I bet on the right one again."

My eyes were already tearing up. Now, I was crying.

"You're the man now, Cruz. Go get Venn. Quix will tell you where. I'll hold on until you bring him in—alive or dead; it'll be justice either way."

My emotions went from sorrow to anger. "Then you hold on, G. I'll be back."

Perspective

Ripley: You started this. Show me everything. I can handle myself.

Corporal Hicks: Yeah, I noticed.

Aliens

EXCERPT FROM: *You'll Never See Starlight Again (Liquid Cool, Book Ten)*

I had to thank the man himself, Wilford G., for introducing me to her. He loved his gambling. Cascade City was in Old Metro, the ancient part when

Metropolis was just a city, not a supercity yet. That's where I drove, and every mile of sky-traffic I passed reminded me more and more of The Man, Wilford G.

Wize Gal owned a casino-restaurant-club, appropriately named Wize. It was a high-end gambling place and a fine restaurant where even the waitresses wore business suits. Her father, Wize Guy, was the previous owner, but he'd retired to warmer, sunnier climates, and he didn't care he had to learn a brand-new language at his age to live there. His daughter ran all his businesses now.

The establishment was huge and upscale but catered to all—from the booshy elite to the Average Joe and Jane, as long as you dressed with class. Male and female valets were all seasoned professionals, but I still parked in a secure parking structure way down the street.

She was a certified paralegal—but as good as any full attorney—smart, relentless, cutthroat. But she had no desire to be a real one. Wize Gal was my legal counsel whenever I needed it. I needed it now.

When I got inside, it was as bustling and noisy as always. People were gambling, drinking, dancing, and watching large monitors on the walls and ceilings everywhere of every sport, fight, or race worth betting on. One didn't have to wonder why her legal work was a hobby rather than her main career. She was rolling in money fit for royalty by the hour, whether or not she came into the office.

A waitress escorted me to her grand office in the center of the establishment. Casinos had more surveillance than Fort Knox, so she was waiting for me. She was a petite brunette dressed in a sharp purple business suit. When I stepped in, her head jerked back as she stared at me with a wrinkled brow and pursed lips.

"Who are you?"

"Don't you start too."

"I take that to mean everyone isn't liking the new black suit look."

"I like it. That's all that matters."

"So, Mrs. Cruz hasn't seen you yet."

I sat down in the plush chair in front of her large silver desk. "Did you receive it?"

She didn't miss a beat as she swiveled to the side and grabbed a heavy tablet. She laid it on the desk in front of her. "Received the file thirty minutes ago. The Council of Corporations. You're working for them now?"

"Maybe," I said.

"It's going to take me longer than thirty minutes to review a non-disclosure agreement of this size. My legal advice is not to sign it."

"Wize, just make sure I won't be selling my soul, giving over my kids, wife, or any family member, or my business or any genetic material, and I'm good."

"Will you be good? From what I gleaned, you'll be privy to the most secret of Council proprietary information. Why would you be good about that?"

"Because in this rare case, I agree with them. It should remain the most secret of secrets."

"What's the play, Cruz? You don't trust the Council of Corporations any more than I do or any sane person."

I said her name. "NeuroDancer."

Wize Gal's charm and playful smirk disappeared. "The mystery mind control stripper-singer-actress diva. Didn't you kill her years ago? But still on the case. Another fatal flaw you have in common with the former G-Man. You won't let it go."

"How can you let go of something like that?"

"G-Man said the same about the Venn case."

"And he was right."

"He was, and it cost him his life. Are you willing to make the same trade?"

"I won't have to."

"Listen to me, Cruz. I'll give you your due. You're slightly more intelligent than the average biped, but this is the Council of Corporations. You think they don't know you're only doing this to find out what they have so you can destroy it?"

"I know."

"What do you think they'll do? Just because you're friends with the chief of police and head of the police union, and are friendly with the local beat cops doesn't mean they can make you disappear. Are you hearing me, Cruz? You're a one-man show, and your cyborg sidekick doesn't count."

"Don't let PJ hear you calling her that."

"I'm serious Cruz. The last time I warned you not to do something, who were you sitting next to?"

Wize Gal knew how to hit below the belt.

"Wilford G. is dead, and you're walking a path to join him."

"Then let me ask you the reverse," I said. "Why are they doing this, then?"

"They're using you. They think you know something and will manipulate you to get that information."

"Wize, I need to know what they know. I'm not stupid. If I need to bring the entire Metro PD into this, I won't hesitate a second."

"You think they'll ever let you dial even the first digit of 9-11? Also, as your legal counsel, I'm obligated to tell you that knowingly planning to breach a corporate non-disclosure agreement is a felony. You can be prosecuted and will. They'll send you to jail, seize your business, seize your legacy properties. Since we're in a casino, let's go with that analogy. They hold all the cards. You have none in this game."

"I hear you, Wize. I do."

"I don't think you do. Are you signing this document?"

"Yes."

"Then you don't hear me. Is your will in order?"

"Oh, please stop."

"You're wearing the right color suit."

"I'll be fine."

"Give me until tomorrow to fully review it."

"Thanks."

"Okay, Cruz. You know, my father was a real-life gangster in his youth."

"I heard some rumors."

"You know why he's sitting on his fat butt on a lounge chair on a sunny beach resort? Because he listened to someone. They told him to walk away from the gang life. He did. So he didn't end up dead. If he hadn't, I'd be dead. He was the one who saved me from self-destructive, suicidal teenage years. I'm a successful businesswoman because of my father. He gets to sit on his fat butt, retired and smiling with endless drinks all day, and playing poker all night. I run his business empire and do my legal stuff on the side to keep myself amused."

"Wize, the one thing I'm not is stupid."

"Cruz, do you think you're untouchable? A guardian angel, or two of them, sitting on your shoulders. Luck runs out eventually. I know. This isn't the only casino I own."

"Maybe it's not luck."

"You have skill and street smarts. No doubt about it. But luck runs out for all of us."

"If we're not careful," I said.

"Will you be careful?"

"I will."

"I'll have the document couriered over to your office tomorrow morning."

"Send it to my residence instead. I'll be working from home."

"What happened to your offices?"

"We had a visit from the Council."

"And?"

"And a guy claiming to be with Metro's Police Intelligence Division."

"Still not hearing the reason you're not working out of your place of business. I don't work from home. I work at my business. Why aren't you?"

"It's only for a few days while the place is swept for listening devices."

"I see. Gifts from the Council."

"Probably."

"The people you wish to partner with."

"They're hiring me."

"They're distracting them."

"I'm fooling them."

"Interesting word choice. Fool. Okay, Cruz, I have to get to some actual work. I'll have the agreement to you tomorrow morning for your signature. Then I'll deliver it to Council headquarters for you."

"Thanks. Wize, I know you're not happy with my decision, but if we're the good guys, then let's be the good guys and not simply say the words. Despite all jokes, I'm doing this for Metropolis and beyond, just like G-Man would have done and did for over seventy years."

"Remember, Cruz. G-Man is dead. You're the Man now. But the caveat is that you must be around for a while for it to stick."

"I already promised G-Man that I would. I don't break my promises."

She nodded. "Then I'll see you when I see you C-Man."

I smiled. She told me she'd come up with a nickname for me, just as she did for my posthumous mentor, Wilford G.

Recap

You looked up to others as role models. You received guidance and advice from mentors. Well, it's a two-way street too. You can be in that role for others, just starting their journey, too, if you choose to be.

ELEVENTH MONTH
November
Classic Sci-Fi Actor Birthdays

CHARACTER (ACTOR) SHOW/Movie

November 1: Switch (Belinda McClory) The Matrix

November 4: Bialar Crais / Pilot (voice) (Lani Tupu) Farscape

November 5: T-1000 (Robert Patrick) Terminator 2: Judgment Day

November 5: Jonas Quinn (Corin Nemec) Stargate SG-1

November 5: Quark (Armin Shimerman) Star Trek: Deep Space Nine

November 5: Guy Fleegman (Sam Rockwell) Galaxy Quest

November 9: Tom Paris (Robert Duncan McNeill) Star Trek: Voyager

November 9: Dr. Janet Fraiser (Teryl Rothery) Stargate SG-1

November 10: Dr. Heywood Floyd (Roy Scheider) 2010: The Year We Make Contact

November 11: Sarek (Mark Lenard) Star Trek: The Original Series/Star Trek: The Next Generation

November 13: Boxey (Noah Hathaway) Battle Star Galactica (Original Series)

November 13: Capt. Elizabeth Lochley (Tracy Scoggins) Babylon 5

November 15: Parker (Yaphet Kotto) Alien

November 15: Oracle (Gloria Foster) The Matrix

November 16: Chiana (Gigi Edgley) Farscape

November 16: Laliari (Missi Pyle) Galaxy Quest

November 19: Chakotay (Robert Beltran) Star Trek: Voyager

November 19: Jadzia Dax (Terry Farrell) Star Trek: Deep Space Nine

November 20: Rachael (Sean Young) Blade Runner (Original Movie)

November 21: Sergeant Apone (Al Matthews) Aliens

November 21: Dr. Julian Bashir (Alexander (Siddig El) Fadil) Star Trek: Deep Space Nine

November 24: Reginald Barclay (Dwight Schultz) Star Trek: The Next Generation/Star Trek: Voyager

November 24: Tasha Yar/Sela (Denise Crosby) Star Trek: The Next Generation

November 25: Khan Noonien Singh (Ricardo Montalban) Star Trek: The Next Generation

November 28: Naomi Wildman (Scarlett Pomers) Star Trek: Voyager

November 28: Amy Pond (Karen Gillan) Doctor Who

DON'T FORGET THE FUN

About Fun

"MARTY! WHAT IN THE name of Sir Isaac H. Newton happened here?" — Dr. Emmett Brown, Back to The Future II

One of the biggest mistakes high-achieving planners can make is forgetting to schedule in the fun. We all remember the saying: All work and no play makes Johnny a dull boy.

(I am not referring to Stephen King's The Shining, so erase that from your mind. This is a sci-fi-inspired book, not horror.)

Excerpt From: Biopunk Blues (Liquid Cool, Book Seven)

At the Liquid Cool offices...

My parents arrived; they had driven me to the office. Then, Dot and her parents.

"We did it!" Bia yelled when she came through the door with Bolt, Zip, Handy, Breech—walking with his new bionic legs and other bio-borgs.

She gave me a big hug.

The Eye Candy Crew showed up. Never had all of them been out of the salon together before. Goat Girl was in her professional appearance, but Twinkle also showed up wearing dark glasses.

"Don't take it personally, Mr. Cruz, but if any of your cop friends show up, I'll likely disappear out the door," he said, shaking my hand.

"I won't take it personally at all," I said to him, laughing.

Fraggy also showed up. He told me, and I had to make the announcement.

"Ladies and gentlemen, Fraggy has been promoted. He's the new president of WHO Earth!"

Everyone applauded.

Finally, Phishy returned. Through the door, he came with more sidewalk johnnies, including Sidewalk Sid, and several sidewalk sallies.

"I'm back!" he said. "Cruz!"

"Hi Phishy. Good to see my office is still here in one piece."

"You know what that means." He ran to PJ's desk and turned up the music. "Cruz Control, please." He was looking at my son.

"Why are you looking at my son, Phishy?"

Cruz Jr. descended in his hoverchair and jumped out.

What I saw next was deeply disturbing. It wasn't just Phishy spinning around doing his chicken dance. He had my son at his side doing the same thing. Everyone was laughing and applauding.

"Phishy, what did you do to my son?"

They danced to blues music. But there was nothing sad here. We were having a party. Another case solved! Until the next one.

Recap

It's not just for children and animals. Play is important for adults, too. Fun is essential to your overall emotional well-being. No one can feel bad when laughing and having a good time with family or friends.

The Planners

BE (LIQUID) COOL/MONTHLY PLANNER

MONTH:

SUN	MON	TUE	WED	THU	FRI	SAT

TOP PRIORITIES / GOALS

PEOPLE TO SEE / PLACES TO GO / REMINDERS

NOTES

RATE / ASSESS THE MONTH:

BE (LIQUID) COOL
WEEKLY PLANNER

WEEK:

| M | T | W | H | F | S | S |

MONDAY

TUESDAY

WEDNESDAY

THURSDAY

FRIDAY

SATURDAY / SUNDAY

WEEK'S PRIORITIES / TO DO

NOTES

RATE / ASSESS THE WEEK:

BE (LIQUID) COOL
WEEKLY PLANNER

WEEK:

| M | T | W | H | F | S | S |

MONDAY

FRIDAY

TUESDAY

SATURDAY / SUNDAY

WEDNESDAY

WEEK'S PRIORITIES / TO DO

THURSDAY

NOTES

RATE / ASSESS THE WEEK:

BE (LIQUID) COOL
WEEKLY PLANNER

WEEK:

| M | T | W | H | F | S | S |

MONDAY

TUESDAY

WEDNESDAY

THURSDAY

FRIDAY

SATURDAY / SUNDAY

WEEK'S PRIORITIES / TO DO

NOTES

RATE / ASSESS THE WEEK:

BE (LIQUID) COOL
WEEKLY PLANNER

WEEK:

M T W H F S S

MONDAY

TUESDAY

WEDNESDAY

THURSDAY

FRIDAY

SATURDAY / SUNDAY

WEEK'S PRIORITIES / TO DO

NOTES

RATE / ASSESS THE WEEK:

Week 46: Don't Forget Family and Friends (Part II)

CRUZ: UNTIL I FIGURED it all out, Phishy and Blinky had to stay where I could keep watch. So a week before Christmas, I had the two human ferrets in my Pony again.

EXCERPT FROM: *A.I. Confidential (Liquid Cool, Book Six)*

Phishy snatched it with a look on his face I had seen before. It was like when I threw a piece of chicken to this feral cat as a kid. The cat pounced on that piece of meat as if it had never eaten before and had this look accompanied by a low, guttural growl. The piece of chicken was in a death-lock in its mouth, and if anything came near it, even its mother, it would scratch its eyes out. Phishy's face looked like that.

But it wasn't over. When Phishy's psycho look passed, then I had to witness more craziness. He turned around and was fiddling with the zipper in the groin area of his pants.

"Phishy, I told you never do that again in my presence!" I yelled.

Of course, Wilford was a laughing mess, and Phishy's crew was having a good time, too. Phishy turned around to face me. "Done!" he said.

This time, Wilford G. almost fainted. He was laughing so hard. Phishy's crew was laughing harder.

"Yes, G., fall down, pass out, expire. That would be great. This is what I have to deal with as a street detective. You have Quix and ex-military. I have Phishy and his pants and company."

Perspective

Cruz: "Why am I being laughed at? Laughed at by even my own parents."

EXCERPT FROM: *The Electric Sheep Massacre (Liquid Cool, Book Four)*

"Post-wedding bliss" was supposed to be my watch phrase for the next couple of months. We had fully settled into our new 150th-floor apartment home in the Concrete Mama. Who said one couldn't live in style in Rabbit City? I'd married a famous full-time fashionista with mad interior design skills. The whole place looked like one of those photos out of an haute couture home magazine featuring some gazillionaire in Silicon Dunes or Opus Fields, but it wasn't. It was Rabbit City, and it was all ours!

"Cruz, what's that?"

China Doll was my wife. Women called her China; men called her Doll. Only her parents and I called her by her first name, Dot. Her question pierced the air before I even knew she was in the room with me.

I was about to answer, but as had happened before, I was stuck for a pet name: "Honey?"—no way—I wasn't using that. To me, honey was bee goo, though it was supposed to be healthy and antiseptic. That was no way to address one's significant other for me.

"Cruz, what's that in your hand?"

No, it wasn't anything crude. I had walked back into the bedroom and grabbed it from the back of the top drawer of my new dresser. We had matching his and hers dressers, another wedding gift from one of our million and one relatives. I had managed to keep it hidden for this long.

"Uh, nothing," I replied.

"Cruz, what's that in your hand?"

I had spun around to face her. As the consummate fashionista, with every piece of clothing, every accessory and every piece of jewelry being the trendiest and the most stylish, the color of the day was indigo. Her hair was tied back, with the ponytail carefully resting on one shoulder, with her pearl necklace and colored neck scarf. Her makeup was always perfect but never overdone.

She was across the room with her hands on her hips—a pose any warm-blooded husband knew to fear, like the bubonic plague. Every one of her fingers had a colored ring, and each wrist had multiple bracelets.

The "contraband" in my hand was my old-school electric hair clippers. I had one hand behind my back so she couldn't see them. I was figuring out how I could hide them, but before I could put my plan into action, Dot had marched across the room, grabbing the hand behind my back.

"Cruz!"

I admit that trying to drop the clippers to the floor and kick them under the bed was childish. She bent down and reached underneath for them.

"Cruz!" She stood up with the hair clippers in her hand. She had a scrunched-up nose expression of disapproval. "How could you? You're married to one of the top beauty and image stylists in Metropolis, but you cut your own hair!"

"I was getting rid of them."

"Cruz, this is totally unacceptable. You're a famous detective, and no famous detective cuts his own hair. How old is this?"

Now, she was holding them from the very tip of the handle as if they were radioactive.

"They're not that old."

"Cruz, this thing is ancient. It's spoiling the Feng Shui of our home."

She and my long-time hair clippers were gone from the room.

"Dot, what are you doing with my clippers?"

She reappeared at the doorway, smiling.

"What clippers," she said. It wasn't a question; it was a declaration.

I knew they were plummeting 150 stories to the bottom of the Concrete Mama trash chute.

Husbands of Earth unite! Hide your stuff from sticky-finger wives!

Perspective

I looked at my Pops. "You whacked that laser bullet back at that guy."

EXCERPT FROM: *Liquid Cool: The Cyberpunk Detective Series (Book One)*

In all the pictures you've seen of mass protests or riots, were there ever any in the pouring rain? Never. People were not interested in exercising their right to civil protest in inclement weather. However, I heard something from one of the Concrete Mama sidewalk johnnies that made me think barricading myself in my own place was not such a safe prospect. I heard the police were rioting at City Hall. There were 500,000 police in Metropolis!

We had left the real world and had entered the world of surreality.

"I don't know where you live," I said to Punch Judy.

"We've lived in the same building for over ten years. How can you not know where I live?"

"I just don't."

PJ's place was going to be my safe house. While my place had a meager helping of furniture, every square inch of her place had a piece of modern deco, neon, or fancy something. She may have been an ex-posh gang member, but she was still all posh.

She had turned her living room into a version of her Liquid Cool work area. Thankfully, she hadn't forwarded the phones, but she had to check, listen, and clear out the voicemail every half hour or completely run out of message storage. It was crazy. She could barely keep up.

One of her guest rooms was my space. I had locked myself in there, going on day two, sleeping. I purposely chose the smallest room she had. It was a decent size, with no outside windows. It was more of a closet than anything. I had destroyed my mobile—they can track you with that. Before my fateful "secret" interview, I had Flash load my Pony into a hovercar transport and ship it out of the City.

PJ didn't watch the news. She only read it on her mobile computer. I know she was always reading it, but she said nothing to me about any of it.

Phishy, with his crazy self, had every sidewalk johnny friend he knew, and all their friends, descend on the Concrete Mama like a swarm of ants. They had the lobby and PJ's floor filled to the rim with people—my own civilian security force. Too bad none of them were armed, but it was the gesture that mattered.

"Cruz!"

I told her not to yell but just knock on the door when she wanted me. When I opened the door, there was Dot. That put a smile on my face. Her parents were with her. That took the smile off my face. I came out of my sanctuary, anyway.

"How are you holding up?" she asked as she gave me a hug.

"Me, I'm fine. I have no idea what's happening out there, but that's good. I'm in here, safe and comfortable."

There was a knock on PJ's front door. If I hadn't seen what I saw, I would have thought I was dreaming. Mr. Wan pulled a .357 magnum shooter from his jacket, and Mrs. Wan pulled a smaller version with a silencer from her purse. Did all it take for my psycho parents-in-law to be on my side was our joint stay at the local jail?

Dot yelled at her parents in Chinese, and they yelled something back but kept their eyes on the door. PJ approached the door, carrying her favorite shotgun. She pressed the button on the door display and gave out a huff as she turned to all of us. "It's stupid man." She opened the door, and there was Phishy, smiling.

Dot's parents put away their guns after PJ closed and locked the door again. Phishy strolled to me.

"It's crazy out there, Cruz."

I held up my hand. "I don't want to know. For me, ignorance is bliss."

"You need to know what's going on," Dot said.

"I can't do anything about anything, so why know? Wait, did something happen at Eye Candy?"

"No, everything is fine. The reporters leaked that I was your girlfriend, and then so many people showed up there, looking for me. I had to leave. I couldn't work with all those people and reporters staring at me through the windows."

"I'm sorry."

"Why are you sorry? It's great. Prima Donna is signing up everyone as clients, and Goat Girl and Cyan are signing up everyone for our new anti-robot union. Everybody is happy. And Prima Donna says thank you."

"She's welcome."

"What's the plan?" she asked.

They had all encircled me. Now, PJ, too.

"Plan? We wait it out."

"This could go on for weeks or months," Dot said. "You really don't know what's going on."

"No."

"Then how can you have a plan?"

"The last I heard was the police were rioting at City Hall. That's it."

Dot's parents started shaking their heads, along with PJ. Phishy was grinning. "It's a lot more than that," Dot said.

"More than rioting?"

"Cruz, you're not an ostrich. Get your head out of the dirty mud, look up, and know what's going on around you."

"As long as they leave you, my Pony, and my place alone, I'm good."

"And the office!" PJ interjected.

"And the office."

"You listed me ahead of the Pony, so I guess I'm good."

I smiled at her.

Now, there was frantic knocking at the door. Both PJ and Phishy ran to the door.

"Don't touch my door," PJ yelled at him as she grabbed her shotgun again. "Okay."

Phishy pushed the display button.

"Phishy," one of the sidewalk johnnies said, standing in front of the door.

"You can't be in and out of my place," PJ scolded Phishy.

"I may need to come back in after I see what they want."

She unlocked the door for him. "No. Stay out."

The door opened, and Phishy stuck his head out. He pulled it back in and ran to me.

"Cruz, there are police downstairs."

"Where?"

"They're pushing their way into the lobby. A lot of them."

"Oh no," Dot said with a scared look.

Her parents had their weapons drawn again.

"Cruz, get your guns," PJ commanded.

"I can't," I said. "They took away my gun license, and I can only use them in my place, not someone else's."

"Stop being foolish," she said. "They're coming for you."

I ran into my room for my gun case.

"Phishy!"

As I pulled my gun case from under the bed and opened it, I asked when he appeared, "You know places like Mad Heights?"

"Mad City? What about it?"

"They got those animal gangs there."

"And lots more, too. Much more dangerous."

"Are there people who just hang around in the darkness?"

"Darkness where?"

"Like in the back alleys."

"Ghouls? How do you know about them?"

"What are they?"

"Night people. They're gangs that hang in the dark with their night-sight."

"What do they do? Just hang out in the dark?"

"No, they get people."

"What does that mean?"

"How do you know about them?"

"Never mind. We'll talk about this later."

Recap

Wouldn't it be such an uninteresting place without all of them?

Week 47: Don't Be So Serious

CRUZ: I LOVED MARTIAN cow people! I was already practicing my new lines: "I may not eat beef, but when I do—it's Martian beef!"

EXCERPT FROM: *I, Alien Hunter (Liquid Cool, Book Five)*

Five days. That Martian space freighter was now only five days away.

Strangely, the Concrete Mama had never had a building party before. But it was having one now. I invited everyone! I had Hellspawn #1 (Dot's father) playing the music, blasting it through the hallway of our 150th floor. I had

Hellspawn #2 (Dot's mother) as chief hostess. Cruz Jr. had his cool hat on and a new hoverstroller. I had hired some college kids to make sure no one ever had an empty glass. My Ma and Pops had flown down and arrived an hour ago to join the festivities. Dot and I would never, ever have to buy diapers out of our own pocket again—well, it was going to be our pocket, but that pocket had a massive inflow of new cash. We would never be Silicon Dunes or Opus Fields rich, or even Elysian Heights rich (where her parents lived), but rich enough for us. I had successfully hunted down my alien with a vid-call. I loved Martian cow people! I was already practicing my new lines: "I may not eat beef, but when I do—it's Martian beef!"

PJ lived in the Concrete Mama, too, so she was there, of course, hanging out with Dot. They were teaching Cruz Jr. to dance. He was looking at them with confused eyes, wondering what I would say as a baby: "What the heck is wrong with these big people? Why are they trying to get me to move like this?"

Everything couldn't be better. The space freighter would soon be here on Earth and then I was done with the ET watchers forever. I hadn't even looked at the data pebble yet. I had lost all interest—I got my big payday. All I wanted to do was relax and have fun.

I was already a hero to the Concrete Mama for dealing with our Rabbit City hoodlum problem. With this building party, I would achieve super celebrity status. I was moving through the smiling, laughing, dancing crowds, shaking hands (wearing my see-through surgical gloves, of course; it was, after all, hundreds of people!) I noticed our doorman was talking to PJ. He knew she was my secretary. They were now looking at me. Oh no, I said to myself. What now?

PJ had come to the party with a new boyfriend. They were always shorter than her and spoke some other language—she only liked foreign men, she had told me. She moved to me with the boyfriend following her like a puppy.

"PJ, it's a party. There's no working at a party."

"You're the boss, and there's no break for the boss. Someone wants to talk to you in the lobby."

"PJ. It's my party. I'm not going down to the lobby."

"The man only wants five minutes."

"PJ."

"And he'll pay."

I was tempted, but I had already gotten a bunch of money, so I could pretend that I was above such monetary considerations. "Have him make an appointment to come to the office like everyone else. This is where we live. In fact, why is a client coming to our personal residence and not the office?"

"Mr. Cruz, I'd be happy to explain."

I turned, and there was a smiling android looking at me.

Perspective

"Yes," I said. "This is the Liquid Cool Detective Agency. He's Liquid. I'm Cool."
— Cruz

EXCERPT FROM: *I, Alien Hunter (Liquid Cool, Book Five)*

All this time, the husband and wife clients were watching me silently. PJ stood there with her bionic arms, suppressing a smile. I walked around to my chair behind my desk, sat down again, and opened the top cabinet. First, my hand pulled out the little fedora I recently bought from Harry's Haberdashery. Mine was tan, but I didn't want Cruz Jr.'s to be the same—his was pinstripe black. I removed his skullcap and placed his hat firmly on his head, and then I got the other item. His little Sherlock Holmes Jr. plastic magnifying toy. It was the only toy that he didn't put in his mouth. My son was now "in uniform," and he became all serious. He tapped the magnifying glass toy a couple of times against his leg, and then he was done. He looked up at our potential clients. I looked at them too. "You both can have a seat now," I said.

The husband burst out laughing. The wife's eyes narrowed, giving me a disapproving stare. "Thank you, PJ," I said. She grinned, turned, and left my private office, closing the door behind her.

The door opened suddenly. "Oh, this is Mr. and Mrs. Cosmos." She disappeared again.

"Thanks, PJ." I gestured again to them, to the chairs, as I sat.

The man was still laughing. The wife punched his arm, and he quieted down. They slowly sat down in the chairs. Cruz Jr. was watching them intently. The clients noticed and looked at me.

"How can my business partner and I help you?"

"Business partner?" the wife asked.

"Yes," I said. "This is the Liquid Cool Detective Agency. He's Liquid. I'm Cool." I looked at my son, who was looking at me now. "Isn't that right, Liquid? You're the one who excretes massive amounts of liquid—nasty!" Cruz Jr. grinned with his toothless baby mouth.

"Do you always allow babies to carry guns in your office?" she asked.

"My business partner isn't a baby. He's a toddler. How can I help? I don't think you came all this way to talk about youth and guns."

They looked at Cruz Jr. again. "Is he going to sit there watching us?" she asked.

"Are you all going to be saying something inappropriate to me?"

"Well, no—"

"Then let's get on with it. He can't even talk yet."

"Shoot them," Cruz Jr. said.

The wife's eyes narrowed, and the husband laughed.

"Pretend you didn't hear that," I said.

"We were told you were a professional, Mr. Cruz," she said.

"That assessment will be made entirely by you. Usually, I'm judged by how I solve my cases, not by the behavior of my toddler son. But it's your choice, of course. Let me call my secretary back in, and she can refund you your retainer—"

"Hold on a minute." The man made a "hold" gesture with his left palm. "That's not what my wife meant. We came a long way, and we're not going all the way back in this storm for nothing." He turned to his wife now. "Stop alienating everyone. We need to hire him."

She gave a heavy sigh.

"What's the problem, Mr. Cosmos?" I asked.

Recap

Whether it's the world of Liquid Cool or our own, a sense of humor can take you far—and keep you sane.

Week 48: Schedule Spontaneity

"SECOND STAR TO THE right and straight on till morning." — Captain Kirk, Star Trek: The Undiscovered Country

EXCERPT FROM: *The Electric Sheep Massacre (Liquid Cool, Book Four)*

Some things were universal on this planet. The hovercab dropped me off, and the street looked like so many others that I'd been to in Metropolis. Not the seediest, but you knew you weren't in a decent neighborhood, either. It looked as if there was no one over 30 on the street, which to them meant I was a senior citizen with one foot in the grave.

British fashion was no different from any other supercity, but with youth, it was all over the place. I had gotten used to seeing Beatnik fashion; now, I was seeing punk fashion—spiky hair, lots of black, but always with some color. Flowers on the lapel also looked to be a common part of UK kid fashion.

Here, VL was every bit as big as in the Americas, but here, even I was having a tough time figuring out where the VL scene ended and where the drug culture began.

"Where's the Refinery?" I asked a young couple wearing silver clothes and long scarves wrapped around their necks and hanging down to their knees.

They laughed at me. "Don't you know?" they said and walked off.

I quickly learned that it was a game after asking five other people the same question and getting giggles or being outright ignored.

"Hey, can you help out an American?" I asked another.

The man almost fell over, laughing. "No!"

Okay, so that was a lousy opening line.

"Where do I go to get some information?" I asked a woman cradling a robot cat in her arms.

"What kind of information?"

"I want to get to the Refinery."

"Don't you know?"

"I don't. That's why I'm asking."

"I wish I could help you, but yesterday's information is today's trash."

"What does that mean?"

"The Refinery isn't a place. It's a party. A party on the move. Only the Refinery knows where the Refinery is."

It was almost the end of the day, and it had taken half of it to find out what the Refinery was; it wasn't a place with a fixed location. Then, it took me hours to find this traveling group of VL party-goers. I had a headache.

Someone had pity on me, finally, and told me to follow them. It was three of them. Two women with cat ear attachments—I didn't know what that signified—and a guy wearing a bowler hat.

They all locked arms, the guy with me, and they skipped down the street. I wanted to die. Me, skipping down the street with a bunch of kids with cat ears. They could blackmail me with this CCTV footage because I knew I looked ridiculous.

Around the corner and to the end of a short street we went. We skipped right into a crowd moving down a main street. Most of the crowd was on hoverchairs plugged into their VL helmets. Each VL chair user had people around their chair; on the edges of the crowd were muscular punks with baseball bats wearing colored shades—reds, blues, greens, purples, etc.

"Old timer," the boy said, letting my arm go, "the Refinery."

They all disappeared into the crowd, and I stood as the crowd slowly moved in front of me. I honestly could not see the end. I looked the other way, and I couldn't see the beginning. It was a sea of people, a moving town of hardcore VR users. There were also go-go bots everywhere—slim humanoid female robots wearing neon wigs, bikinis, and knee-high boots—dancing as they walked. All adding to the wild party atmosphere. We didn't have anything like this in Metropolis.

Perspective

"Stuff your eyes with wonder, live as if you'd drop dead in 10 seconds. See the world. It's more fantastic than any dream made or paid for in factories." — Ray Bradbury, Fahrenheit 451

EXCERPT FROM: *I, Alien Hunter (Liquid Cool, Book Five)*

I didn't go into work. I had called PJ, and she informed me that Liquid Cool was swarming with reporters. I thought being called Meteor Man was bad. Now, I was the Metro P.I. involved in the Proof of Alien Life Case. Free Earth had so many people surrounding their city to get "insight" into talking to the aliens that all of them, sane and insane, were barricaded inside.

"Cruz, why did you have me stay home today? I have to work."

"In this?"

The news switched from district to district. Eye Candy was under siege from media and onlookers, too. I imagined the entire world was now ET believers.

"You have a point there." She looked at Cruz, Jr., who was lying on his back on our bed, wiggling around. "He wants his hoverchair."

"Cruzie, you need to start walking."

"Cruz Jr., ignore him. I'll get your chair." She pulled his hoverchair to the bed. Personally, I didn't like hoverchairs for babies. It made them think they were adults since they were hovering at adult level. When they started walking, they'd think they were going backward in life. "When I was 1 and 2, I was all the way up there; now I'm 3 and 4, and I'm down here on the ground with smelly feet and possible isopods."

She put him in the hoverchair, and already he was smiling. "Why are we home, Cruz? Are we hiding?"

"All I want to be is a private detective, but it's like I'm a galactic secret agent. This whole case isn't just crawling with Martians, but government agents too, and I'm sure Up-Top megacorp operatives, and there's talk of military spaceships, ETs, and ET artifacts. It's too much."

"It's too much? What do you mean? That's the case."

She was monitoring Cruz Jr. in his hoverchair. He flew right up to my face, and he playfully touched the side of my head and then hovered away. "No, Dot. This is not the case. That's the problem. They're trying to keep me away from the real case, but I'm on to them. They want secret agents. We'll give them secret agents."

She looked at me with her hands on her hips. "What?"

"Pack your bag, Mrs. Cruz. You, me, and Cruz Jr. as of this instant, are galactic superspies. We're going to break this whole case wide open. Let's get going. Mission one: get out of the Concrete Mama undetected by everyone."

"Superspies, Cruz?"

"I find myself being pulled further and further away from the kind of detective work I want to do. It's like the OGs when I was a hovercar restorer. Who were the happy ones? The ones who kept a low profile had their own stable of classics that they could manage and wash by hand weekly without any robots. The unhappy ones had all the prestige and fame, had a big staff, ran major racing teams, and oversaw merchandising and marketing globally. They were miserable. They never saw their classic vehicles, never even got a chance to sit in one to breathe in that new minty smell. They were cut off from what they loved and why they got into the biz to begin with.

"I want to be a street detective—it may be small, but I want small. Look at all this. I got the Mayor and chief in my office. I'm known by rich spacemen and Martians and the Council of Corporations. I keep this up, and I won't be in charge of my life anymore—all of them will. I don't want to be the PI to the uber-governments and megacorps of Earth and Up-Top. I am a Metro PI who has Average Joe and Jane clients, an occasional corporate, and an occasional government. That's it. I can control that. This I can't control; no one can. I keep complaining about it. I'm taking back my persona.

"Dot, you could have taken your skills on the road and left Earth to pamper those Up-Toppers. Could have made tons more money, but your life wouldn't be your own. You'd spend more time on shuttles bouncing from the space colonies to the lunar colonies to Mars and all over again. Who cares if you have the big money and big money friends if you're a miserable wreck? If it's not you. Eye Candy is great because you're there, and the Up-Toppers fly down to you! Yeah, I'm taking back my persona."

"Good for you, Cruz. But your vehicle is bright red, and everyone knows what it looks like. How do you suppose you'll get us out of here undetected?"

"Ever wondered how I'm able to disappear so readily when you've had your people looking for me?"

"Umm?" She smiled. "Cruz, what are you playing at?"

"You have wondered. Let's go."

Recap

When all you do is live by a plan, an occasional act of complete spontaneity can be so liberating and refreshing.

Week 49: Vacations!

"WELCOME TO JURASSIC Park." — *Dr. John Hammond, played by Richard Attenborough*

EXCERPT FROM: *Write Me a Murder on Jules Verne's Island (Liquid Cool, Book Nine)*

The smartest thing I did for our vacation was get us "premium check-in." You had to go through all kinds of background checks and pay a fee, but it was well worth it. We could bypass all the crazy, winding lines of people at the regular check-in counters. Why everyone didn't do it was beyond me.

What we couldn't bypass was security. We went through the scanning arches and luggage check-in as security personnel checked our tickets. Ordinarily, our luggage would be sent on its way, but neither Dot nor I believed in lost luggage. We kept our mountain of luggage with us and would pay the fee to physically watch it loaded onto our flight. The lines weren't that bad. We had gone through the entire thing in less than fifteen minutes and were headed to our departure gate.

"Please tell me you got the VIP waiting area upgrade," Dot said.

"Well, isn't the Cruz family VIPs?"

She smiled, reached over with her free hand, and squeezed my chin. Kat laughed at us.

The VIP lounge was a secluded area away from the "mere mortals" of the departure gate. The seats were bigger and better, equipped with their own entertainment centers—music and TV. Lots of vending machines for cold and hot food and drinks. I even bought us all our own headphones. The screen was on a swivel arm. Dot found a movie as I situated both Cruz Jr. and Kat in one chair. Dot would watch them, and I'd watch our mountain of luggage. We'd gotten to the airport and through everything a lot quicker than we thought. Better to be early than late, but we had an hour to go before boarding.

Everything around us seemed normal. The wife and kids were watching their movie. I watched our luggage and kept a roving eye on our surroundings. Inside the VIP waiting area was also an All-Vacationers Travel Hub—the fun, lively commercial area of travel agents. Their glass-walled office was filled with changing holo-screens of travel destinations and live bands of smiling performers. We made sure to sit as far away from them as possible, and they were why Dot had quickly grabbed the kids' attention with TV.

The purpose of the hub was to entice travelers with a sea of vacation offers. Deals offered were better than you could ever get on the Net, or so they said. Your bags were already packed, you were already regretting coming back to your day job—what better way to get you to buy a vacation add-on or switch to a whole new travel itinerary altogether?

That's when I saw him. A clean-cut kid with blond hair wearing a light jacket and tie. He clearly was looking at me and seemed to be getting up the nerve to approach me. I didn't like it. I had no weapons to shoot anyone if needed.

The kid came out of the office and made a beeline for me. He smiled, then did a Japanese bow.

"Are you Mr. Cruz?"

"I am."

"Please, sir, may I speak with you?"

"Why? What did I do?"

"Oh, no. You have done nothing wrong, sir. May I simply speak with you privately?"

My wife and I glanced at each other, then looked at him suspiciously.

"It will only be a moment, sir, I assure you. I work for a company that represents one of our travel destinations."

"Which one?" Dot asked him.

"Jules Verne's Island."

"We did want to go there," she said, "but it's far too expensive."

"Mr. Cruz, only a moment of your time. I'll even give a discount voucher for your time."

"Sure, I'll listen. But I don't want my luggage to get stolen."

"Oh, no, sir. I will take care of you."

The kid waved to someone, and I saw a young security guard run to us. He told the guard to watch our luggage cart.

"Cruz, what have you done?" she asked. Of course, my wife stood from her chair and was suspiciously watching me, and so were my kids.

"Nothing," I replied.

I followed him into an office with clear glass walls all around. My wife and kids watched as we talked. The young man was a great salesman. He presented his case well, was prepared for all my objections, made me multiple offers I couldn't refuse, including bribes, and closed the deal.

We walked back out to the wife and kids.

"Cruz, what's going on?" she asked.

"Dot, Mr.—"

"Mr. Vec, ma'am," the young man said.

"Mr. Vec has an offer for us I think we should consider."

"Cruz, we're on vacation, and our flight will be boarding within the hour."

"Dot, I'm going to just come out and say it. The owners of the island want to change our vacation plans to Jules Verne's Island to take charge of a situation until police authorities arrive. We don't have to do anything but enjoy our vacation. The authorities will arrive and be off on their way. We'll still be there to enjoy all our vacation days to the fullest. We both want the Asian vacation, but ten countries and fourteen days with our avalanche of luggage and two kids? That means ten flights and ten more times at the airport. We both want simple, and this is it."

"All expenses paid, ma'am," Vec added.

"What's the situation, Cruz?"

I looked at Vec for a second. I turned to her. "There's been a murder on the island, or they think it is. It could be he just...expired."

The look on my wife's face was a cross between confusion, outrage, and incredulity.

"We wouldn't have to do anything. I wouldn't have to do anything," I told her.

"No!" Dot said.

"They don't have the personnel to manage the situation properly until the authorities arrive."

"No."

"The scene is sealed up. It's at a hotel. It's nothing dangerous."

"No."

"Actually, as a private detective, I'm not allowed to investigate a murder. Forget those books and movies. It's illegal."

"No."

"Every year, this group of authors rents the entire island for the month. They have normal security, of course, but the island doesn't have its own police of any kind. They have to be called in from the mainland."

"No."

"My role would be to simply be there. That's it. It was on our list to visit one day, so here's our chance. A free vacation. Cruzie, Kat, can we say 'free!'"

"No."

"Since these authors have rented the island, no one else is there besides hotel and grounds staff. We'd have the entire island practically to ourselves. There are only five authors on the island, and they stay in their rooms most of the time."

"No."

"Yes, one of them might have murdered someone. The murdered man is an author, too. But you see, this is just a writer-on-writer thing, so there's no danger."

"No."

"So, free vacation for us and the family. Then there are the perks. On-demand massage, spa, sauna, full gym, zero-gravity swimming pool."

Vec held up his tablet. As he pushed a button, the screen changed. The kids were watching closely, too.

"Laser golf, holo-tennis courts, bike path encircling the island for running, biking, or hover-biking."

Vec displayed live-action demos on his tablet.

"Famous Jules Verne's amusement park all to ourselves," I said, "including steampunk-themed hoverchair transportation."

"Mommy, amusement park," Cruz Jr. said.

"Scuba diving, mini-floating islands for sunbathing, family hydrofoils for boating, para-sailing, and waterskiing."

Vec showed her on his tablet.

"And! The island has its own mini-mall. Of specific interest are its fashion stores featuring the latest styles from around the world."

Dot took the tablet from the man.

"Styles for adults and children—of all ages."

Vec and I stood quietly as Dot finished viewing images and demos on the tablet.

She looked at me.

"Yes."

I raised my hand in triumph. "Kids! Mommy said yes! We're going to have so much fun!"

She pointed the tablet at me.

"Cruz, we're on vacation! No working!"

"I can't work. I'm a private citizen. I'm not allowed to investigate the police's case. They'd put me in jail."

"Ma'am, all the owners want is his presence," Vec said. "This is beyond the scope of island staff. The owners simply want peace of mind and will graciously compensate you for your wonderful time on the island. Mr. Cruz won't have to do a thing."

"Cruz, I am putting you on notice. No working cases! This is our vacation. Our first vacation as a family."

"Dot, I can't investigate a police case. I'm a private citizen. Private detectives can't go running around solving murder mysteries. That's all Movie-Town fakery. The one thing I can promise you is there will be no investigating by me on this vacation."

Welcome to my Liquid Cool Cozy Murder Mystery on Jules Verne's Island.

Perspective

"Scotty, beam us down." — Star Trek

EXCERPT FROM: *The Moon is a Good Place to Die (Liquid Cool, Book Eight)*

From Earth, when you could see it, the Moon was always so beautiful. But to approach the planetoid for real, its image literally filled your entire field of vision. It was breathtaking. From the upper level of Run-Time's double-decker spacecraft, I stared out the observation lounge. It was large enough for all hundred-plus passengers as we began our final descent. I sat in the front row in the center of older wealthy business types and younger wealthy vacation hoppers. Tourism was big, big business for the Moon—those uber-wealthy who could afford it, but there were plenty of Earthers for once-in-a-lifetime visits.

For a while, there was nothing else visible on the big, beautiful white rock. Then, the structures came into view. The main center dome looked to be made of a slightly glowing opaque silver material covered in lines of flashing lights. Surrounding the main structure was a network of connected smaller domes, not all the same size. We saw antenna towers, dishes, and what looked to be missile launchers. Other spacecraft landed and departed from the outermost dome spaceports. We had arrived on the Moon, and all of us were in awe.

I had always thought Metro International was a behemoth of a structure, but the Moon spaceport was far larger, which was tiny compared to the main Lunar Colony mother dome. I would soon learn the proper nomenclature.

There was, however, bad news. Run-Time's craft had been recalled to one of the Space Station Colonies. Run-Time said it was routine, but I didn't necessarily believe him. Run-Time ran his businesses professionally and efficiently. Never a wasted move or expense. He didn't want to worry me. They know I'm here, I thought to myself, as the passengers and I prepared to exit the craft.

"Are you sure about this?" he asked.

"I'll be fine. I want people to think I'm here all alone."

"But you are."

We chatted a bit more. We were each trying to convince the other that everything would be okay. Neither of us was all that successful.

"Don't let anything happen to you up here, Cruz. I don't want your wife after me. The Moon isn't a good place to die."

"You're the second person to tell me that."

"Then listen to us."

He pressed a card in my hand before I disembarked from the spacecraft. All the other passengers were already gone; I was the last one. I put the card in a pocket and held my pacifier (I'll explain later) in the other. One of the flight crew had gotten me a push trolley for my suitcases. My best friend and I exchanged hugs.

"You look good in your lunar outfit," he said.

I had changed out of my trademark tan fedora and slicker for a new outfit—a white fedora and white slicker.

"I'm Up-Top now," I said. "When in Rome, dress as the Romans."

I was on my way. My foot was about to touch the surface of the Moon for the first time in my life. When it did, stepping down from the Let It Ride spacecraft's floating stepladder, I smiled. An automated people mover waited.

The mover was like pods we had on Earth, only these didn't use hovertech, but some type of maglev (magnetic levitation) tech. I watched the spacecraft for a while as I raced away. Behind me, a giant transparent barrier closed. I could see Run-Time's spacecraft clearly. There was no delay. It launched and flew out of the spaceport dome into space. On Metropolis, I had my own team, my connections, contacts, associates, my weapons, my Pony. Here I had two suitcases and a giant pacifier in my mouth.

Recap

We can't visit other galaxies, solar systems, and planets, but there are countless places on Earth you can explore every day and still not see them all in your lifetime.

Also, the occasional "stay-cation" counts too.

TWELFTH MONTH
December
Classic Sci-Fi Actor Birthdays

CHARACTER (ACTOR) SHOW/Movie

December 2: Boothby (Ray Walston) Star Trek: The Next Generation/Deep Space Nine/Voyager

December 3: Pris (Daryl Hannah) Blade Runner (Original Movie)

December 3: Aiden Ford (Rainbow Sun Franks) Stargate Atlantis

December 6: Elizabeth Weir (Torri Higginson) Stargate Atlantis

December 7: Private Drake (Mark Rolston) Aliens

December 9: Major General Hank Landry (Beau Bridges) Stargate SG-1

December 9: Worf (Michael Dorn) Star Trek: The Next Generation/Deep Space Nine

December 10: Count Baltar (John Colicos) Battle Star Galactica (Original Series)

December 11: Jango Fett (Temuera Morrison) Star Wars: The Prequels

December 11: John Crichton/Farscape; Lt. Colonel Cameron Mitchell/Stargate SG-1 (Ben Browder)

December 13: General Chang (Christopher Plummer) Star Trek: The Undiscovered Country

December 15: Daniel Jackson (Michael Shanks) Stargate SG-1

December 15: Harry Kim (Garrett Wang) Star Trek: Voyager

December 16: Colonel Tigh (Terry Carter) Battle Star Galactica (Original Series)

December 18: Apoc (Julian Arahanga) The Matrix

December 20: Lt. Ezri Dax (Nicole de Boer) Star Trek: Deep Space Nine

December 21: Mace Windu (Samuel L. Jackson) Star Wars: The Prequels

December 25: Rod Serling creator of original anthology television series, The Twilight Zone

December 28: Lt. Uhura (Nichelle Nichols) Star Trek: The Original Series

December 31: Commandant Mele-On Grayza (Rebecca Riggs) Farscape

THE FINAL STRETCH

Almost There!

"YUB NUB, EEE CHOP YUB nub..." — Ewok celebration finale, Star Wars: The Return of the Jedi

You've reached month twelve and the final three weeks. Excellent!

You can do a final sprint to the end or keep your steady, focused pace across the finish line, but you're almost there!

The Planners

BE (LIQUID) COOL / MONTHLY PLANNER

MONTH:

SUN	MON	TUE	WED	THU	FRI	SAT

TOP PRIORITIES / GOALS

PEOPLE TO SEE / PLACES TO GO / REMINDERS

NOTES

RATE / ASSESS THE MONTH:

BE (LIQUID) COOL
WEEKLY PLANNER

WEEK:

M T W H F S S

MONDAY

TUESDAY

WEDNESDAY

THURSDAY

FRIDAY

SATURDAY / SUNDAY

WEEK'S PRIORITIES / TO DO

NOTES

RATE / ASSESS THE WEEK:

BE (LIQUID) COOL
WEEKLY PLANNER

WEEK:

| M | T | W | H | F | S | S |

MONDAY

TUESDAY

WEDNESDAY

THURSDAY

FRIDAY

SATURDAY / SUNDAY

WEEK'S PRIORITIES / TO DO

NOTES

RATE / ASSESS THE WEEK:

BE (LIQUID) COOL
WEEKLY PLANNER

WEEK:

M T W H F S S

MONDAY

TUESDAY

WEDNESDAY

THURSDAY

FRIDAY

SATURDAY / SUNDAY

WEEK'S PRIORITIES / TO DO

NOTES

RATE / ASSESS THE WEEK:

Week 50: Accomplished

MCCOY: I PREFER A DOSE of common sense! You're proposing that we go backwards in time, find humpback whales, then bring them forward in time, drop 'em off, and hope to Hell they tell this probe what to do with itself!

Kirk: That's the general idea.

McCoy: Well, that's crazy!

Star Trek: The Voyage Home

EXCERPT FROM: *Liquid Cool: The Cyberpunk Detective Series (Book One)*

All I had to do was push a button to start the engine of my classic Ford Pony. High-performance, super-charged, advanced nitro-acceleration hydrogen engine. A sleek, bright red muscle-vehicle coupe to make the average person gawk and the mouths of the genuine hovercar enthusiast and collector hang open.

I had found the shell in a junkyard over fifteen years ago when I was in middle school, and it took me a few years to build and restore it, spare part by spare part. I had been upgrading it ever since. No one believed I found and built such an expensive muscle hovercar from scratch, but it was true, and I drove it every day. It was considered a true classic and got me solid offers to part with it almost every week, but you don't sell a classic Ford Pony; it's a purchase for life—like a legacy house. My Pony had been featured (without my permission) in so many hovercar magazines that I lost count.

I coasted out of the alleyway without revving the engine. I wanted no more than a purr out of it. If "they" were coming for me, I had to make my getaway quietly. That's what I did. Not even turning on my car lights, I flew out of the alley, waited for my chance, and drove into the empty sky-lane. I'd stay under the monorail line bridge as long as I could to avoid Run-Time's taxis. Big Brother government had nothing on Run-Time's civilian surveillance of cabbies throughout the city. They were better than any drone army.

Recap

There are two schools of thought when you're in the last stretch of your "project": try to cram in as much as possible or ease off the work. It's your decision and there's no right or wrong answer. By now, you will have completed many of your month-by-month objectives toward your overall goals.

Your Action Mindset will shift to an Accomplishment Appreciation Mindset.

Week 51: Perseverance

"THE BEST WAY TO PREDICT the future is to create it!" — credited to Abraham Lincoln and Peter Drucker (and you don't need a time machine!)

EXCERPT FROM: *Blade Gunner (Liquid Cool, Book Two)*

It was a no-name sleazy bar-restaurant on the outskirts of Wharf City, but in our present mental state and physical condition, it was the same as Heaven. I was sure that to everyone who noticed us as we came through the front door, we looked as if we had walked off some kind of battlefield. My tan fedora and coat were long gone; I had dumped them in the outwash. Besides Phishy, everyone who knew I had been in that tunnel was dead, and I planned to keep it that way.

I wasn't clean and neat because I was a germophobe. I was that way because I had class. I was that way because I was a human being who didn't walk on all fours and wasn't born in a barn. Phishy and I walked in covered in grime and slime, soaking wet, but we sat at a booth in the tiny restaurant part of the bar. Yet, everyone inside ignored us—the bartender serving drinks, the barflies on stools slinging back their glasses of hard liquor, the patrons at booths or tables stuffing their faces with slop. In fact, none of them looked much cleaner than we did. Clearly, no health inspector had ever set foot in this joint.

"Give me your mobile."

Phishy handed it to me without a word.

"I'll get it back to you."

He nodded, trying to smile. Phishy was still shell-shocked.

"For the next few days, I want you to lay low," I said. "Do you have someplace safe to stay?"

He nodded again.

"I don't want to take any chances."

"He knows my name." Phishy lost it, and his eyes teared up.

He was right. Swordplaya and company were gone forever, but the person who killed them probably did know Phishy's name.

"Phishy."

It took him a bit to collect himself.

"We're going to take care of it. I promise. Leave right now and stay with one of your friends you can trust, safe. Get rested up. Get yourself together.

Send word to me, by one of your sidewalk johnny buddies, secretly, when you're settled. In fact, it's better I have your phone." I grabbed the phone and quickly ripped out its disk. "See. It's off. So, if he has it or gets it, he'll think we were washed away, too."

Phishy sniffled and nodded.

"Call a taxi," I said.

"No, I'll walk. I need to be outside for a bit to think and calm down."

"Yeah," I said. "I hear you—but don't take chances."

"I won't."

We stood, and Phishy looked at me for a moment. "Thanks for saving my life, Cruz. I shouldn't have done what I did, but only you could have saved me. I didn't want to die. I don't do real crime. I'm Phishy. All I do is hustle."

"Just get yourself to someplace safe and rest up. Think of it as vacation time."

"Yeah." He flashed a Phishy smile at me.

As he left the bar, I could see he was already returning to normal. I was returning to normal again because now I was having random thoughts of—wedding plans!

"Could I have some napkins?" I asked the bartender.

He glanced up at me for a second, then returned to pouring himself a drink. Was he really going to blatantly ignore me? I watched him with squinted eyes. I stepped to the bar, directly opposite him and crossed my arms.

"Napkins."

"Are you going to pay for them?"

"Do you expect me to pay for napkins?"

"I don't get them for free."

"What kind of place is this? No one charges customers for napkins."

"You're not a customer. You haven't bought any booze or food. My establishment isn't here for your personal hygiene needs, bub."

"Bub?"

"Yeah, bub. Napkins are for paying customers only."

"You're not a 'bub,' you're a bum. I want some napkins to wipe the grime off my face."

"What grime? You look fine to me."

Was he serious? I was a walking dirt mop.

"You know what, bub? Get your napkins from the restroom and get out of here." He pointed to the back of the bar.

A wave of panic came over me—public restroom?

I never ever, ever, ever used public restrooms. I didn't care how clean they were supposed to be. I had a routine in life and made sure I stuck it so I was close to home for any "pit stops." Public restrooms? I'd rather die.

"There or no napkins for you, bub."

I had to get this gunk off of me. I felt as if my skin were crawling. I had to chance it.

I gave the bartender a dirty look as I marched to the restrooms. My girlfriend, Dot, had been counseling me. She'd said I had to get over my phobia of public restrooms, especially if we wanted to travel, and with my new detective job, that could take me far away from the Concrete Mama. She told me she'd tackle her phobia of bridges if I handled my phobia of public restrooms. Besides, she told me, that's where people go to wash their hands. Yes, I agreed with her that that was a very "pro-germophobic" activity, and we would slay our phobias together.

"MEN." I stopped at the door. All my willpower would need to be summoned. I didn't even have gloves to wear. I pushed the door open with my foot and stepped in, preparing myself for what I might see—or hear.

What I walked into was nothing short of a house of horrors. Immediately, I saw him—the man was over 500 pounds, his back to me, straddling, with one fat leg on the lip of the wall urinal, and his two hands, palms out, braced against the wall. It seemed that he was nothing but fat, and all his butt fat was flowing out of his pants to moon me.

It wasn't a restroom. My vehicle was larger, and the man took up half the room—literally; next to the urinal was a toilet with no partition whatsoever. Across was a sink with an empty towel dispenser.

"Who dat?" he said. The man's jelly dough head began to turn to look at me. An explosion of bodily functions.

"Ahh!"

I ran from that restroom so fast, I'm surprised I hadn't reached the necessary velocity for time travel. I was out the door and into the streets; if it had been the desert, there would have been a trailing dust cloud.

Excerpt From: *Blade Gunner (Liquid Cool, Book Two)*

Part Two

What do you think were the chances I would ever set foot near a public restroom after that Restroom of Horror with Jabba the Butt?

There was no nice way to say it. I was having a full-blown panic attack due to my germophobia. This was actually very serious. The doctors had once told my parents that if I didn't grow out of the condition, I might have to live in a hermetically sealed Bubble Colony for those suffering from the same psychosis.

My Pops wasn't having any of that. "He has a phobia, not a psychosis; you're not sending our boy to the moon," he told them, and that was that. No more doctors for me, only counselors—completely useless, the lot of them. My Gramps was the only counselor I'd needed. I'd asked him how he'd quit chain-smoking two packs of cigarettes a day 50 years ago, and he said, "I woke up one day, and said 'I'm not smoking anymore.'—and did it." That's what I did. I said "No" to my germophobia, so it couldn't prevent me from living my life.

Well, I was partially successful. I did live my life, but I had to avoid nastiness. If I found myself in nastiness, there was a chance of having an attack like I was having at the moment. But there was a quick cure that I had availed myself of only a few times before.

The Centers for Disease Control had a base in every major supercity in the world. Command post, research labs, vaccination storage, and, my personal favorite, Decon.

Metro Disease Control hated me. They had threatened to hire extra guards to keep me out the next time. Well, this was "the next time." Thanks to the heavy rain, they wouldn't know it was me until I was inside. I scaled the outer fence like a human centipede.

"Hey, this is restricted property!" I heard someone yell as I bolted across the parking lot.

I saw one and then two other guards giving chase, but I was too fast for them. I outran them and leaped up the steps. I could see a guard at the reception desk notice my face. He turned around to press the button but—

"Ha!" I yelled. I was in before he could lock the doors and sprinted down the hallway.

He clumsily came out from behind the counter. The other three guards ran in, already out of breath.

"Intruder alert!" sounded over the overhead.

I whipped around the corner but glanced back for a second. There were about a dozen of them chasing me now. I knew they'd try to block my path, and already I heard feet running to me from around the corner ahead. I stopped and leaned against the wall. Three more guards barreled around and saw me but couldn't stop in time. I was gone!

There were guards, scientists, and I think the main janitor and the housekeeping lady were chasing me now, too. I was in Decon! There it was! I picked up speed and dived over the railing into the pool.

As my body sank slowly into the pool of decontamination gel, I stripped off as much of my clothing as possible and threw the items as far away from me as I could. I flipped over and saw a full audience watching me from the railing.

"Cruz, you're done!" one of the hulky bodyguards angrily yelled at me.

I simply smiled. My body submerged into the wonderful, beautiful, magnificent gel with its magical decontamination properties to erase all the filth, visible and microscopic, from my body. I would emerge better than a newborn baby after a morning bath. I would emerge as clean as was possible for a living human being.

Recap

Cruz defeated his germophobia and need for CDC gel baths.

We don't need to tell you to persevere to achieve your goals. You've already been doing so over the past 12 months! Doing, not talking about it or dreaming about it, made it possible.

Week 52: Celebration

"A MAN EITHER LIVES life as it happens to him, meets it head-on and licks it, or he turns his back on it and starts to wither away." — Gene Roddenberry, creator of Star Trek

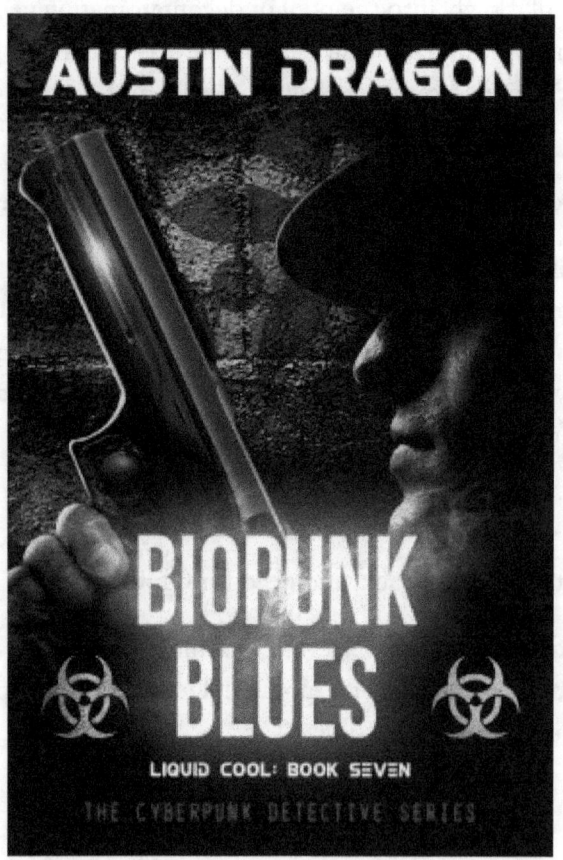

EXCERPT FROM: *Biopunk Blues (Liquid Cool, Book Seven)*

A Freak Show in My Office...

My parents arrived; they had driven me to the office. Then Dot and her parents.

BE COOL

"We did it!" Bia yelled when she came through the door with Bolt, Zip, Handy, Breech—walking with his new bionic legs, and other bio-borgs.

She gave me a big hug.

The Eye Candy Crew showed up. Never had all of them been out of the salon together before. Goat Girl was in her professional appearance, but Twinkle also showed up wearing dark glasses.

"Don't take it personal, Mr. Cruz, but if any of your cop friends show up, I'll likely disappear out the door," he said, shaking my hand.

"I won't take it personal at all," I said to him, laughing.

Fraggy also showed up. He told me, and I had to make the announcement.

"Ladies and gentlemen, Fraggy has been promoted. He's the new president of WHO Earth!"

Everyone applauded.

Finally, Phishy returned. Through the door, he came with more sidewalk johnnies, including Sidewalk Sid, and several sidewalk sallies.

"I'm back!" he said. "Cruz!"

"Hi Phishy. Good to see my office is still here in one piece."

"You know what that means." He ran to PJ's desk and turned up the music. "Cruz Control, please." He was looking at my son.

"Why are you looking at my son, Phishy?"

Cruz Jr. descended in his hoverchair and jumped out.

What I saw next was deeply disturbing. It wasn't just Phishy spinning around doing his chicken dance. He had my son at his side doing the same thing. Everyone was laughing and applauding.

"Phishy, what did you do to my son?"

They danced to blues music. But there was nothing sad here. We were having a party. Another case solved! Until the next one.

Recap

You did it! Take a bow!

Shall we do it again for next year?

BONUS

"The Box"

OUR FAVORITE SCI-FI detective with an attitude, Cruz, had his own unique way of planning and preparing for his own Positive Thinking, Planning, and Action. He has to deal with all those cases, criminals, and clients in his supercity of Metropolis and beyond.

CRUZ: THE ONLY SOUND was that of the rain hitting the window behind me. As I sat behind my desk, I knew I was in trouble from the moment she walked into my office.

PERSPECTIVE

"I offer a toast. The undiscovered country...the future." — Chancellor Gorkon (David Warner), Star Trek: The Undiscovered Country

---

EXCERPT FROM: *Liquid Cool: The Cyberpunk Detective Series (Book One)*

I would put myself in the "box". It wasn't a real box, and it wasn't even a physical thing. It was what I called completely separating yourself from people and any possible distractions to get some major life task done. It was like going off to a secluded island, but you could go anywhere, even your own place. The key was unplugging from everyone and everything to create your own "fortress of solitude" for an indefinite period.

But I found out there was another group of people who liked to put themselves in a "box" away from the outside world and all possible distractions to sit and assimilate a set of knowledge like a machine—gazillionaires. All these CEOs, founders, and innovative genius scientists of the greatest corporations seem to do it in their quest to come up with the next "big thing." Unlike normal people, they had island retreats, lunar strongholds, or personal flying cities to go to, but it was the same concept—cut yourself off from humanity with a ton of books and no access to the Net.

So, the original idea was not my own. Monks did that long before the Greeks invented money, and there could be gazillionaires. Solitude was a must, and often, some quasi-fasting was involved. There was absolutely no answering the video-phone, texts, or emails. For the hardcore, nakedness was sometimes also involved. They said the purpose of all this was to get to your most primal state so your "inner child" would not only emerge but go wild. Well, I wasn't doing the complete full Monty nakedness in my place. No clothes except for my boxers was what I did.

Regular eating and sleeping also went out the window. When this primitive process of hyper-knowledge consumption was over, they had a flurry of new ideas for their next robot, machine, computer program, vehicle, or spaceship. I couldn't knock the process when it worked for me, too.

I had done it before when I was much younger when I wanted to know everything there was about classic hovercars and restoring them. I don't think I left my place for three whole months, as I consumed every piece of data about hovercars, the technology to make them, the technology to keep them running, and all those ninja tactics that would set me above anyone else doing what I was doing. I was in my twenties and was in all the top classic hovercar clubs in my neighborhood and beyond. Every other member of those clubs was at least in their fifties, so I was the "child prodigy". But I wasn't a genius. I simply channeled my OCD tendencies into something productive.

BE (LIQUID) COOL: 52 Weeks of Witty, Pithy, and Profound Sci-Fi Based Inspiration For Positive Thinking, Planning, and Action!

Hopefully, it helped you on your journey of transformation or action with a smile or chuckle along the way.

APPENDIX

ABOUT SELF IMAGE

HYSY versus HOSY ("How You See Yourself" vs. "How Others See You")

Do you see yourself as how you really are, how others want you to be, or, even deeper, how you think others want you to be?

The dynamic of How Others See Us and How We See Ourselves could be an important self-psychological consideration. People can go way overboard in self-analysis, but examining our motivations for our proposed life goals can be a healthy exercise. Starting an advanced exercise routine to become the next Mr. or Ms. Olympia may not be a valid motivation unless you're quitting your day job to become a professional bodybuilder. Is it really for health or low self-esteem? Planning to run a mile or two daily, every other day, or even just walking before or after work to achieve a sustainable, healthy lifestyle might make more sense.

People may not see us the same way that we see ourselves. Your behavior, personality, appearance, and more will lead people to form an image of you that you may not share.

SELF-IMAGE

Self-image is the mental picture we have of ourselves. It includes what we describe of ourselves, such as physical appearance, intelligence, talent, selfishness, kindness, etc. These characteristics form a collection of our perceived assets (strengths) and liabilities (weaknesses).

The positive must come from within you. Others can help, but no one can do it for you.

Here are some questions you can ask yourself to assess your self-image:

- What do you like about yourself?

- What would your friends say?

- What could improve your self-image?

ABOUT PERSONALITY VERSUS Character

What is the difference between character and personality?

Personality is the combination of qualities, attitudes and behavior that makes a person unique. Character is the set of moral beliefs and mental qualities that make a person different from others.

Personality is the external person everyone sees with their own eyes in terms of your behavior and actions.

Character is the internal "you" that governs your behavior and actions regarding right and wrong.

About Visual Mind Maps

You can organize information and ideas in different ways, like using a physical planner or journal, or specific online software. Another tool that may be helpful to some is using mind maps.

A mind map is a way to diagram words, ideas, and information, often drawn on a blank page, easel board, or dry eraser board.

More Blank Planner Pages

BE (LIQUID) COOL / MONTHLY PLANNER

MONTH:

SUN	MON	TUE	WED	THU	FRI	SAT

TOP PRIORITIES / GOALS

PEOPLE TO SEE / PLACES TO GO / REMINDERS

NOTES

RATE / ASSESS THE MONTH:

BE (LIQUID) COOL
WEEKLY PLANNER

WEEK:

M T W H F S S

MONDAY

TUESDAY

WEDNESDAY

THURSDAY

FRIDAY

SATURDAY / SUNDAY

WEEK'S PRIORITIES / TO DO

NOTES

RATE / ASSESS THE WEEK:

NEED MORE MONTHLY AND Weekly Planner Pages?

Download free from my website:

https://www.austindragon.com/monthly_planner_page

https://www.austindragon.com/weekly_planner_page

REVIEW REQUEST

DEAR READER,

I hope you enjoyed **BE (LIQUID) COOL**.

Can You Write Me a Review?

If you enjoyed **BE (LIQUID) COOL: 52 Weeks of Witty, Pithy, and Profound Sci-Fi-Based Inspiration For Positive Thinking, Planning, and Action**, I'd greatly appreciate an honest review on one or more of the following sites:

REVIEWS ARE THE BEST way for readers to discover good books. My writer's motto is simple: "Readers Rule!" Thanks so much.

Always writing,

Austin Dragon

ABOUT THE AUTHOR

AUSTIN DRAGON IS THE author of over 20 books in science fiction, fantasy, and classic horror. His works include the sci-fi detective **_LIQUID COOL_** series, the epic fantasy **_FABLED QUEST CHRONICLES_**, the international futuristic epic **_AFTER EDEN_** Series, the classic **_SLEEPY HOLLOW HORRORS_**, and the upcoming **_PLANET TAMERS_** military sci-fi series. He is a native New Yorker but has called Los Angeles, California home for more than twenty years. Words to describe him, in no particular order: U.S. Army, English teacher, one-time resident of Paris, ex-political junkie, movie buff, Fortune 500 corporate recruiter, renaissance man, futurist, and dreamer.

He is currently working on new books and series in science fiction, epic fantasy, and classic horror!

http://www.austindragon.com/books

www.ingramcontent.com/pod-product-compliance
Lightning Source LLC
Chambersburg PA
CBHW070042080526
44586CB00013B/885